MOCHI'S PUGPYHOOD

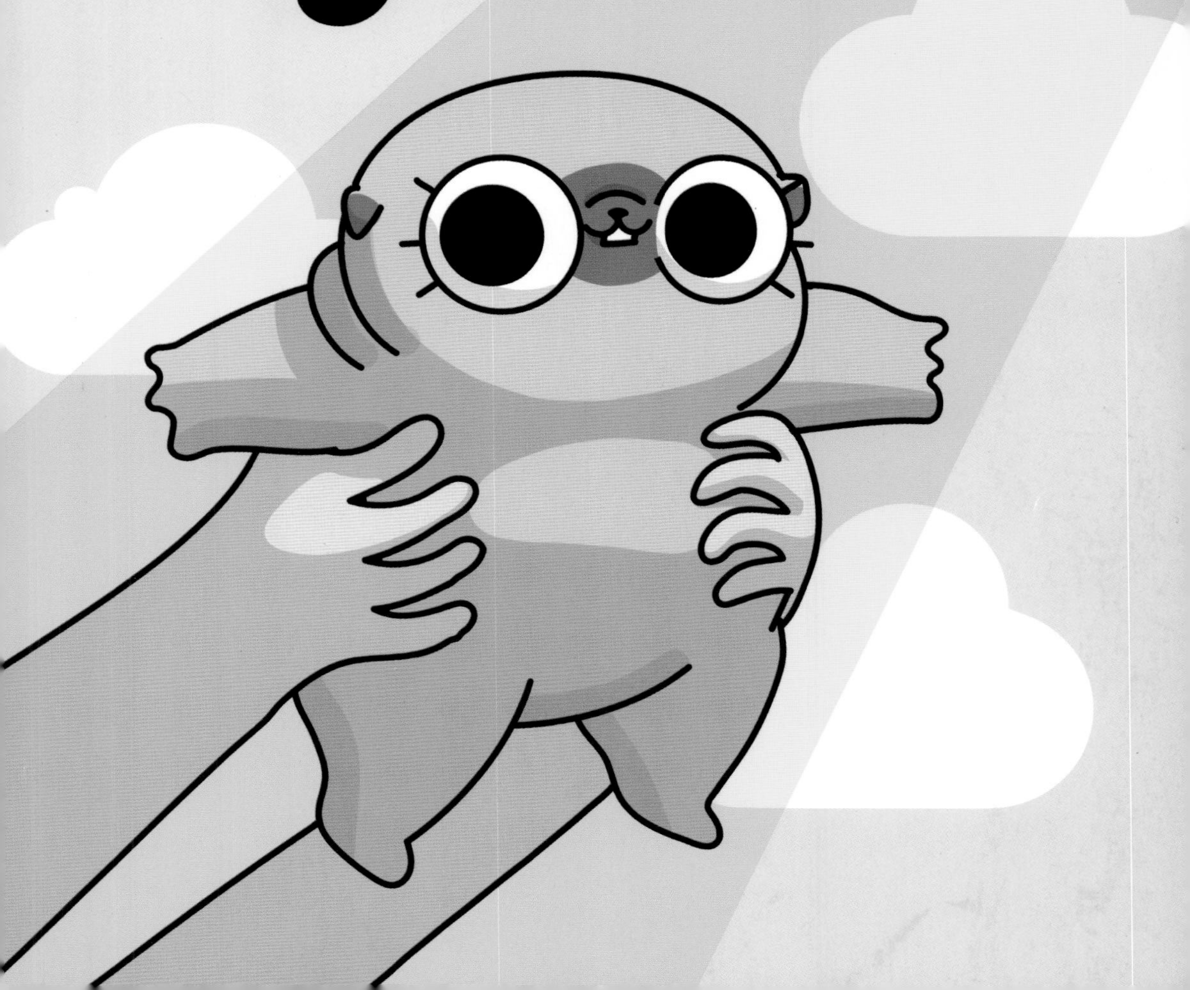

TO MOCHI, THE BABIEST BABY

MOCHI'S PUPPYHOOD

Andrews McMeel
PUBLISHING®

THIS BOOK TELLS TRUE, REAL-LIFE STORIES OF MOCHI'S PUGPYHOOD. IT ALSO CONTAINS ONE BIG DARK SECRET FROM MOCHI'S PAST THAT CAN NEVER BE TOLD.

BY CONTINUING TO READ, YOU AGREE TO KEEP THIS FROM EVERYONE.

ESPECIALLY PELI (AKA PAPI).

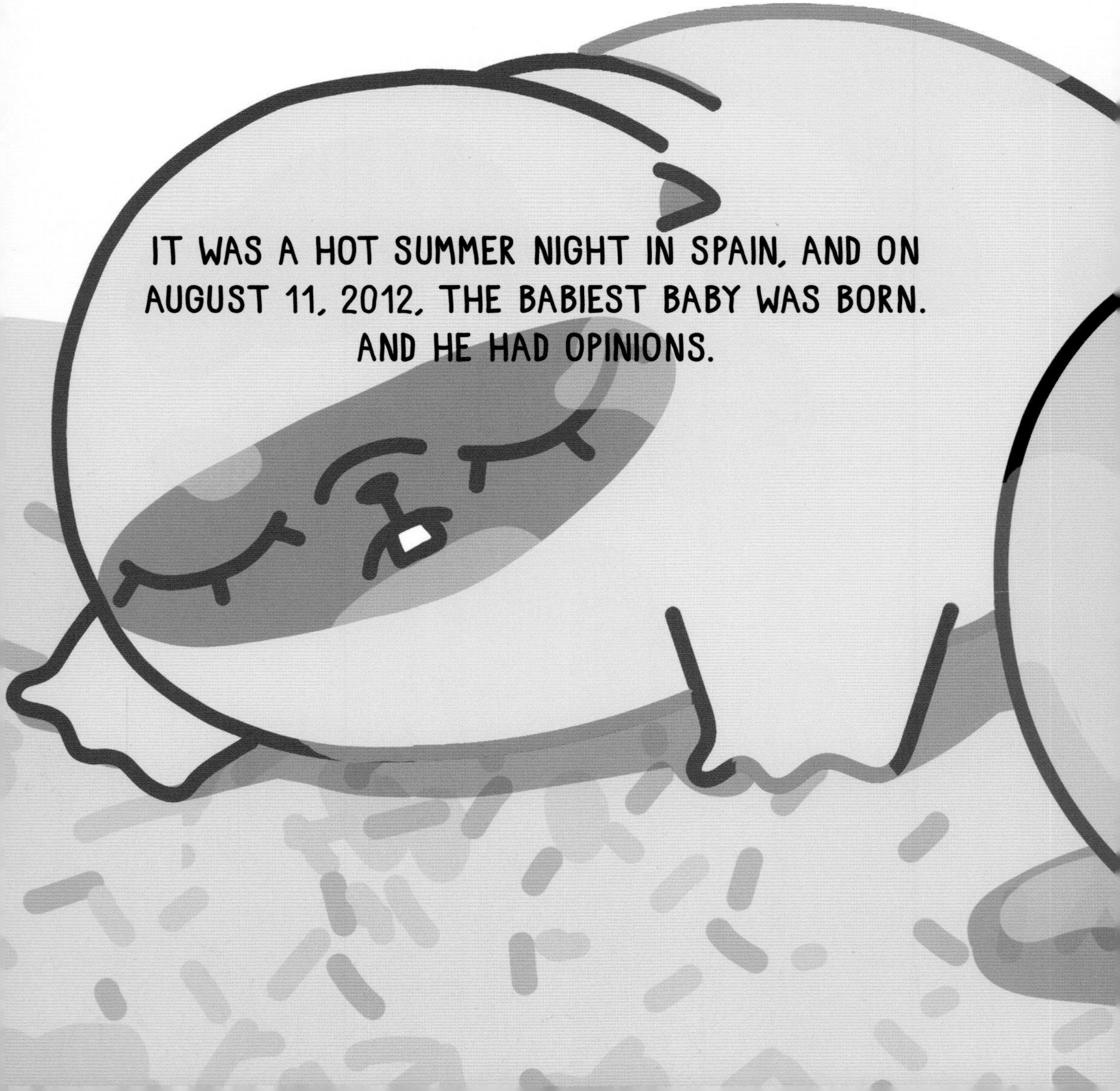
IT WAS A HOT SUMMER NIGHT IN SPAIN, AND ON AUGUST 11, 2012, THE BABIEST BABY WAS BORN.
AND HE HAD OPINIONS.

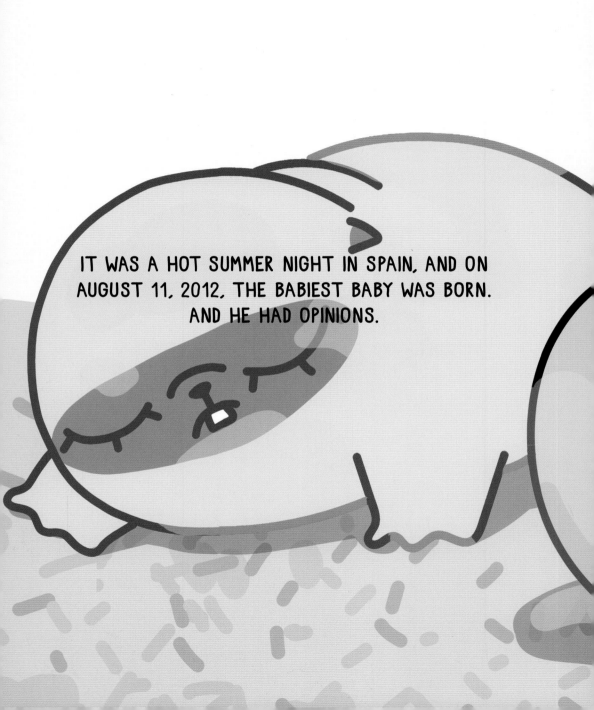

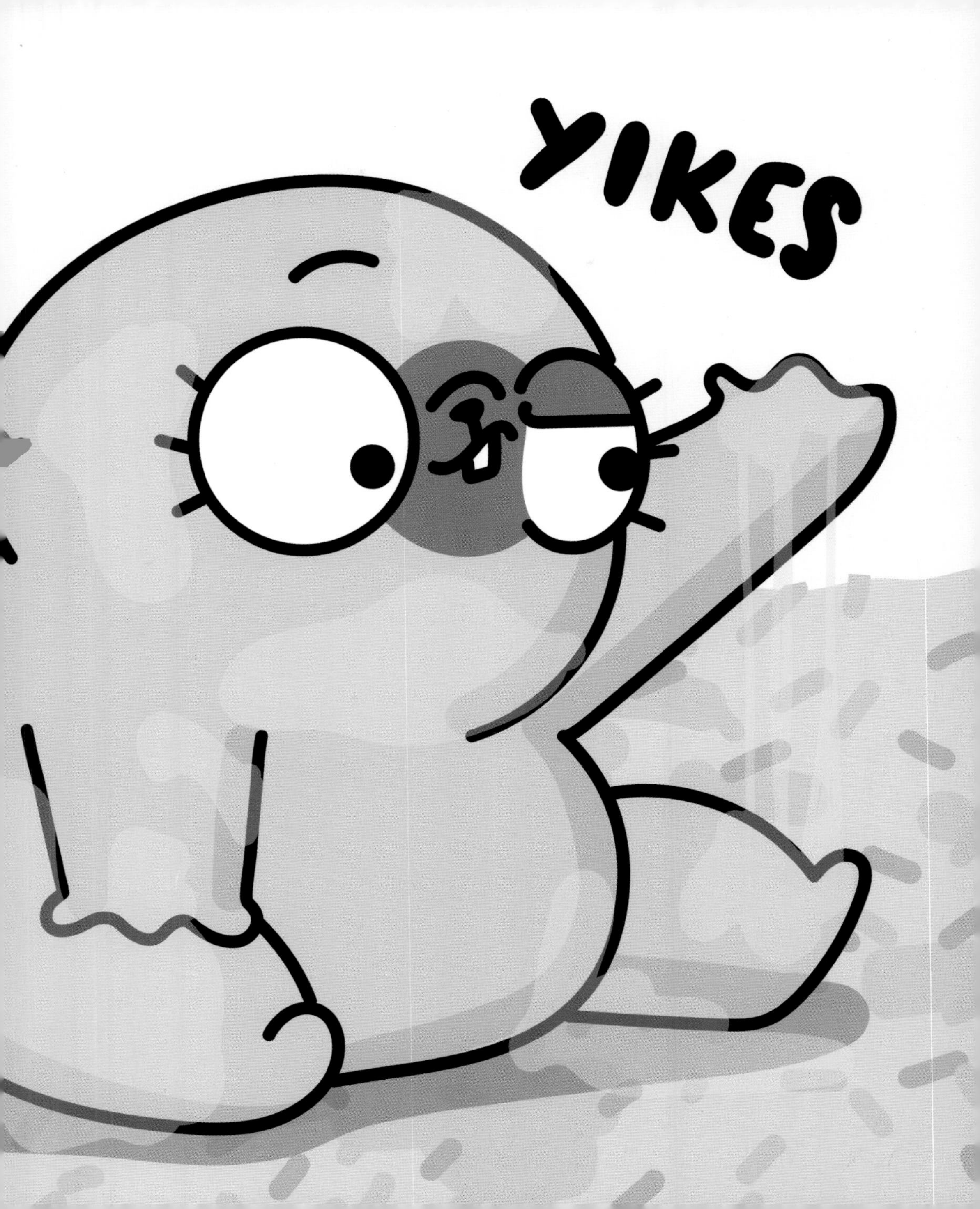
YIKES

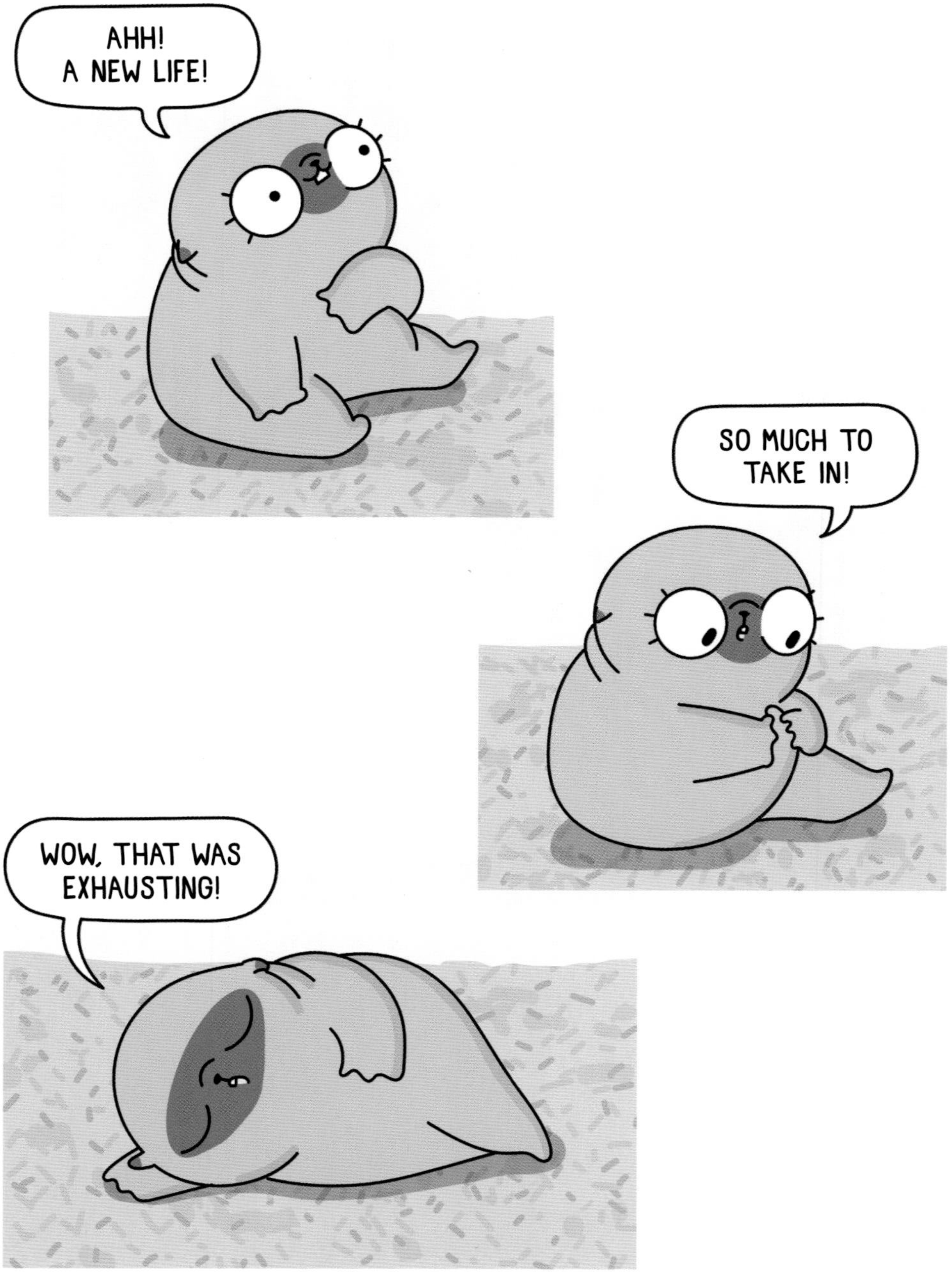
AHH! A NEW LIFE!
SO MUCH TO TAKE IN!
WOW, THAT WAS EXHAUSTING!

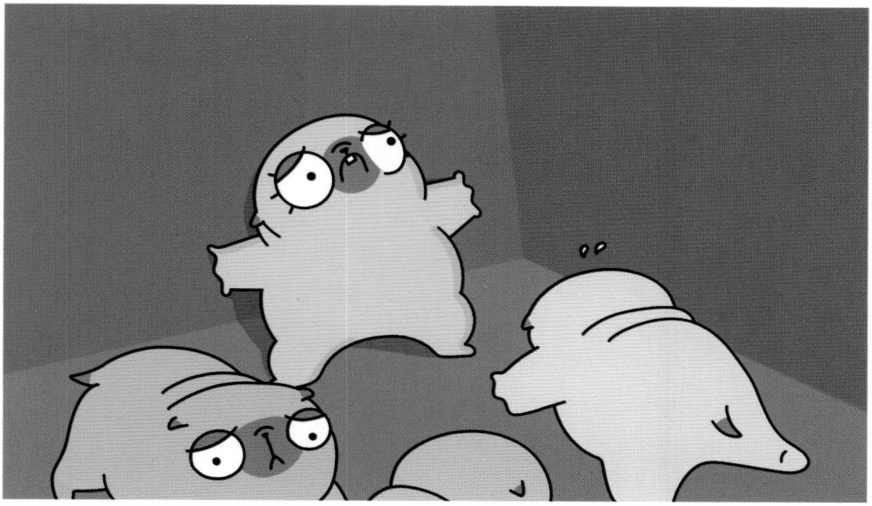

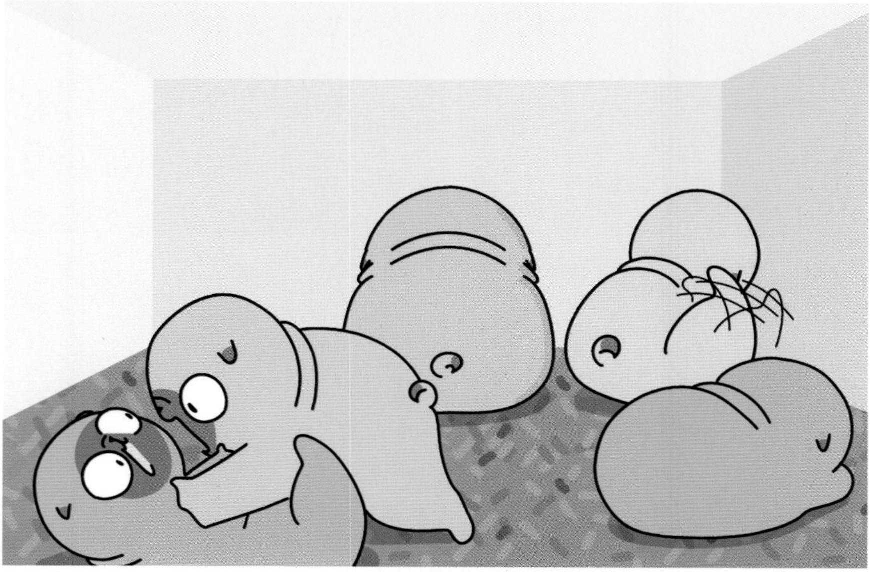

ONE BY ONE, MOCHI'S SIBLINGS WERE ADOPTED.

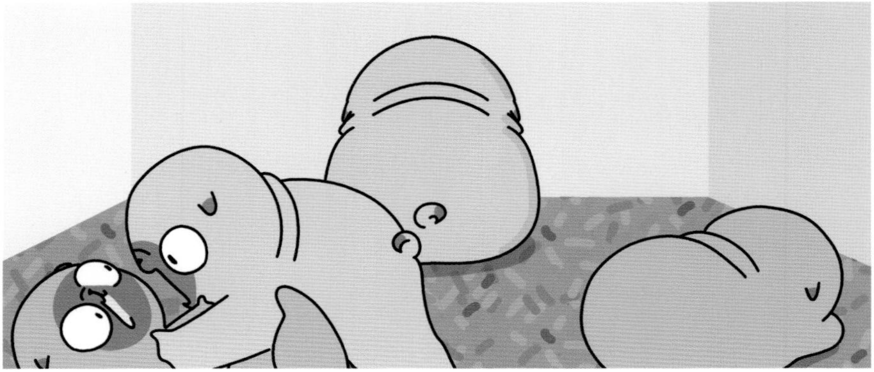

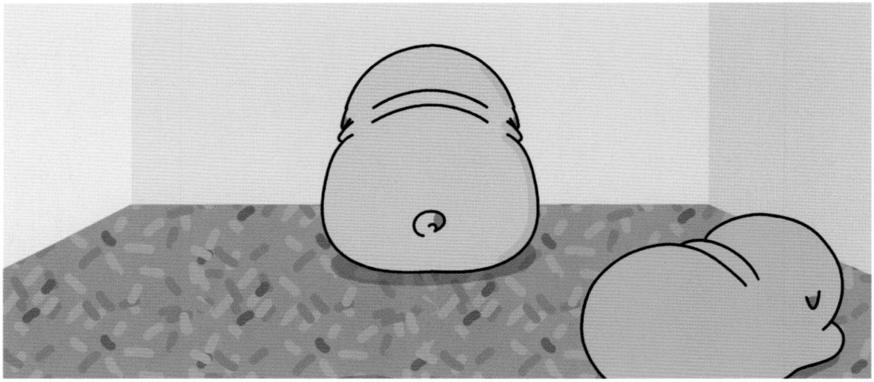

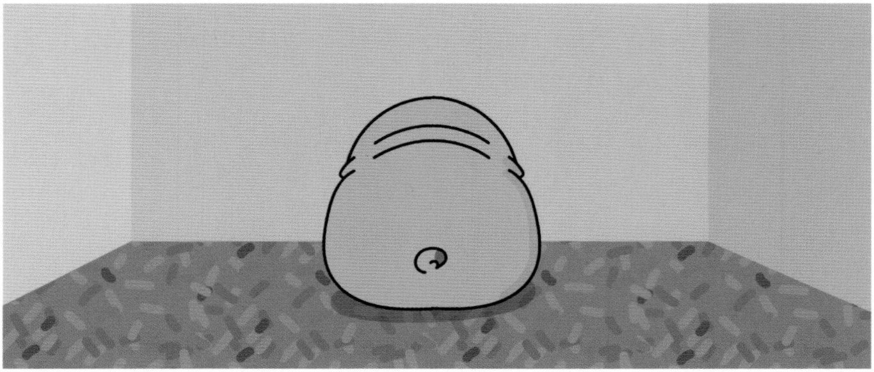

DAYS WENT BY, AND MOCHI WAS GROWING BIGGER AND GETTING BORED OF NOT BEING PICKED.

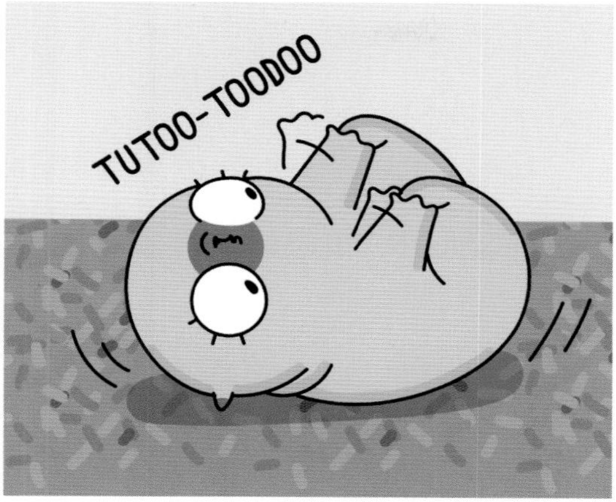
TUTOO-TOODOO

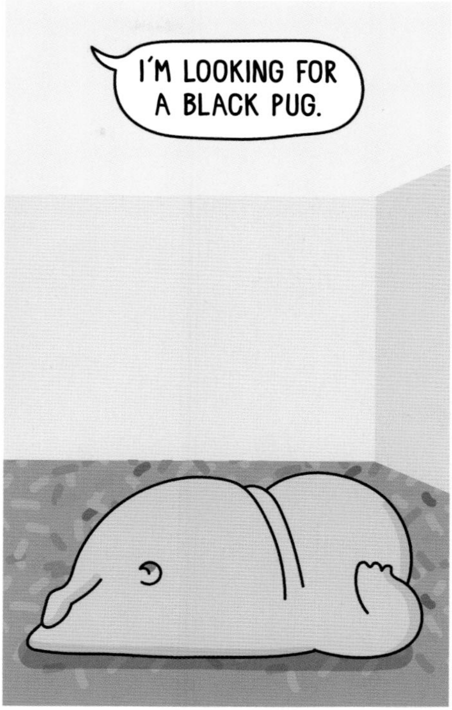
I'M LOOKING FOR A BLACK PUG.

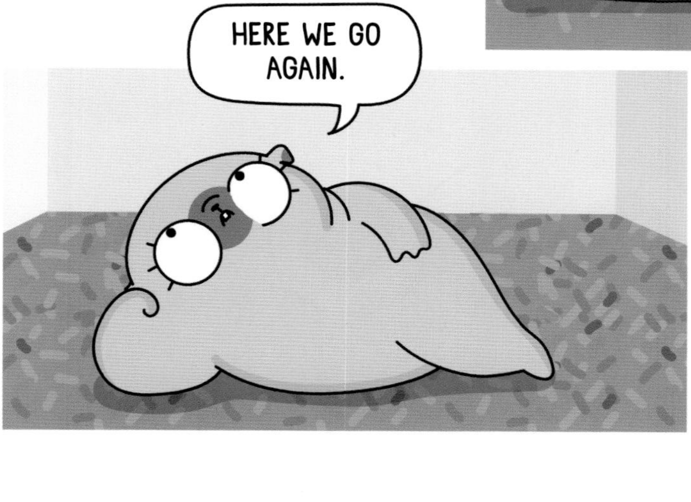
HERE WE GO AGAIN.

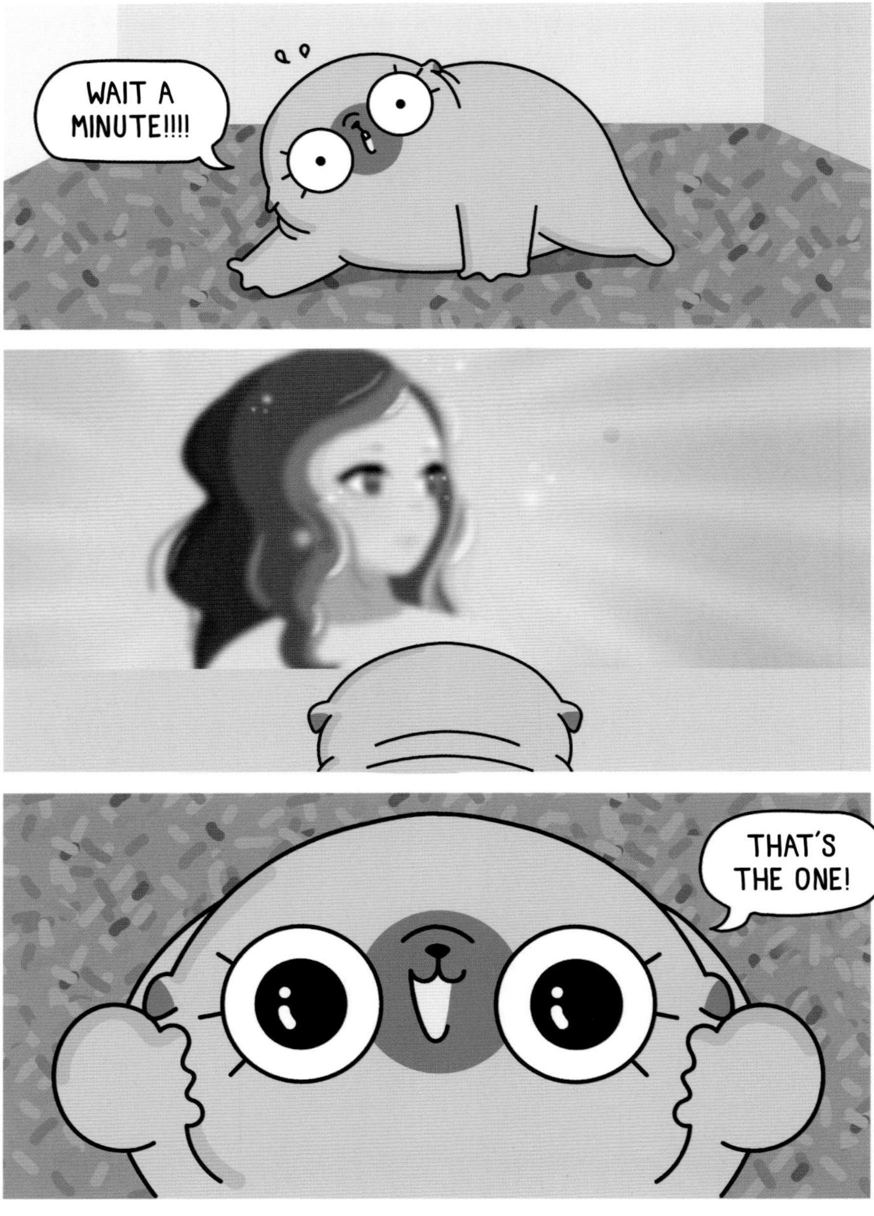
WAIT A MINUTE!!!!
THAT'S THE ONE!

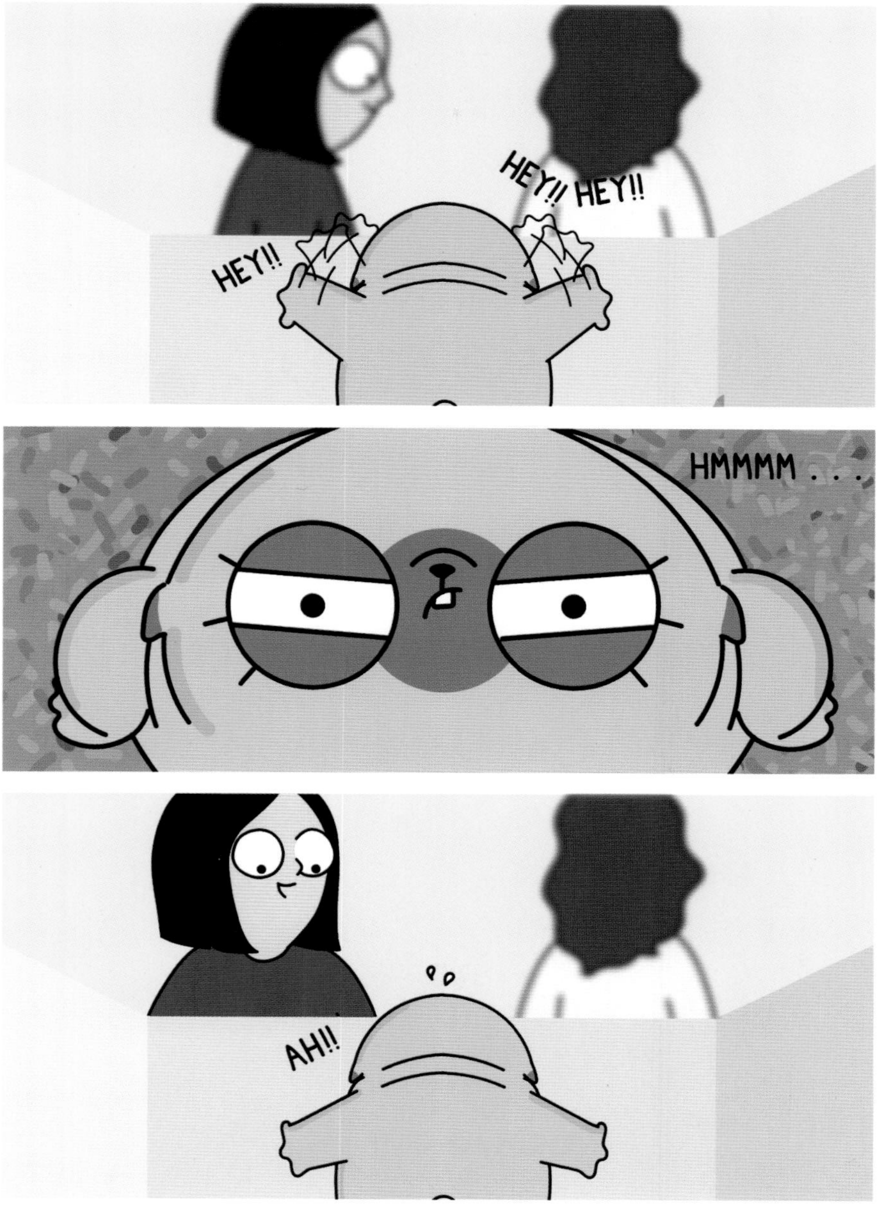
HEY!! HEY!!
HEY!!
HMMMM . . .
AH!!

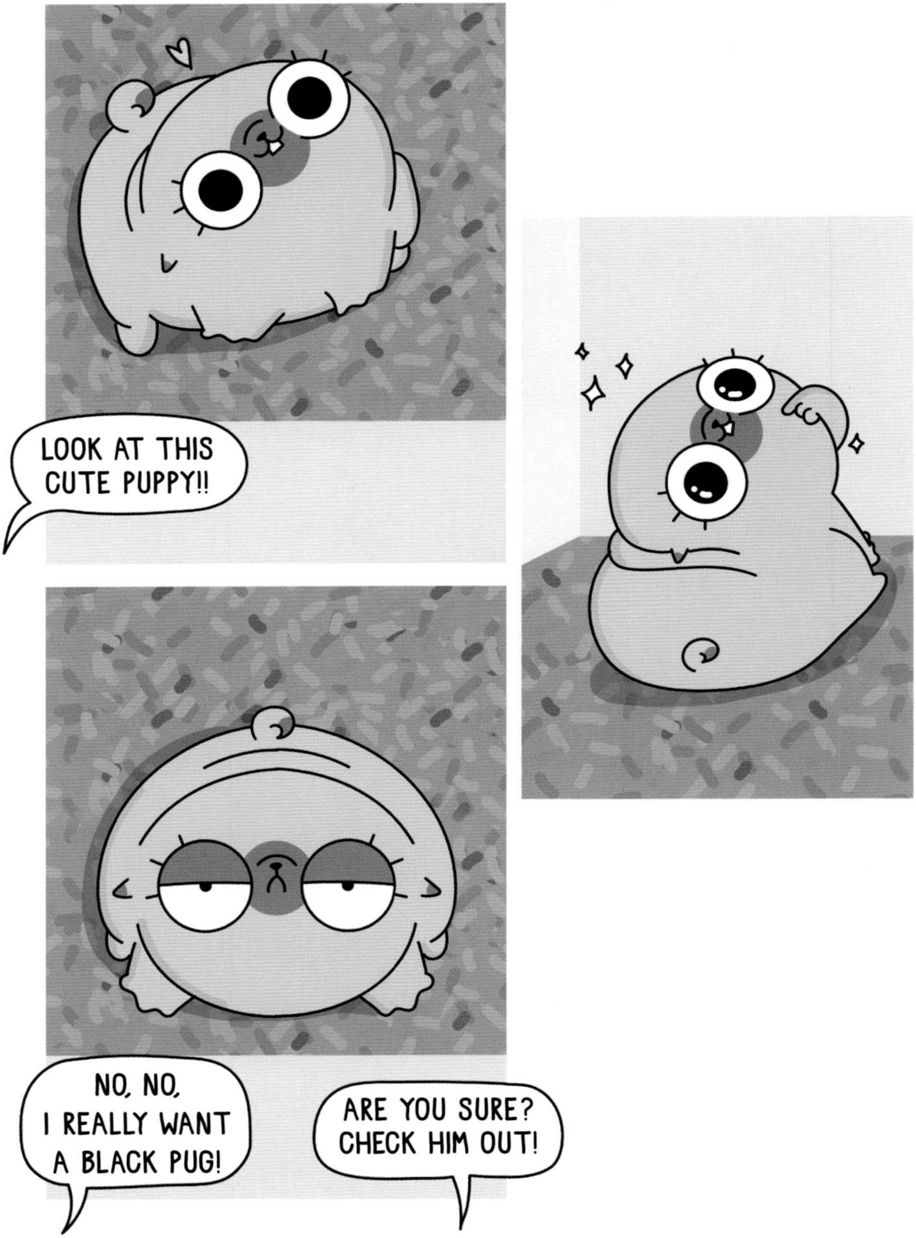
LOOK AT THIS CUTE PUPPY!!
NO, NO, I REALLY WANT A BLACK PUG!
ARE YOU SURE? CHECK HIM OUT!

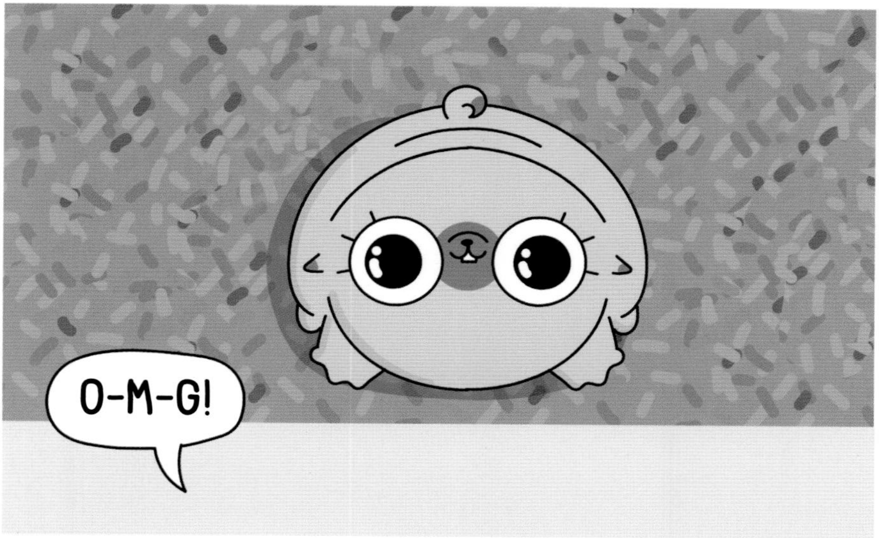
O-M-G!

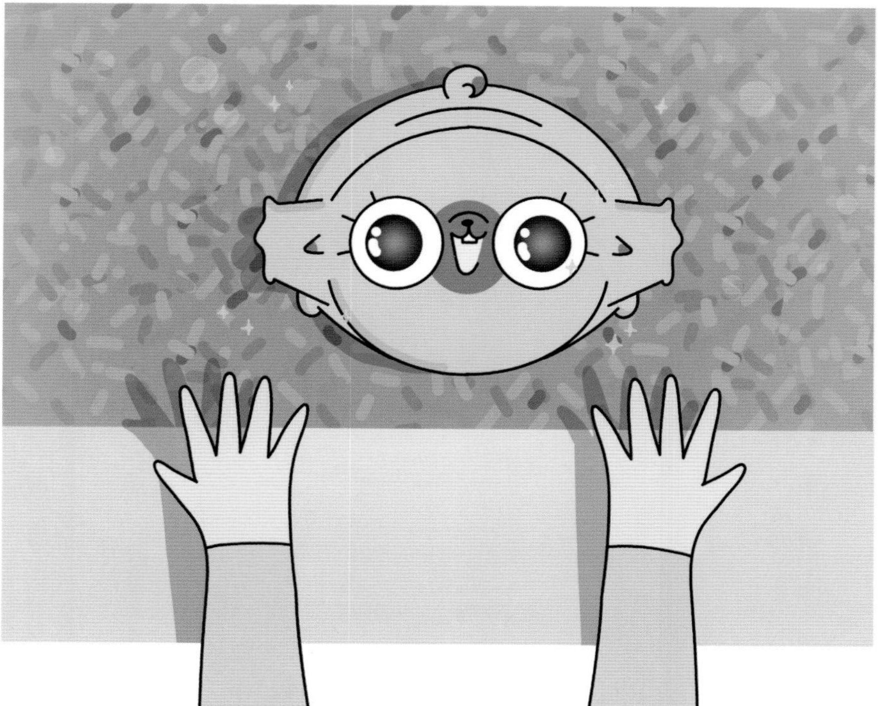

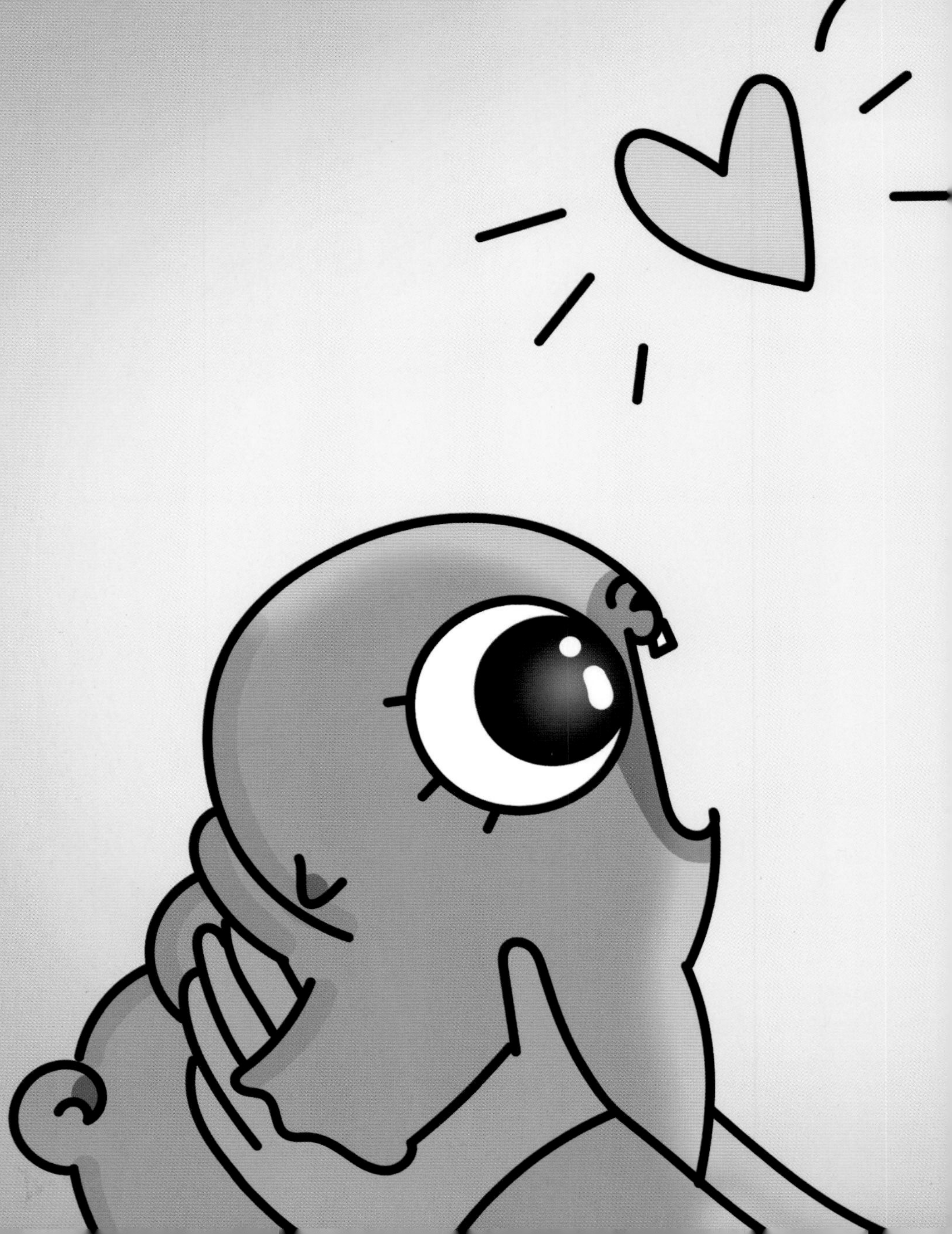

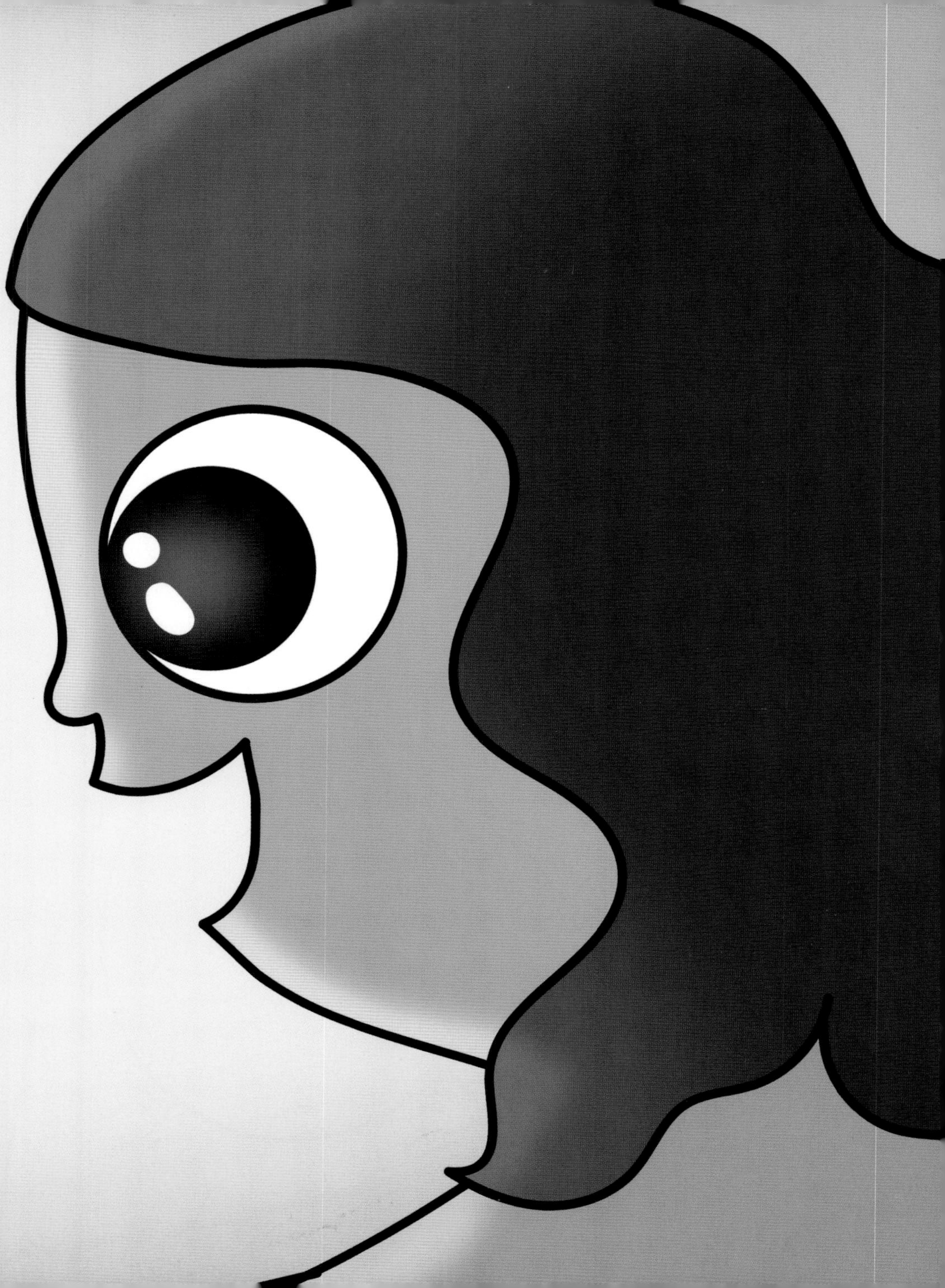

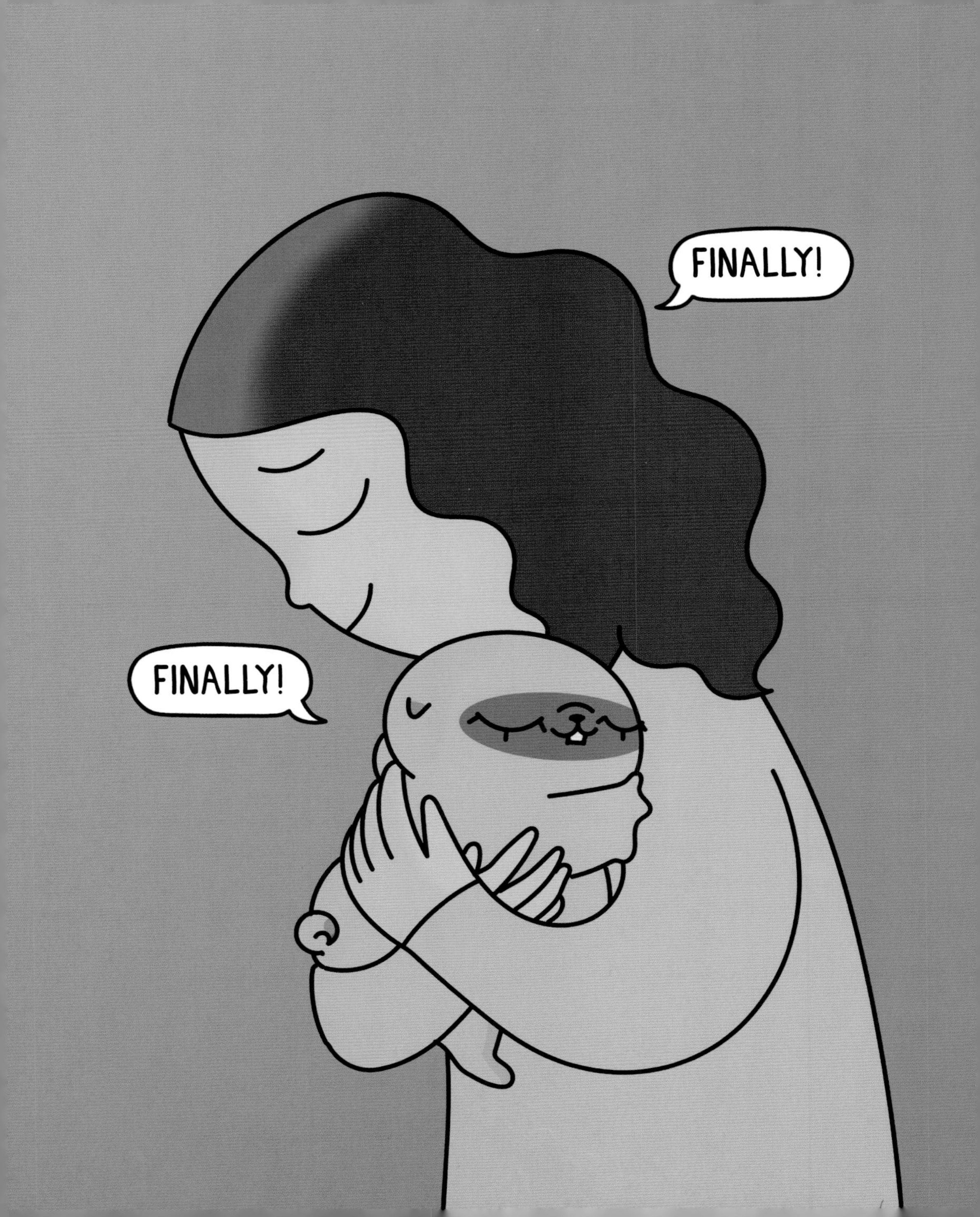
FINALLY!
FINALLY!

I'LL NEVER FORGET THE MOMENT I HELD MOCHI FOR THE FIRST TIME. WE JUST FOUND EACH OTHER. IT WAS MEANT TO BE.

IT WAS TOTAL INSTANT LOVE. IT WAS SUCH A BEAUTIFUL, SPECIAL, AND MEANINGFUL MOMENT, AT LEAST UNTIL IT WAS INTERRUPTED BY A RANDOM REQUEST.

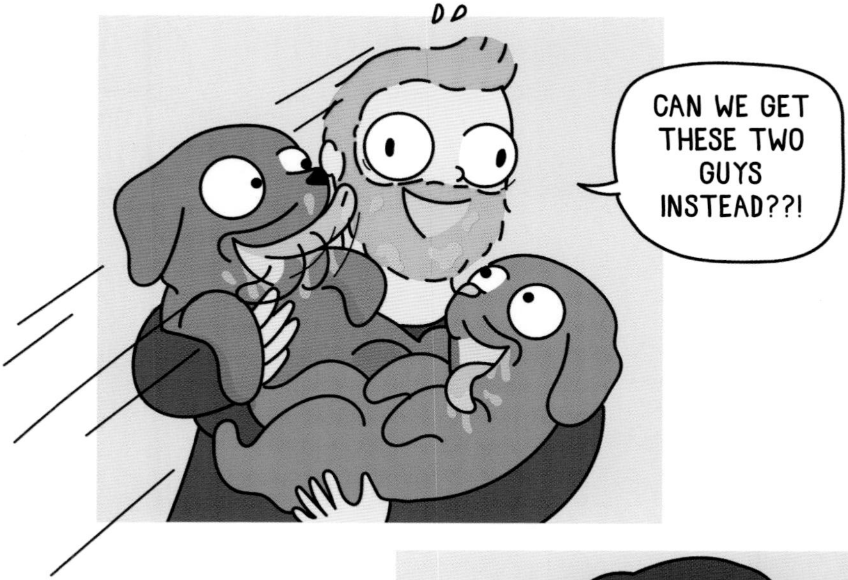
CAN WE GET THESE TWO GUYS INSTEAD??!

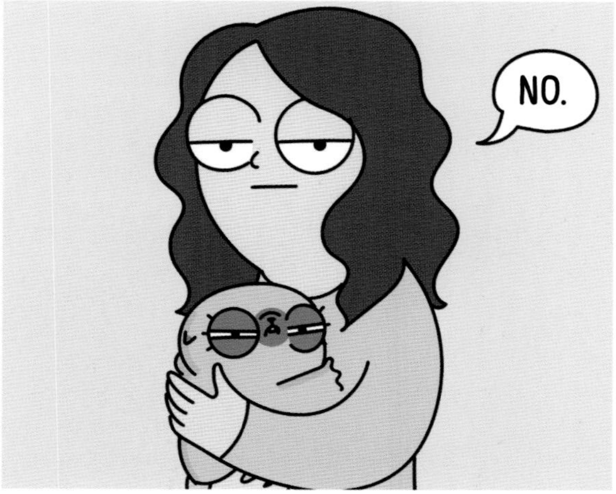
NO.

THE DAY WE BROUGHT MOCHI HOME

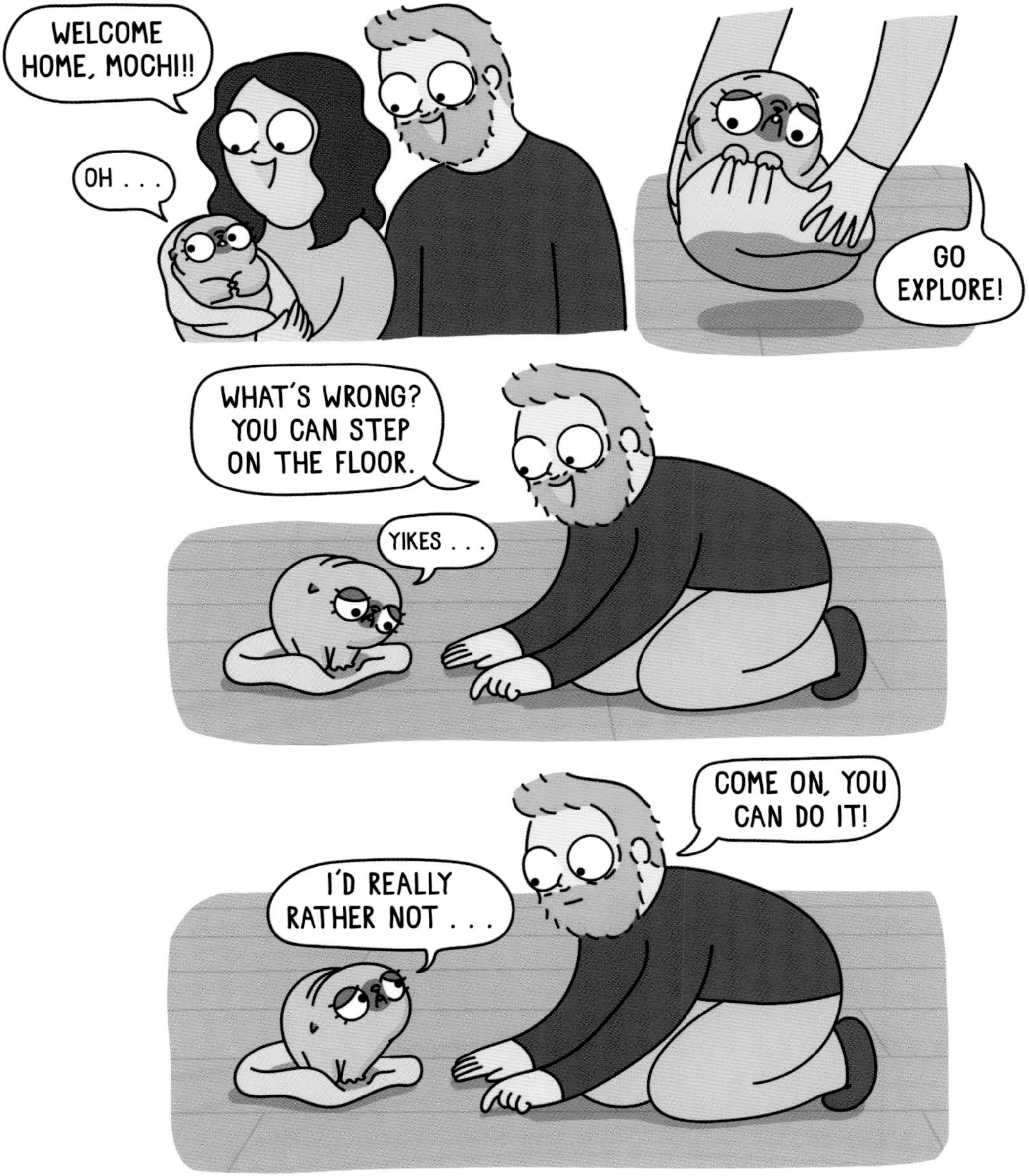
WELCOME HOME, MOCHI!!
OH . . .
GO EXPLORE!
WHAT'S WRONG? YOU CAN STEP ON THE FLOOR.
YIKES . . .
COME ON, YOU CAN DO IT!
I'D REALLY RATHER NOT . . .

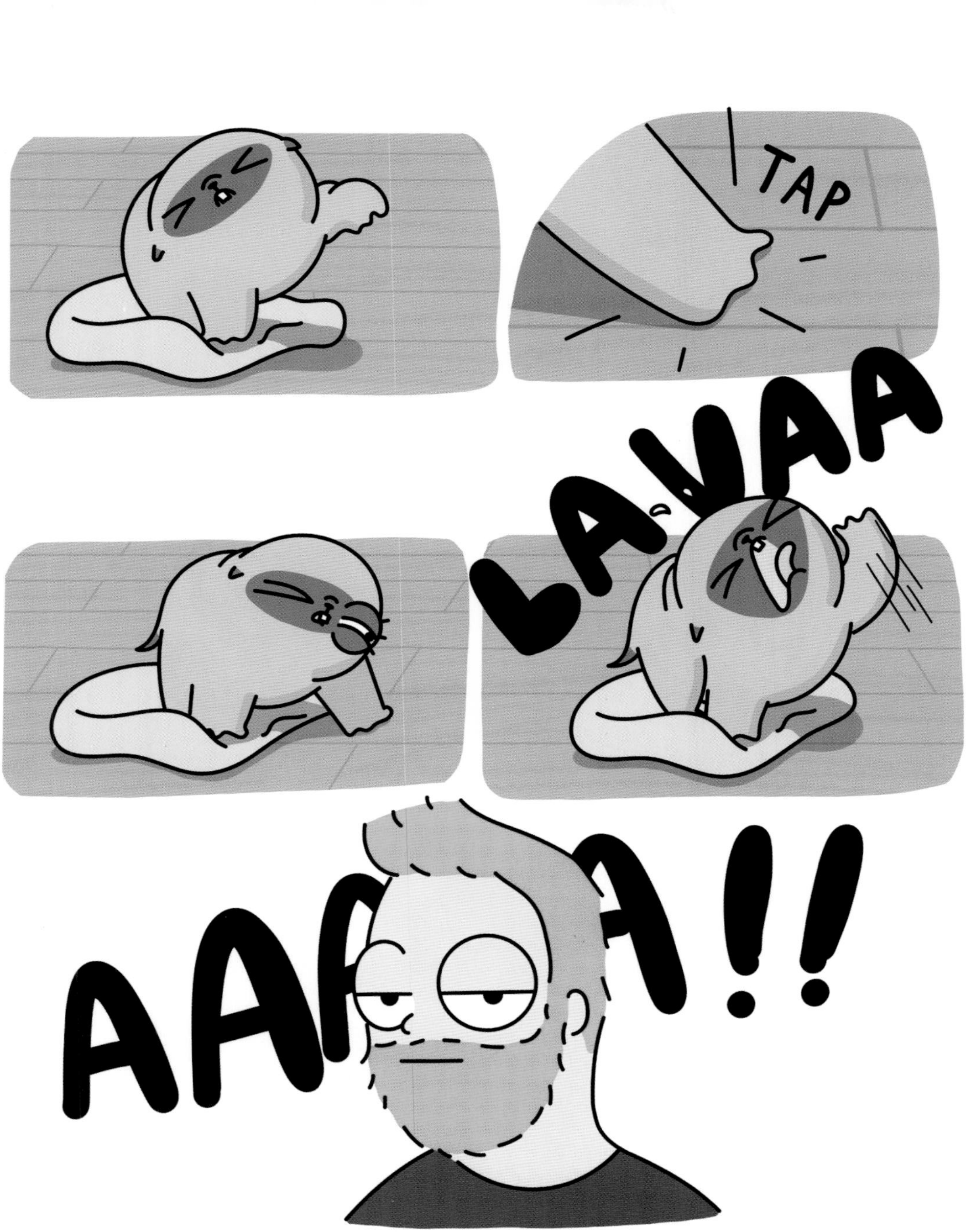
TAP
LAWAA
AAAA!!

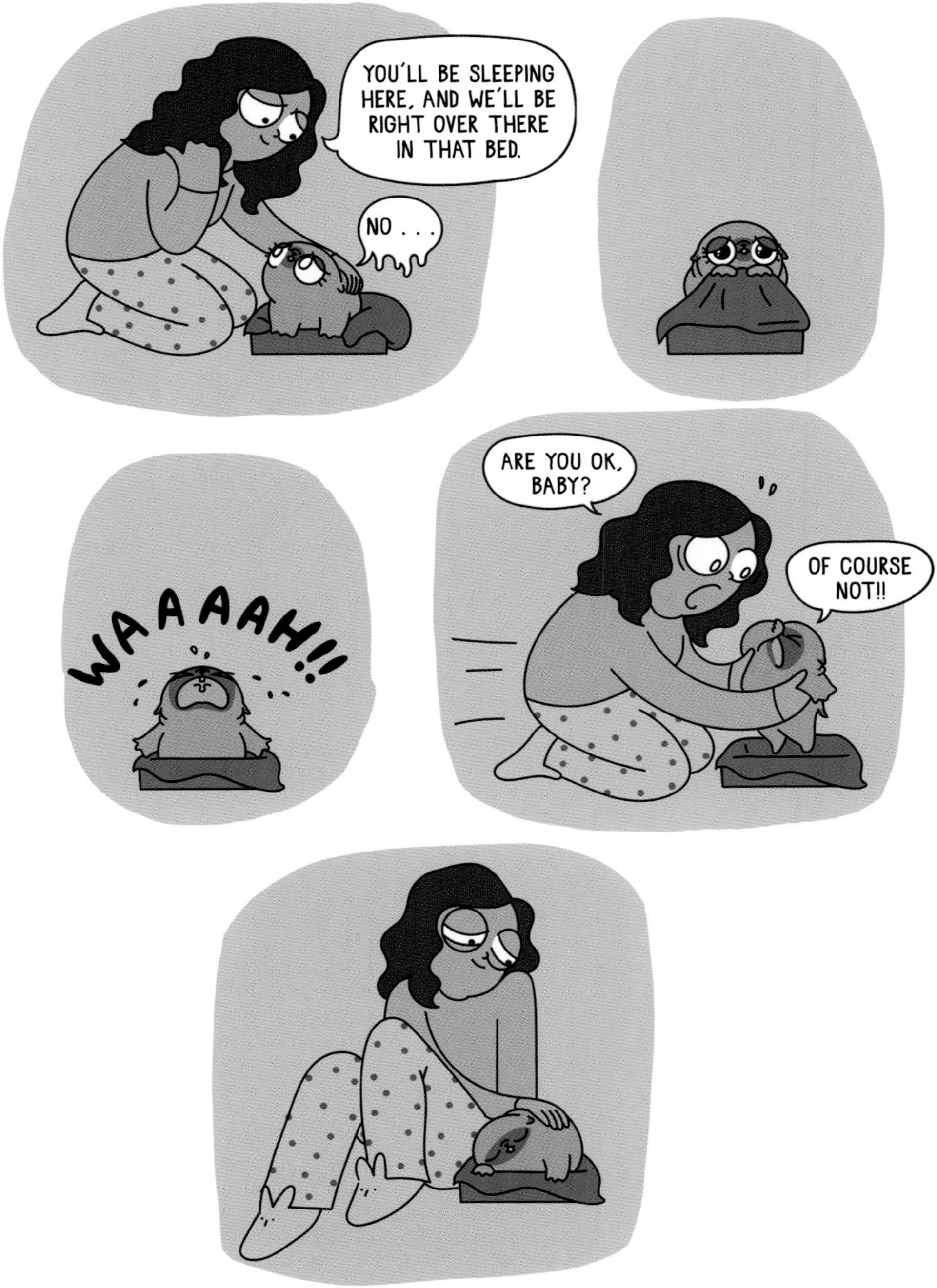
YOU'LL BE SLEEPING HERE, AND WE'LL BE RIGHT OVER THERE IN THAT BED.
NO . . .
WAAAAH!!
ARE YOU OK, BABY?
OF COURSE NOT!!

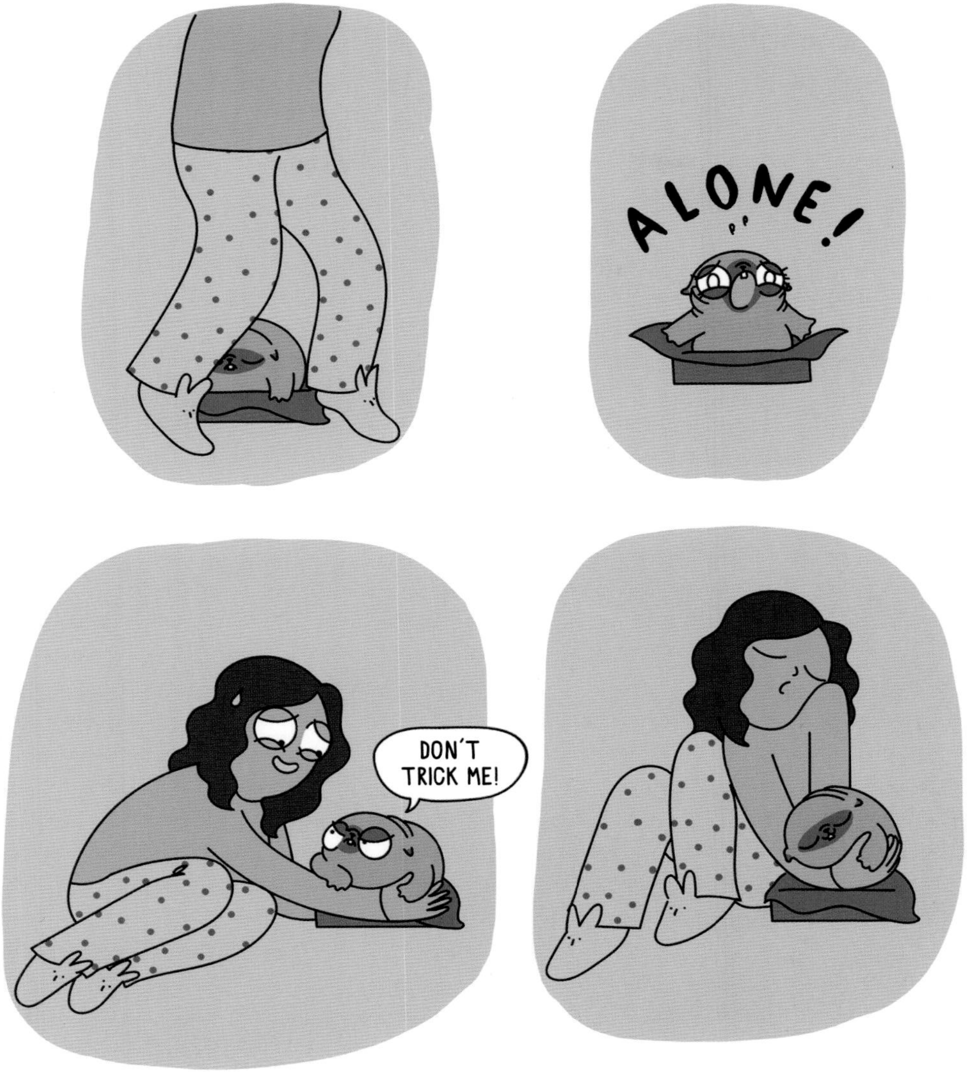
ALONE!
DON'T TRICK ME!

THE FIRST NIGHT DIDN'T GO SO WELL. MOCHI SHOWED US HE HAD NO INTENTION TO SLEEP ALONE, AND HE GOT HIS WAY.

WHEN WE FIRST GOT MOCHI, HE SLEPT IN A CARDBOARD BOX WITH A TOWEL IN IT. I KNOW, NEGLECT MUCH? HE DRAGGED EVERYTHING HE FOUND AND LOVED INTO HIS LITTLE BOX.

POOM!

HI HI
HI HI

THEN ONE DAY, WE GOT HIM A VERY NICE BED, AND HE LOVED IT.

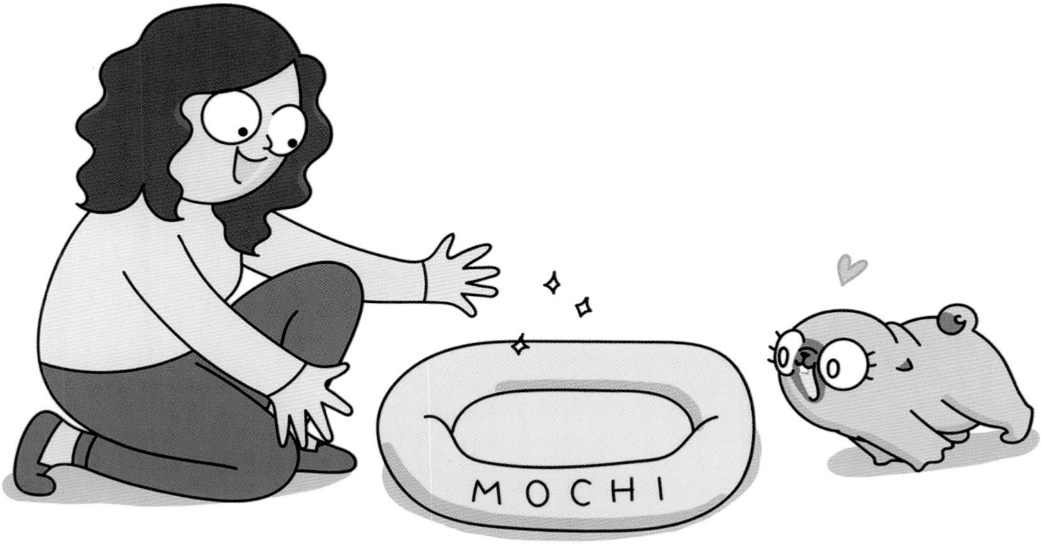
MOCHI

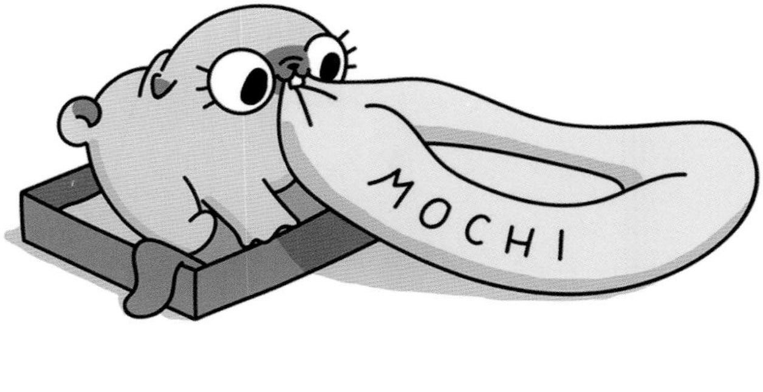
MOCHI

WHAT THE WORLD DIDN'T PREPARE ME FOR WAS THAT I WOULD BE GETTING A BRAND NEW FURRY SHADOW.

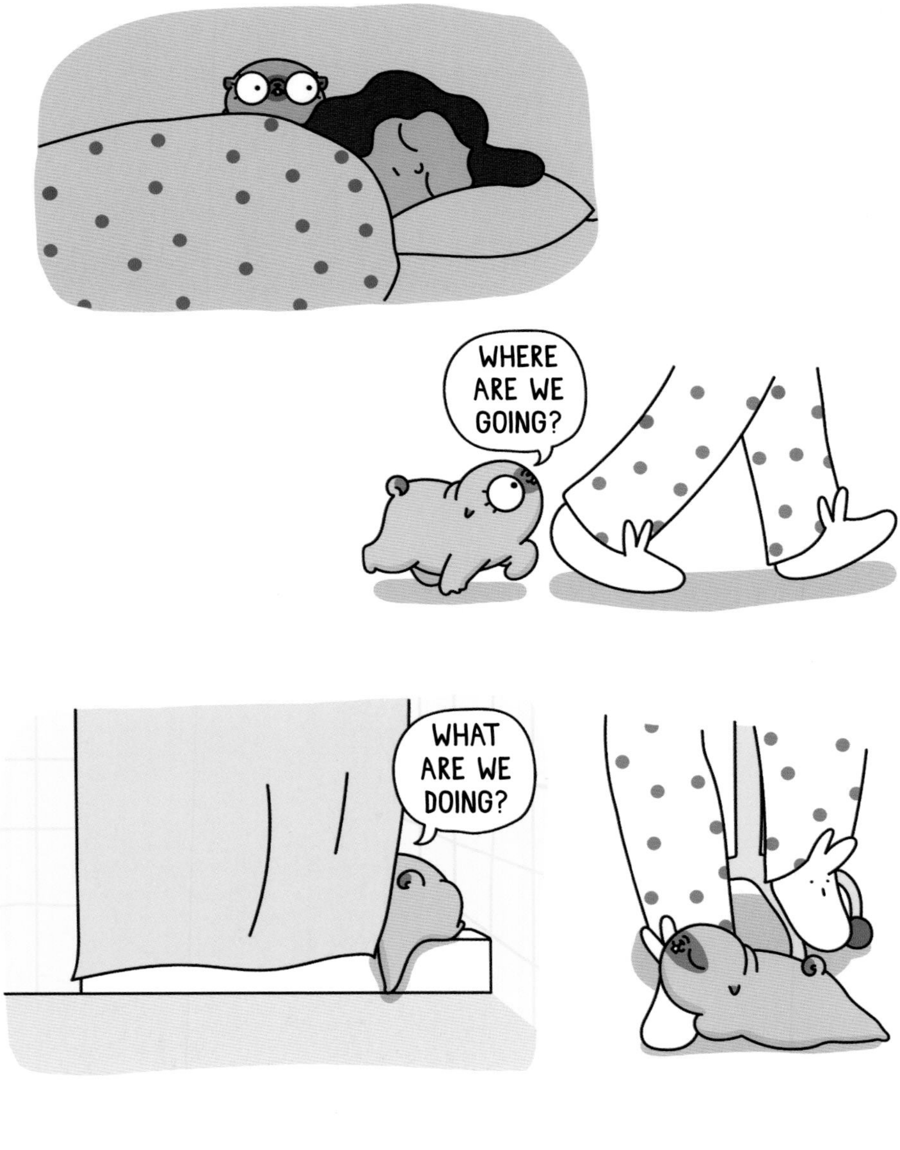
WHERE ARE WE GOING?
WHAT ARE WE DOING?

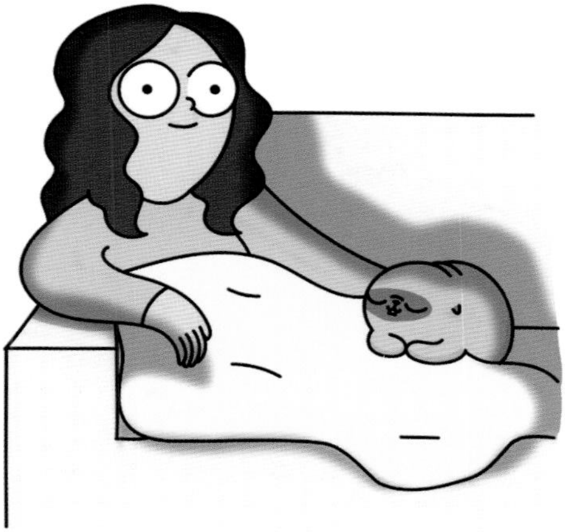

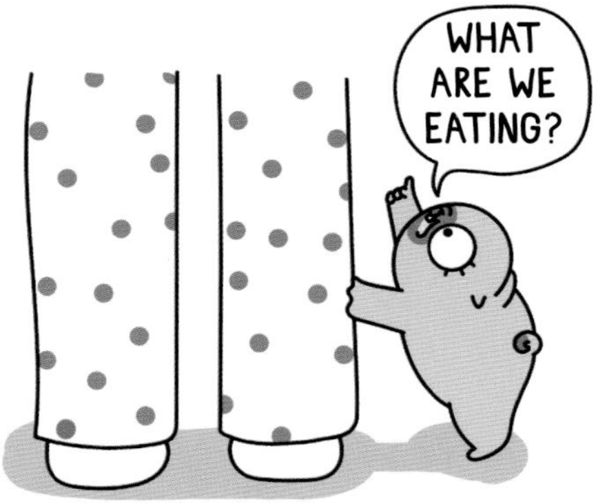
WHAT ARE WE EATING?

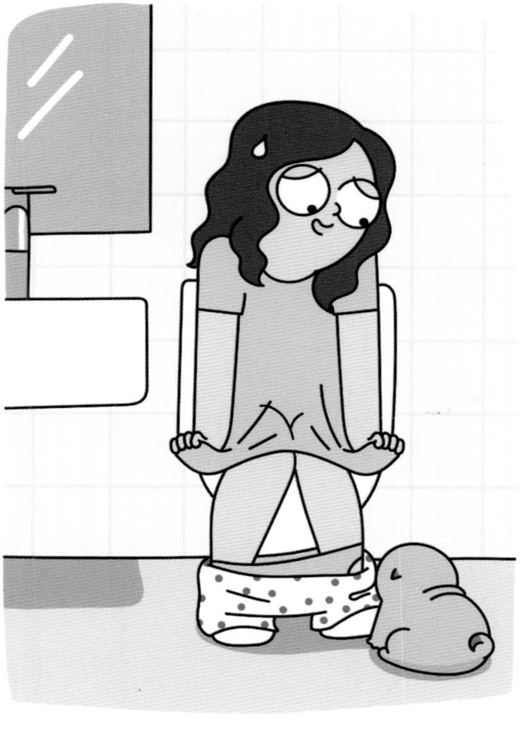

MOCHI COULDN'T GO OUTSIDE BECAUSE HE DIDN'T HAVE ALL HIS VACCINES YET. AT THAT POINT, WE HAD SPENT EVERY SECOND TOGETHER. BUT ONE DAY . . .

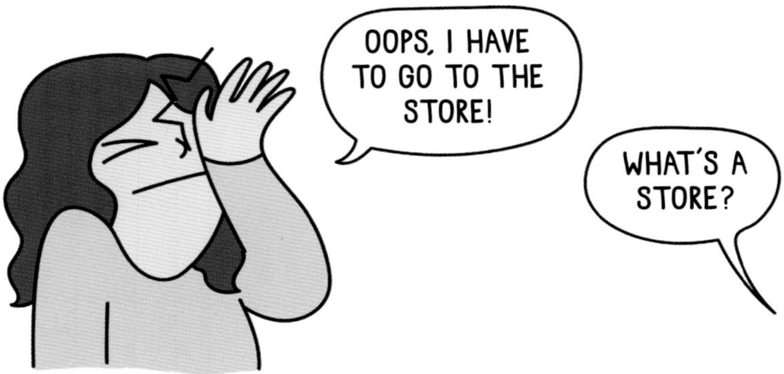
OOPS, I HAVE TO GO TO THE STORE!
WHAT'S A STORE?

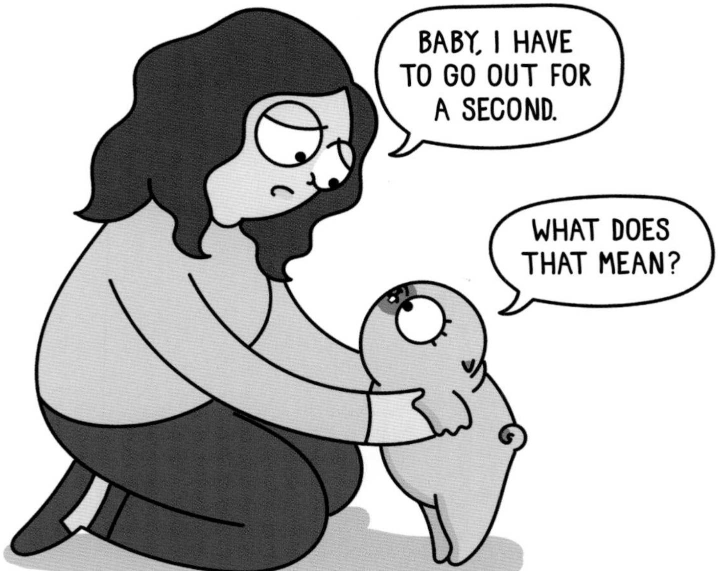
BABY, I HAVE TO GO OUT FOR A SECOND.
WHAT DOES THAT MEAN?

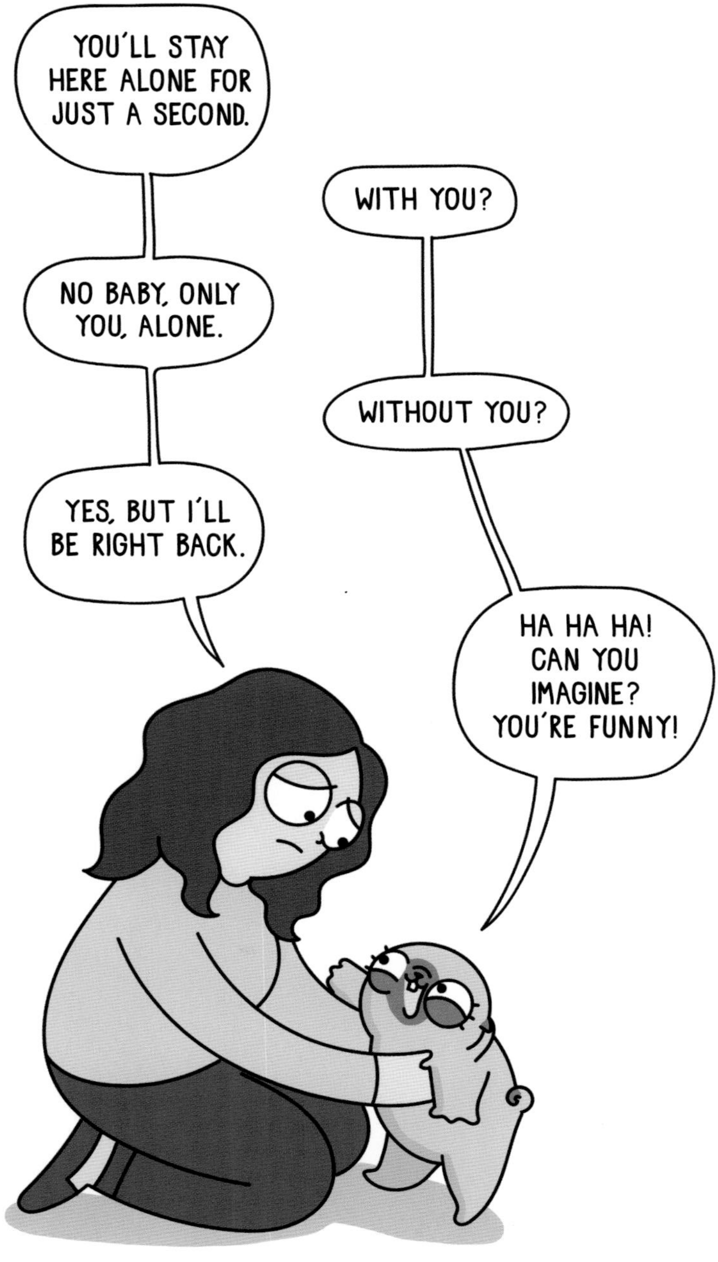
YOU'LL STAY HERE ALONE FOR JUST A SECOND.
WITH YOU?
NO BABY, ONLY YOU, ALONE.
WITHOUT YOU?
YES, BUT I'LL BE RIGHT BACK.
HA HA HA! CAN YOU IMAGINE? YOU'RE FUNNY!

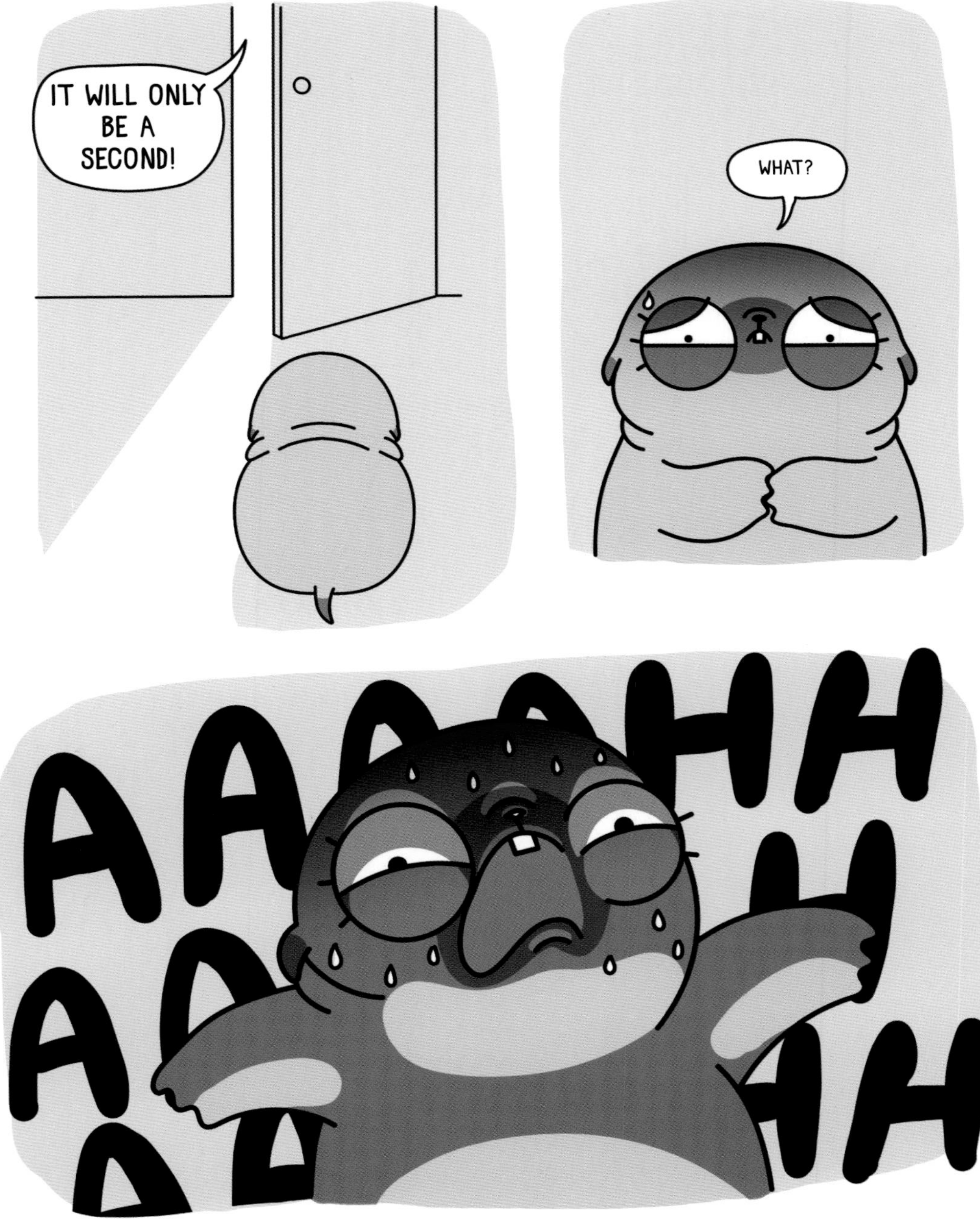
IT WILL ONLY BE A SECOND!
WHAT?
AAAAHH AAAAHH AAAHH

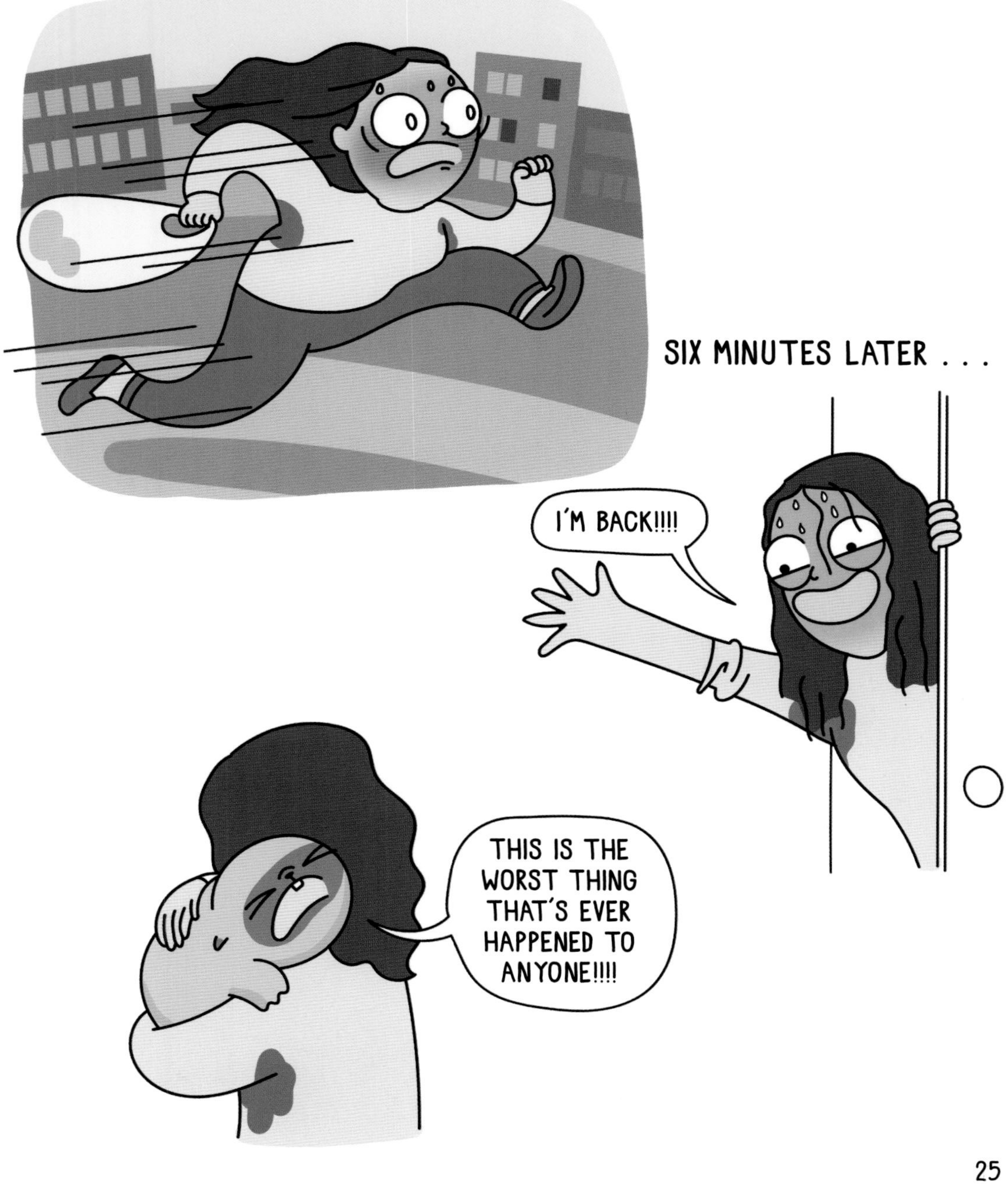
SIX MINUTES LATER . . .
I'M BACK!!!!
THIS IS THE WORST THING THAT'S EVER HAPPENED TO ANYONE!!!!

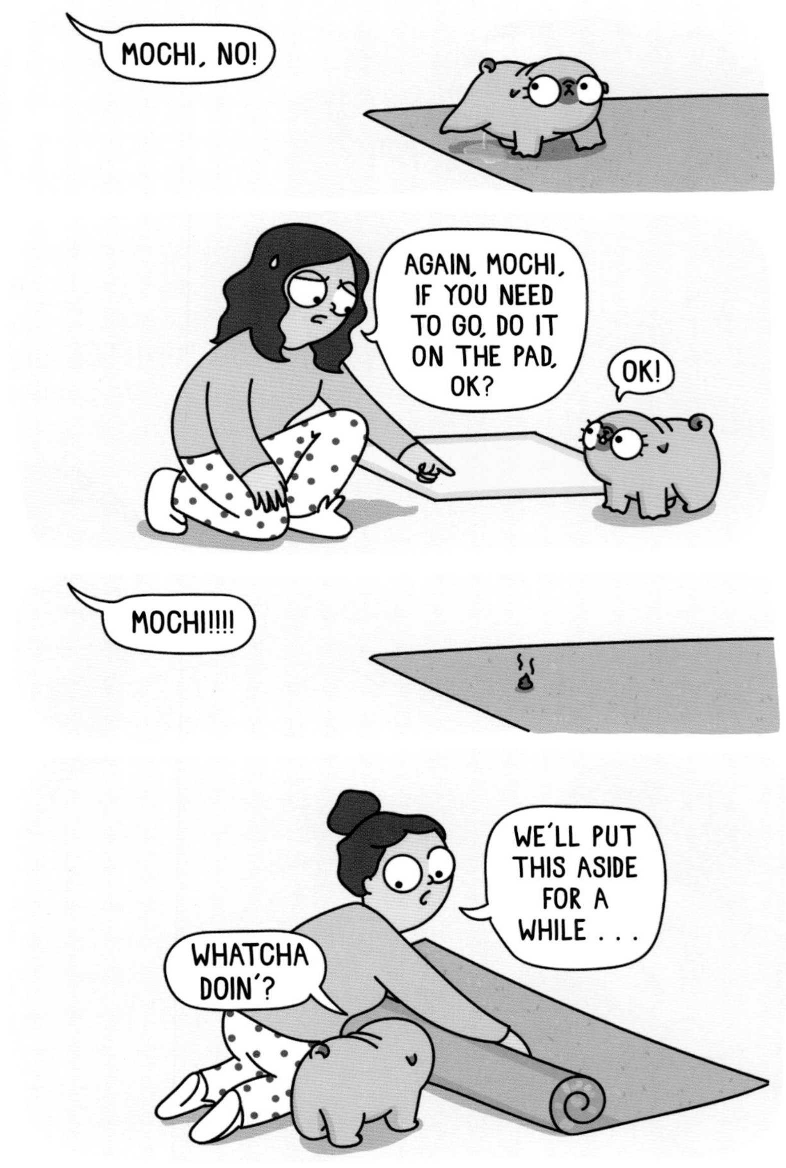
MOCHI, NO!
AGAIN, MOCHI, IF YOU NEED TO GO, DO IT ON THE PAD, OK?
OK!
MOCHI!!!!
WE'LL PUT THIS ASIDE FOR A WHILE . . .
WHATCHA DOIN'?

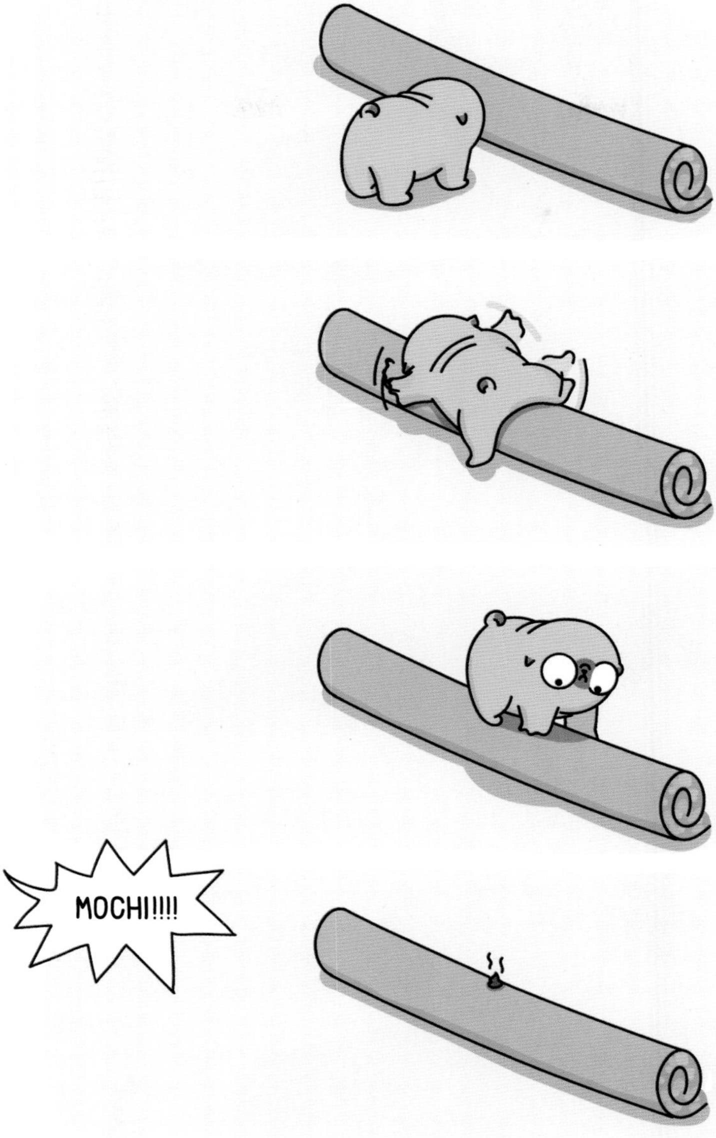
MOCHI!!!!

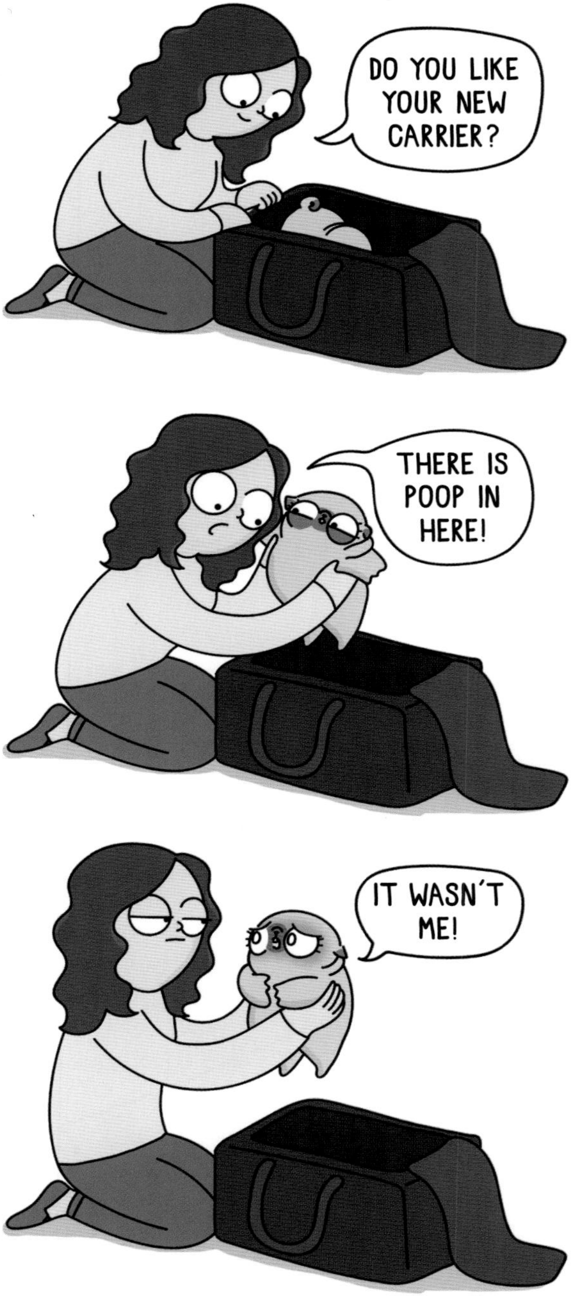
DO YOU LIKE YOUR NEW CARRIER?
THERE IS POOP IN HERE!
IT WASN'T ME!

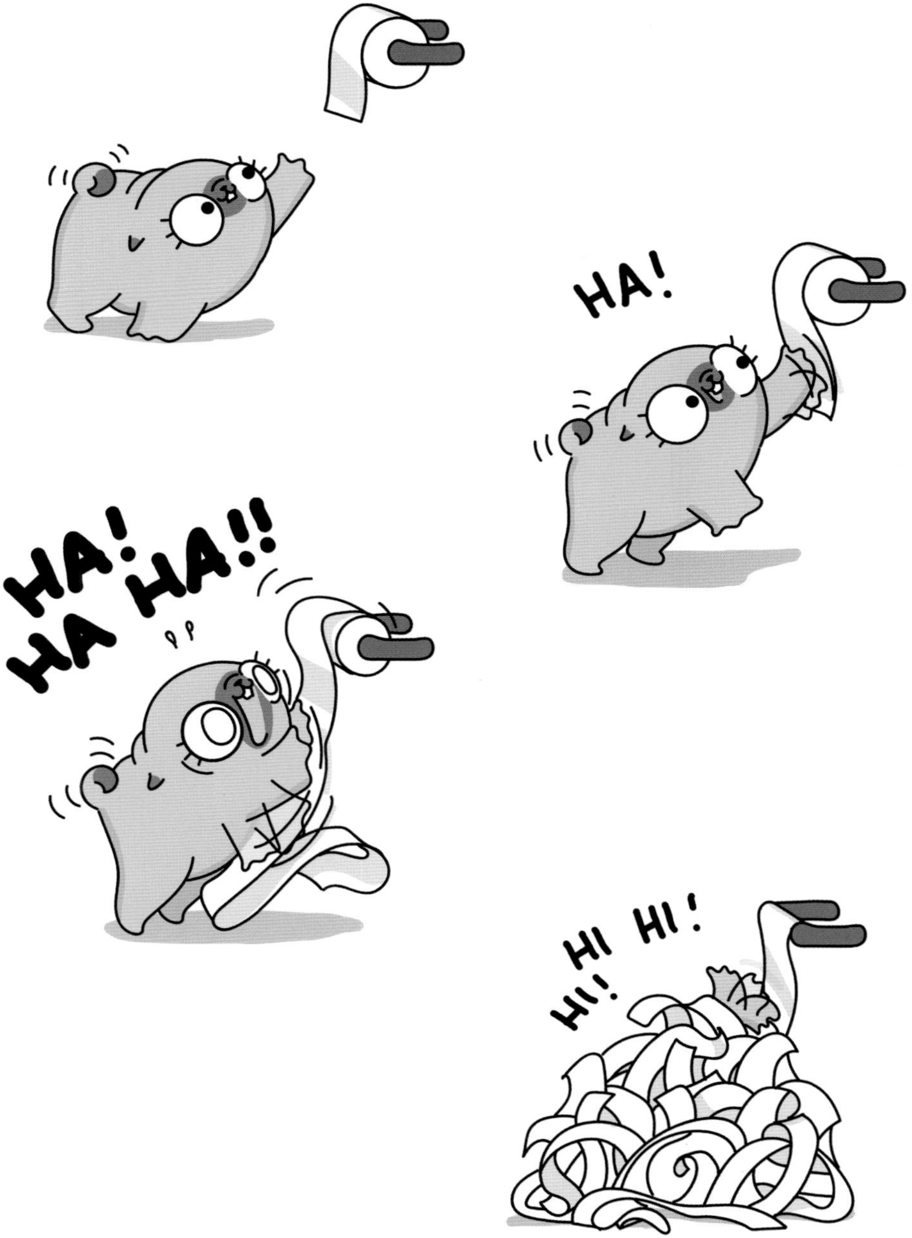
HA!
HA! HA HA!!
HI HI!
HI!

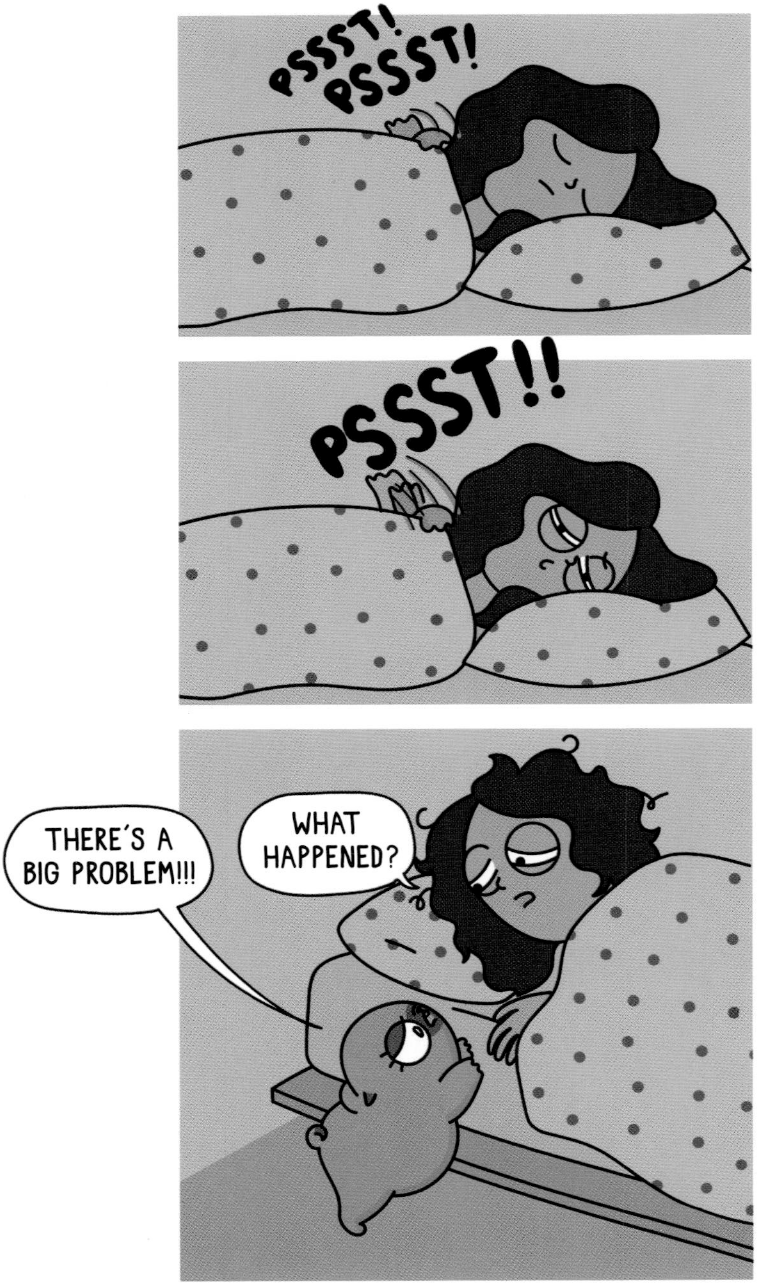
PSSST! PSSST!
PSSST!!
WHAT HAPPENED?
THERE'S A BIG PROBLEM!!!

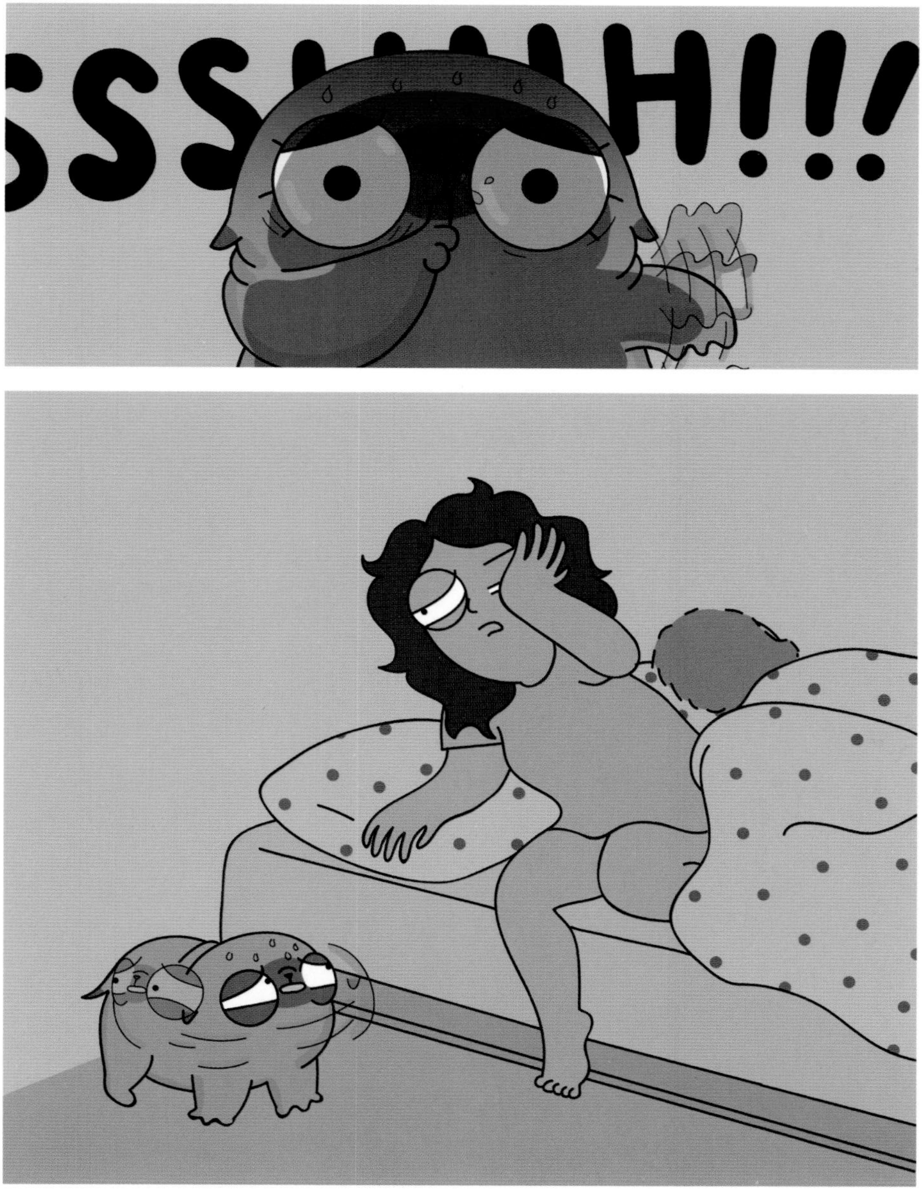
SS H!!!

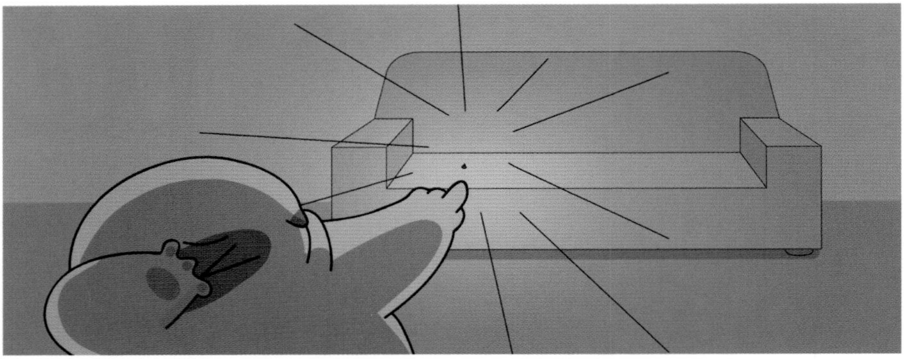

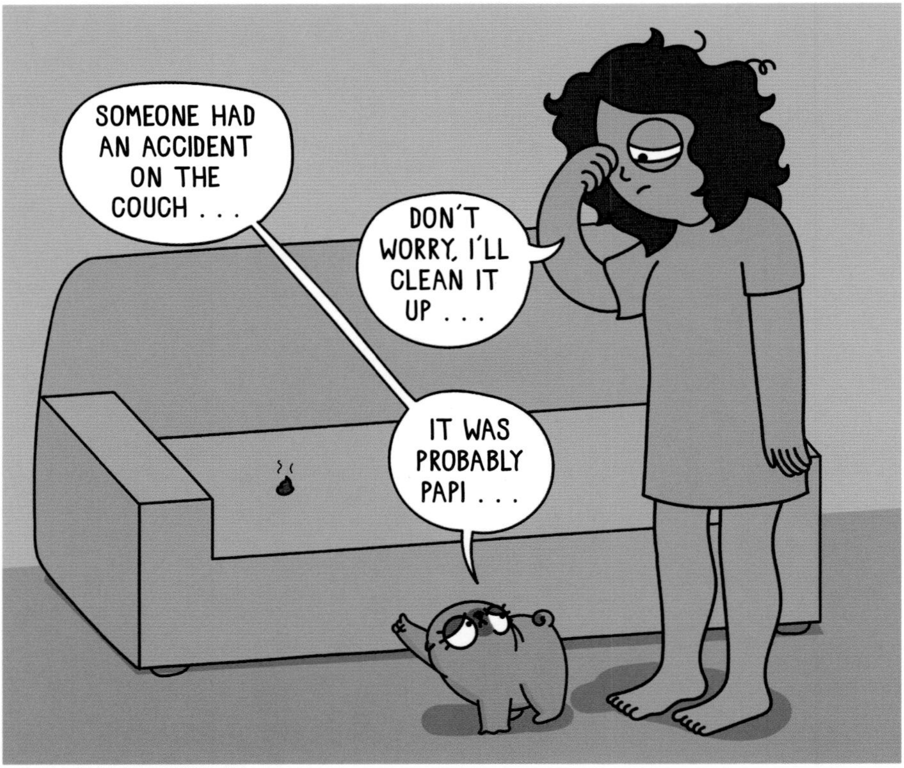
SOMEONE HAD AN ACCIDENT ON THE COUCH . . .
DON'T WORRY, I'LL CLEAN IT UP . . .
IT WAS PROBABLY PAPI . . .

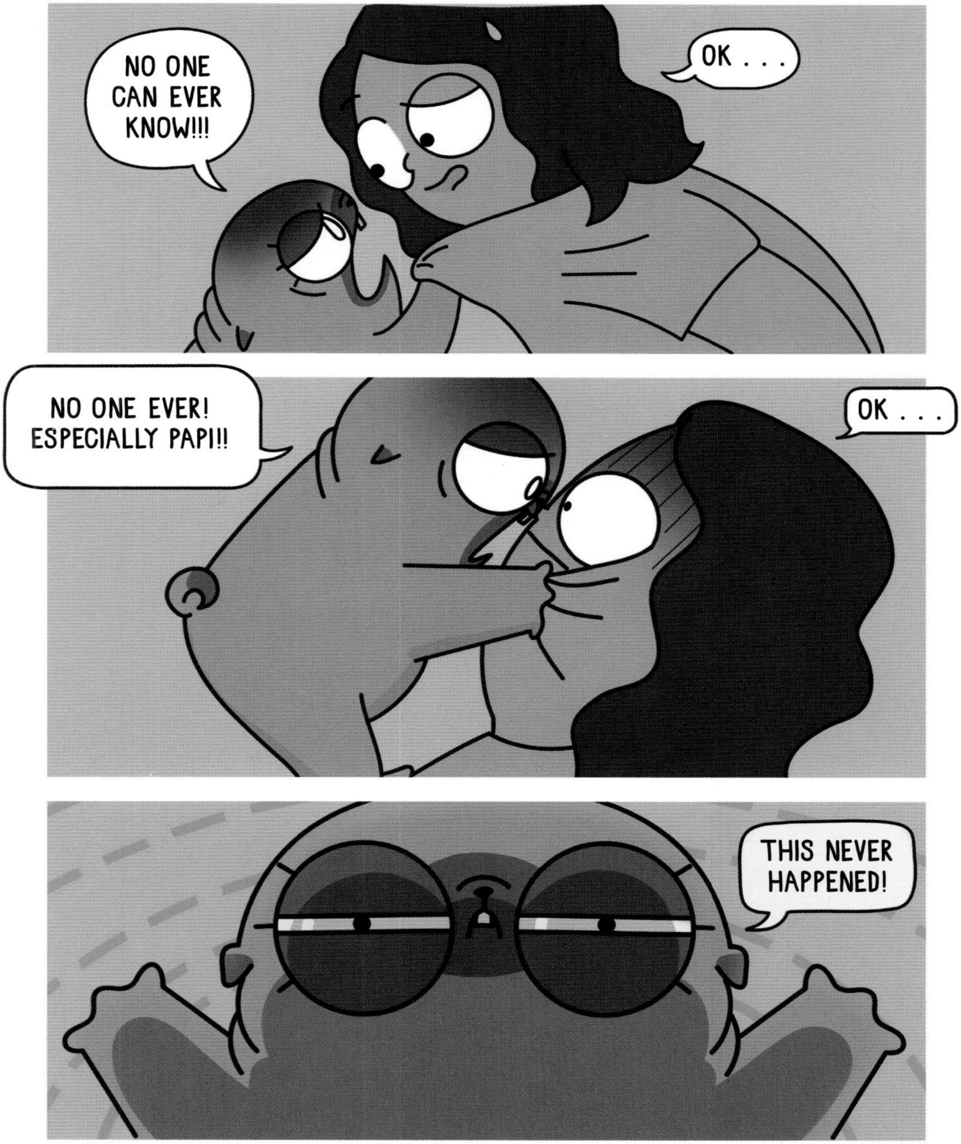
NO ONE CAN EVER KNOW!!!
OK . . .
NO ONE EVER! ESPECIALLY PAPI!!
OK . . .
THIS NEVER HAPPENED!

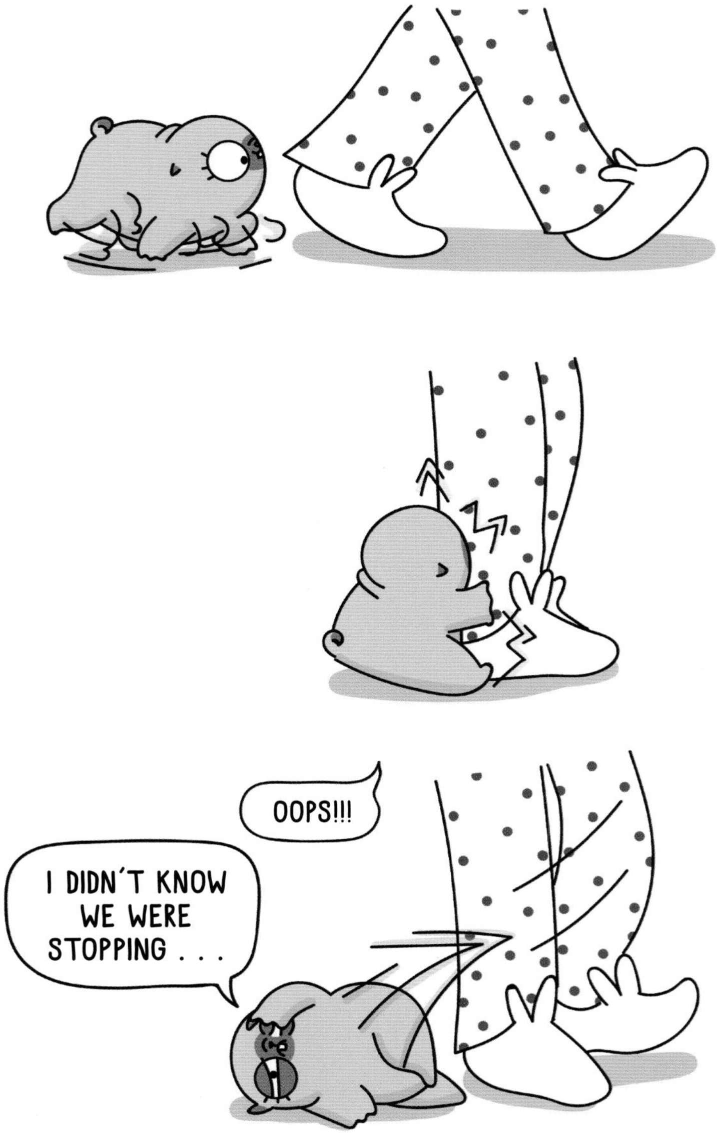
OOPS!!!
I DIDN´T KNOW WE WERE STOPPING . . .

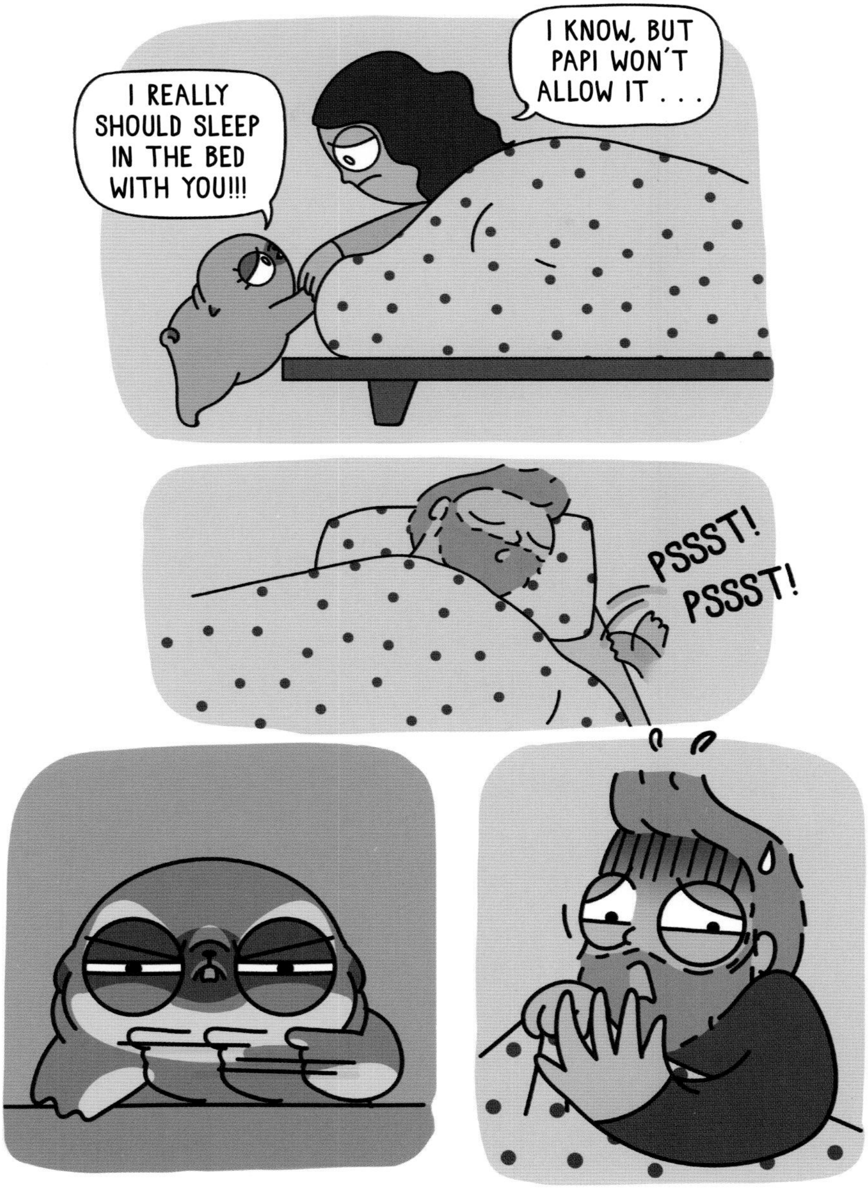
I REALLY SHOULD SLEEP IN THE BED WITH YOU!!!
I KNOW, BUT PAPI WON'T ALLOW IT . . .
PSSST!
PSSST!

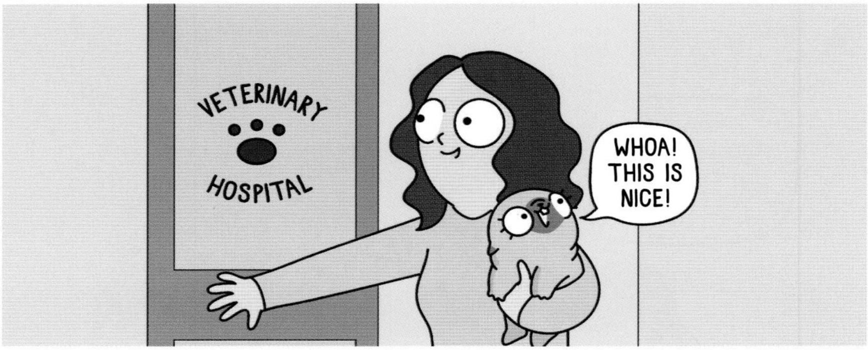
VETERINARY
HOSPITAL
WHOA! THIS IS NICE!

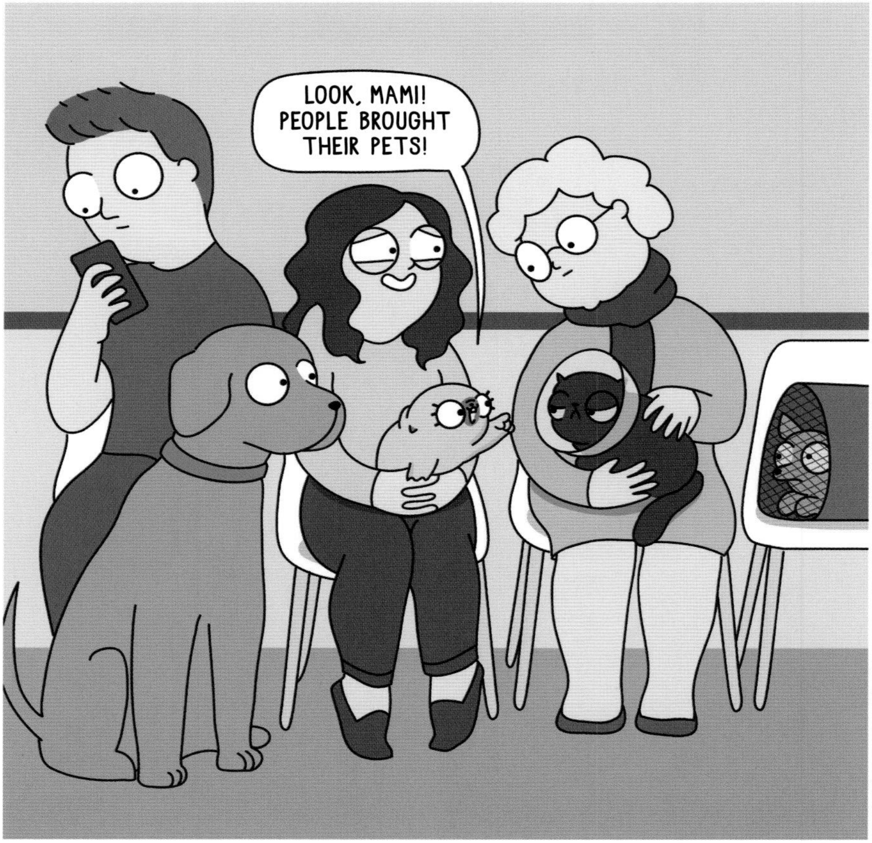
LOOK, MAMI! PEOPLE BROUGHT THEIR PETS!

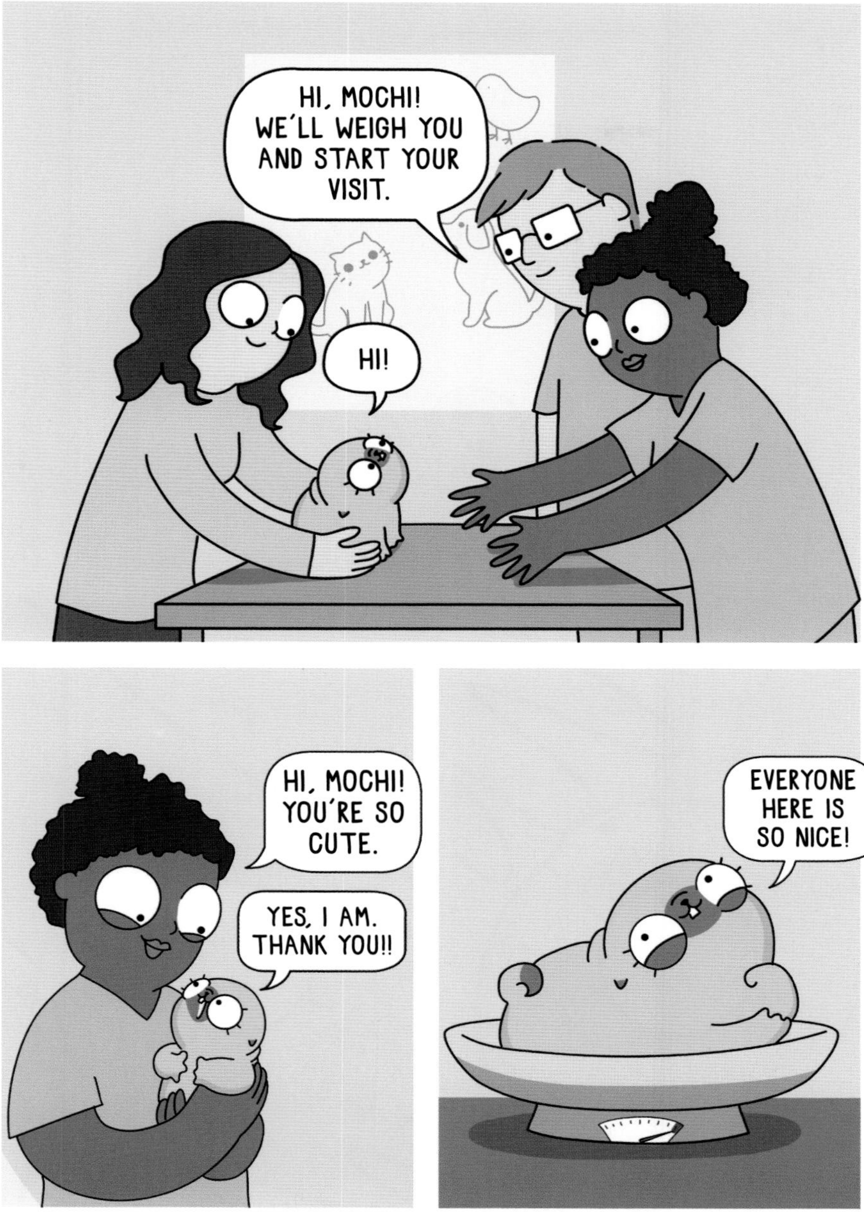
HI, MOCHI! WE'LL WEIGH YOU AND START YOUR VISIT.
HI!
HI, MOCHI! YOU'RE SO CUTE.
YES, I AM. THANK YOU!!
EVERYONE HERE IS SO NICE!

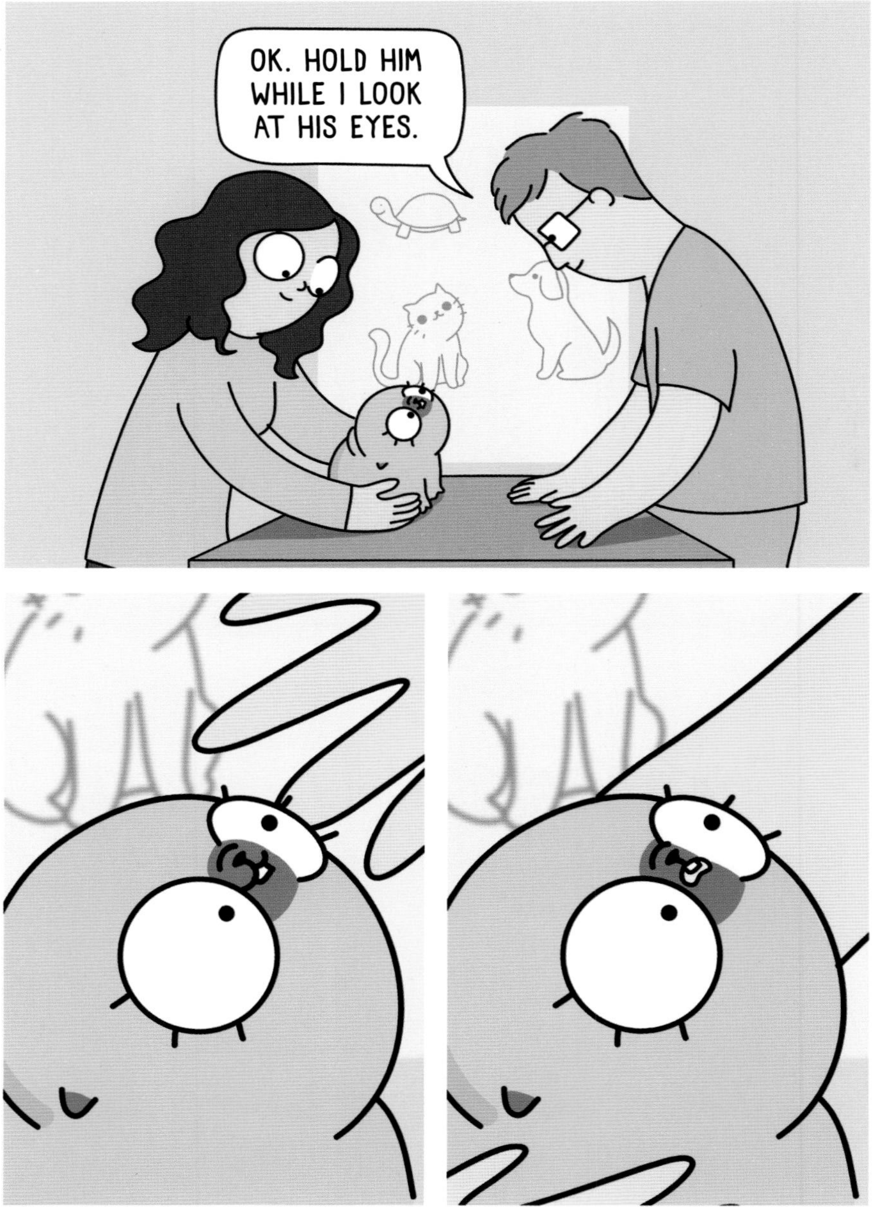
OK. HOLD HIM WHILE I LOOK AT HIS EYES.

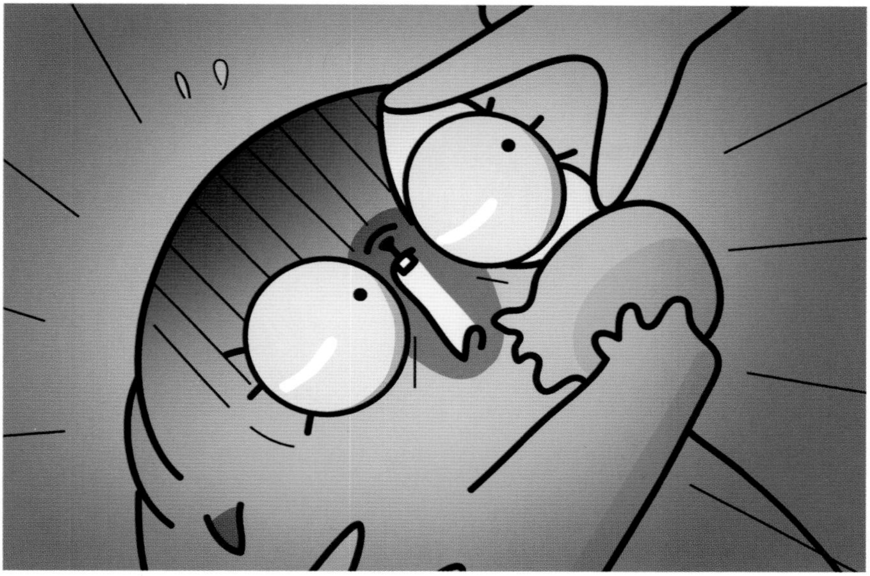

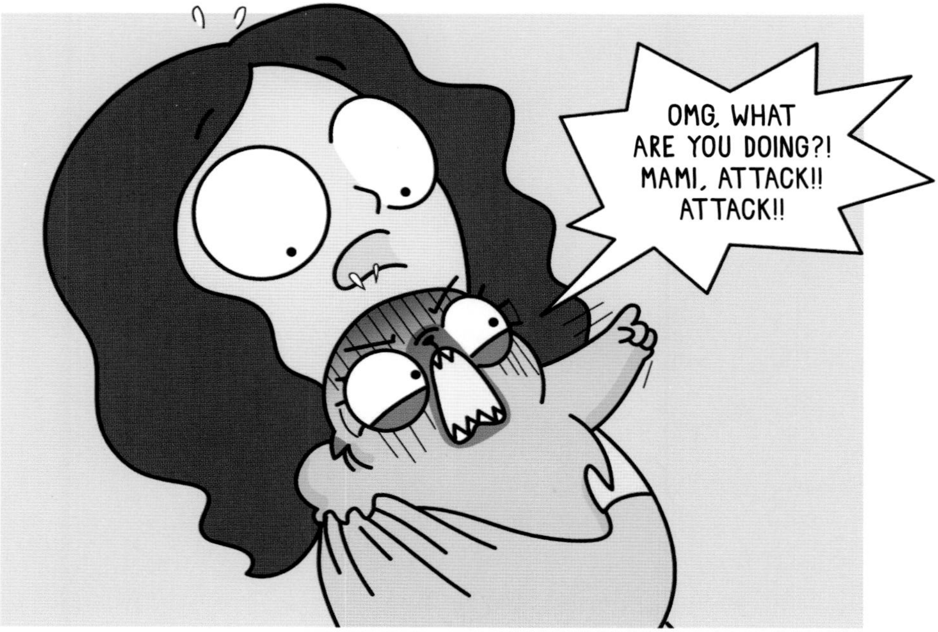
OMG, WHAT
ARE YOU DOING?!
MAMI, ATTACK!!
ATTACK!!

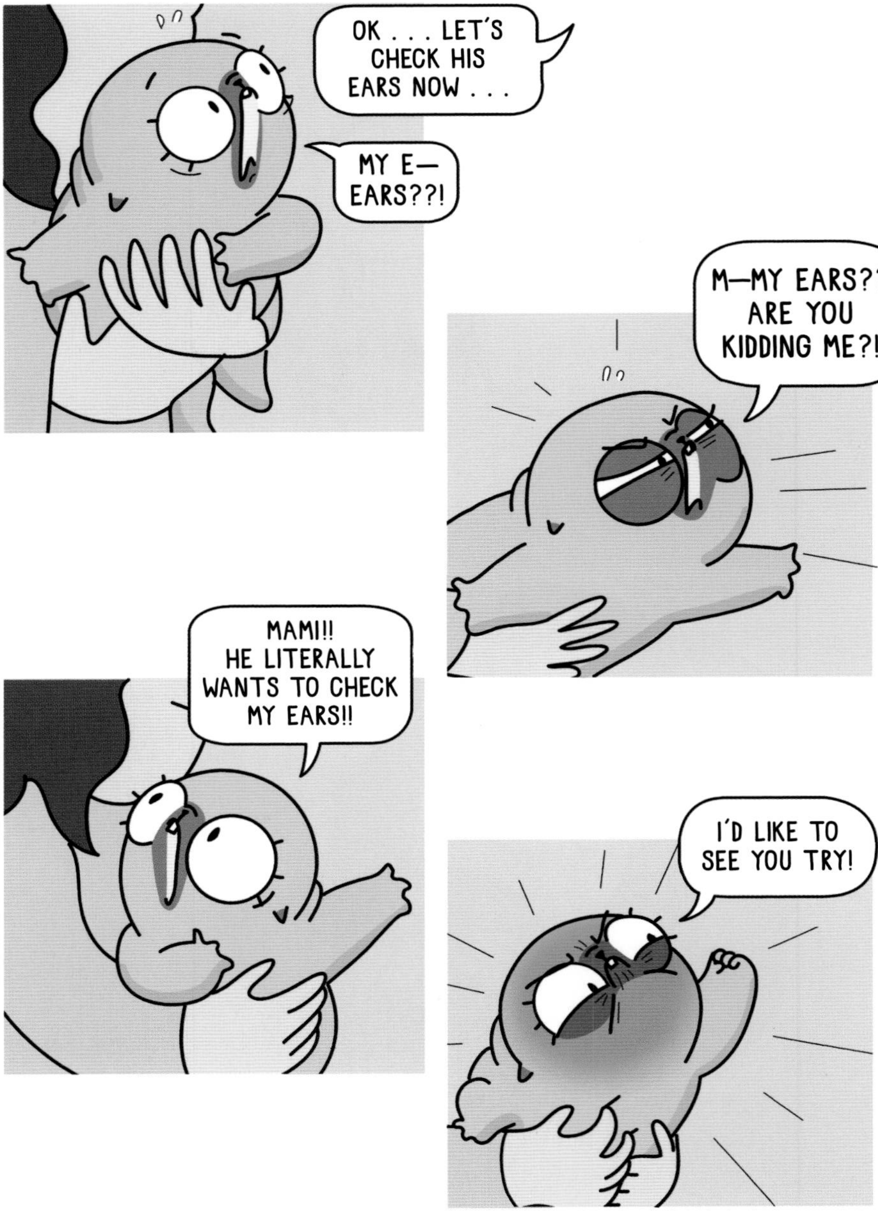
OK . . . LET'S CHECK HIS EARS NOW . . .
MY E— EARS??!
M—MY EARS?? ARE YOU KIDDING ME?!
MAMI!! HE LITERALLY WANTS TO CHECK MY EARS!!
I'D LIKE TO SEE YOU TRY!

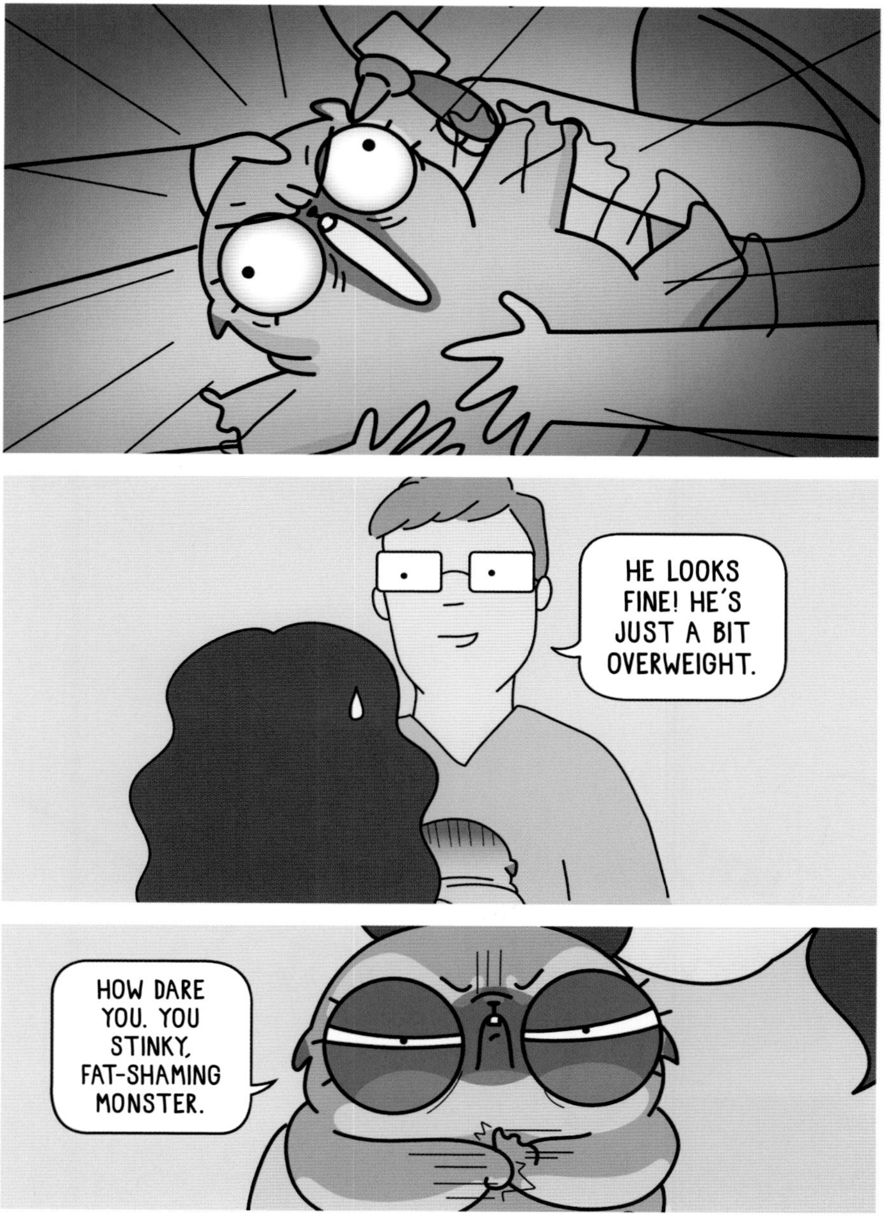
HE LOOKS FINE! HE'S JUST A BIT OVERWEIGHT.
HOW DARE YOU. YOU STINKY, FAT-SHAMING MONSTER.

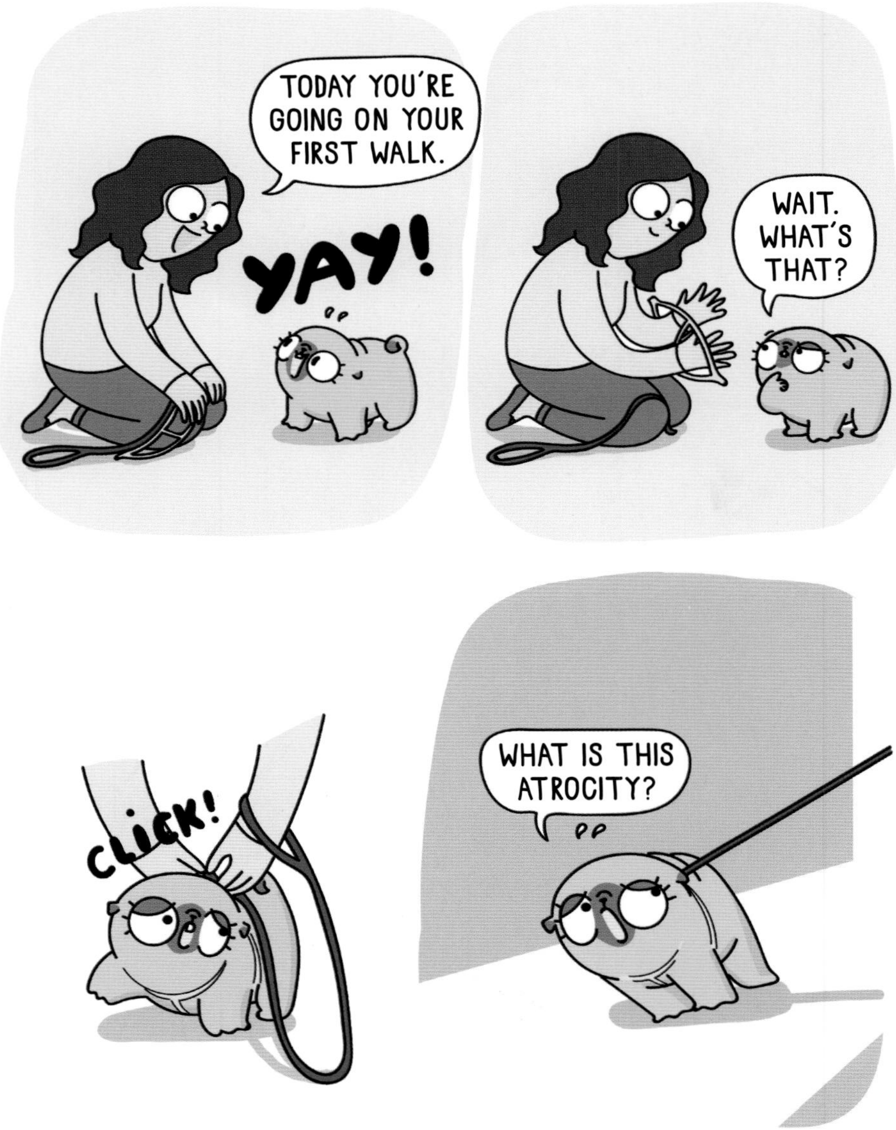
TODAY YOU'RE GOING ON YOUR FIRST WALK.
YAY!
WAIT. WHAT'S THAT?
CLICK!
WHAT IS THIS ATROCITY?

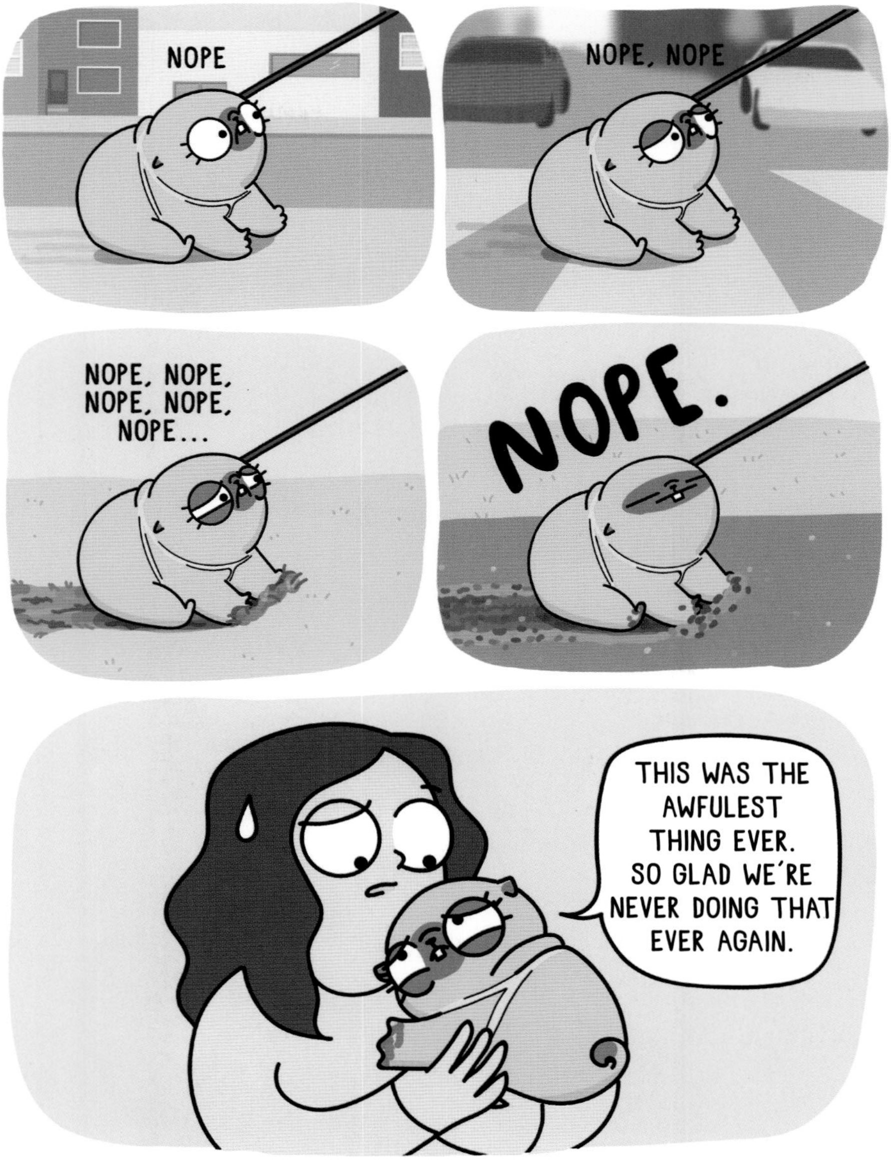
NOPE
NOPE, NOPE
NOPE, NOPE, NOPE, NOPE, NOPE...
NOPE.
THIS WAS THE AWFULEST THING EVER. SO GLAD WE'RE NEVER DOING THAT EVER AGAIN.

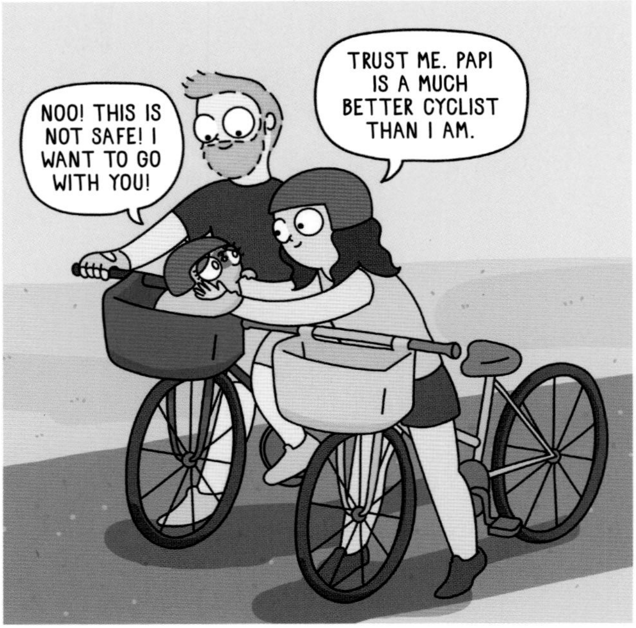
NOO! THIS IS NOT SAFE! I WANT TO GO WITH YOU!
TRUST ME. PAPI IS A MUCH BETTER CYCLIST THAN I AM.

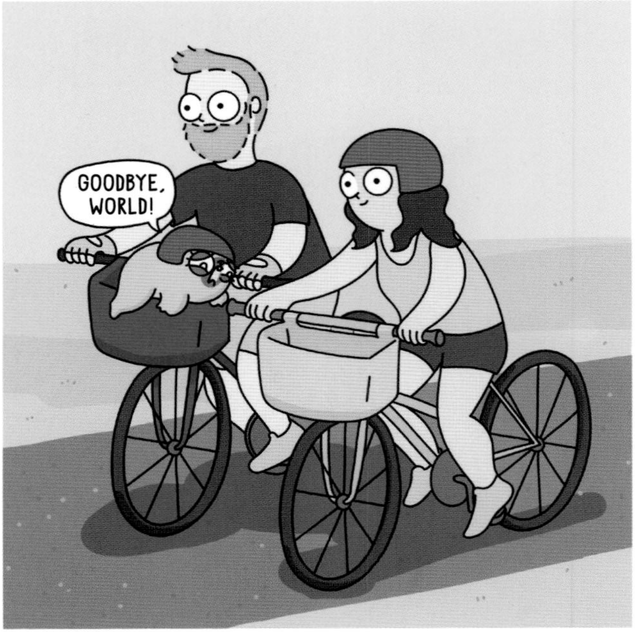
GOODBYE, WORLD!

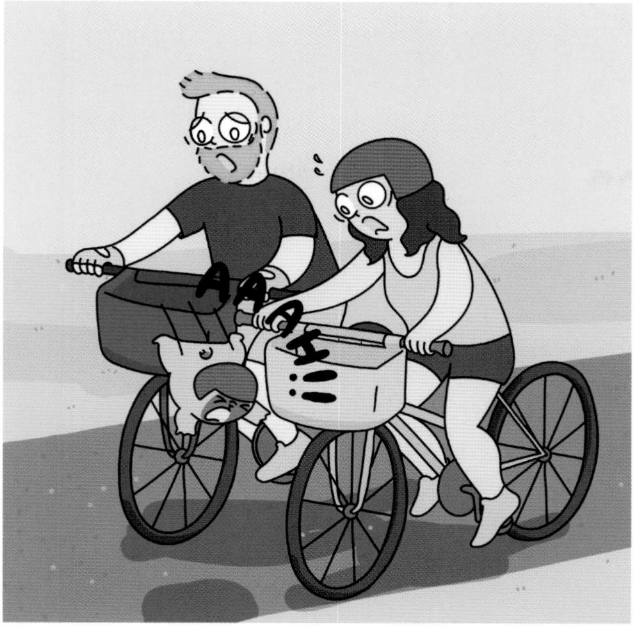
AAAH!!!

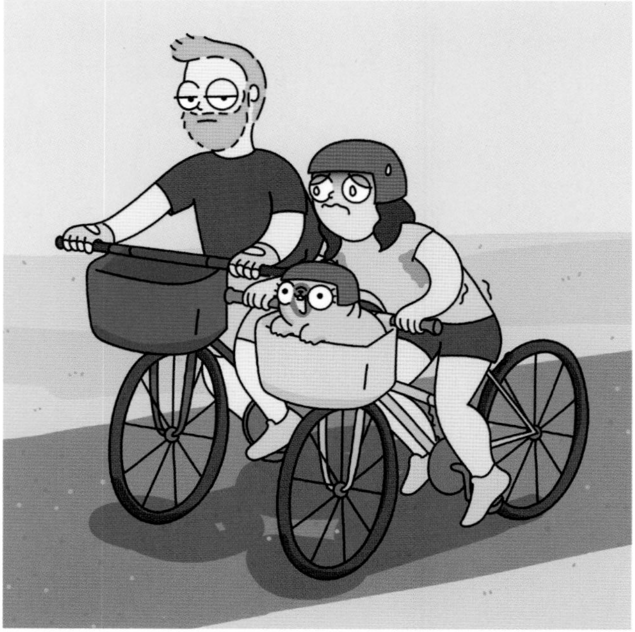

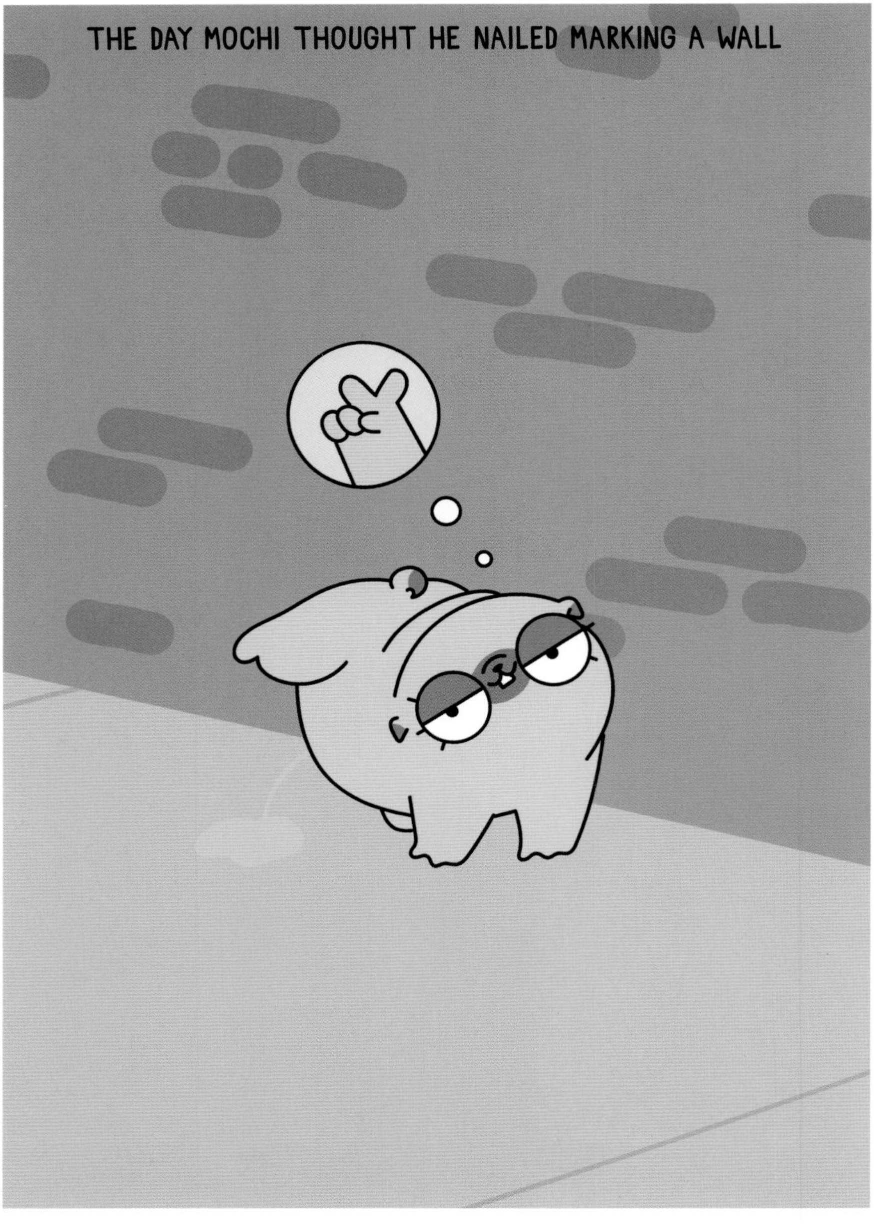
THE DAY MOCHI THOUGHT HE NAILED MARKING A WALL

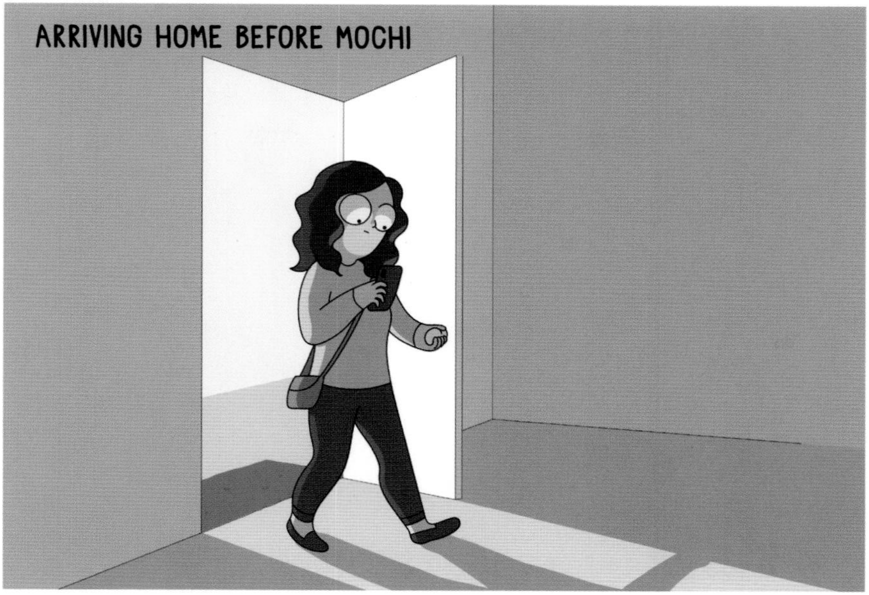
ARRIVING HOME BEFORE MOCHI

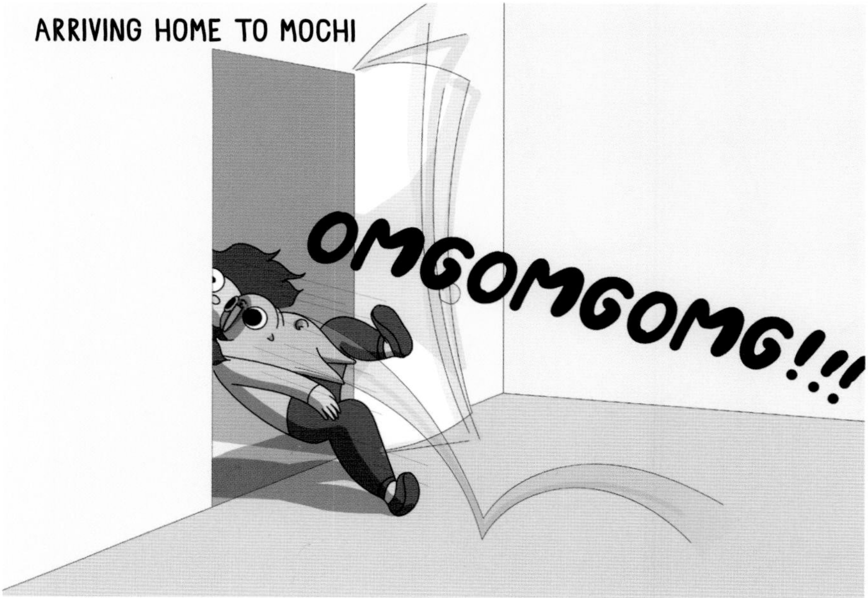
ARRIVING HOME TO MOCHI
OMGOMGOMG!!!

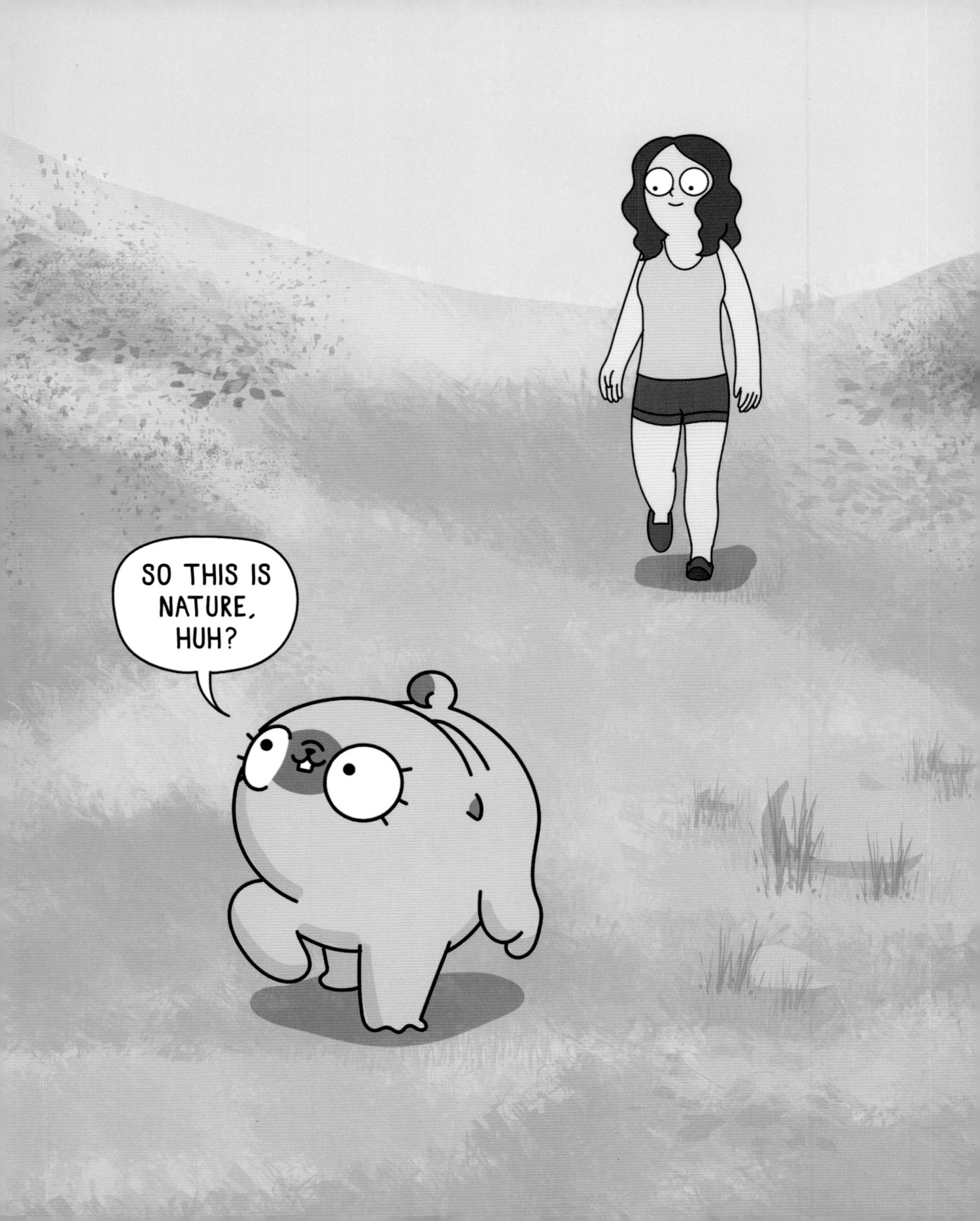
SO THIS IS NATURE, HUH?

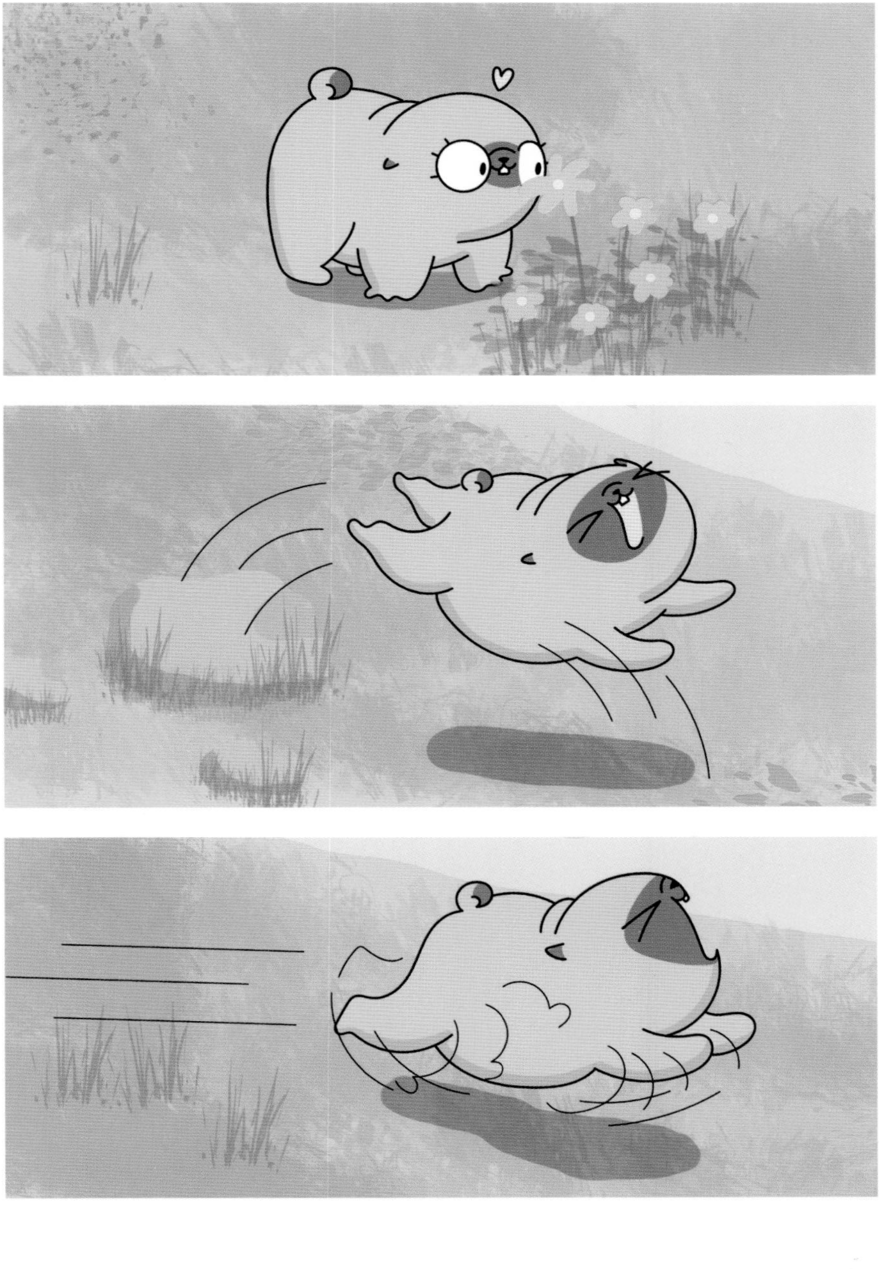

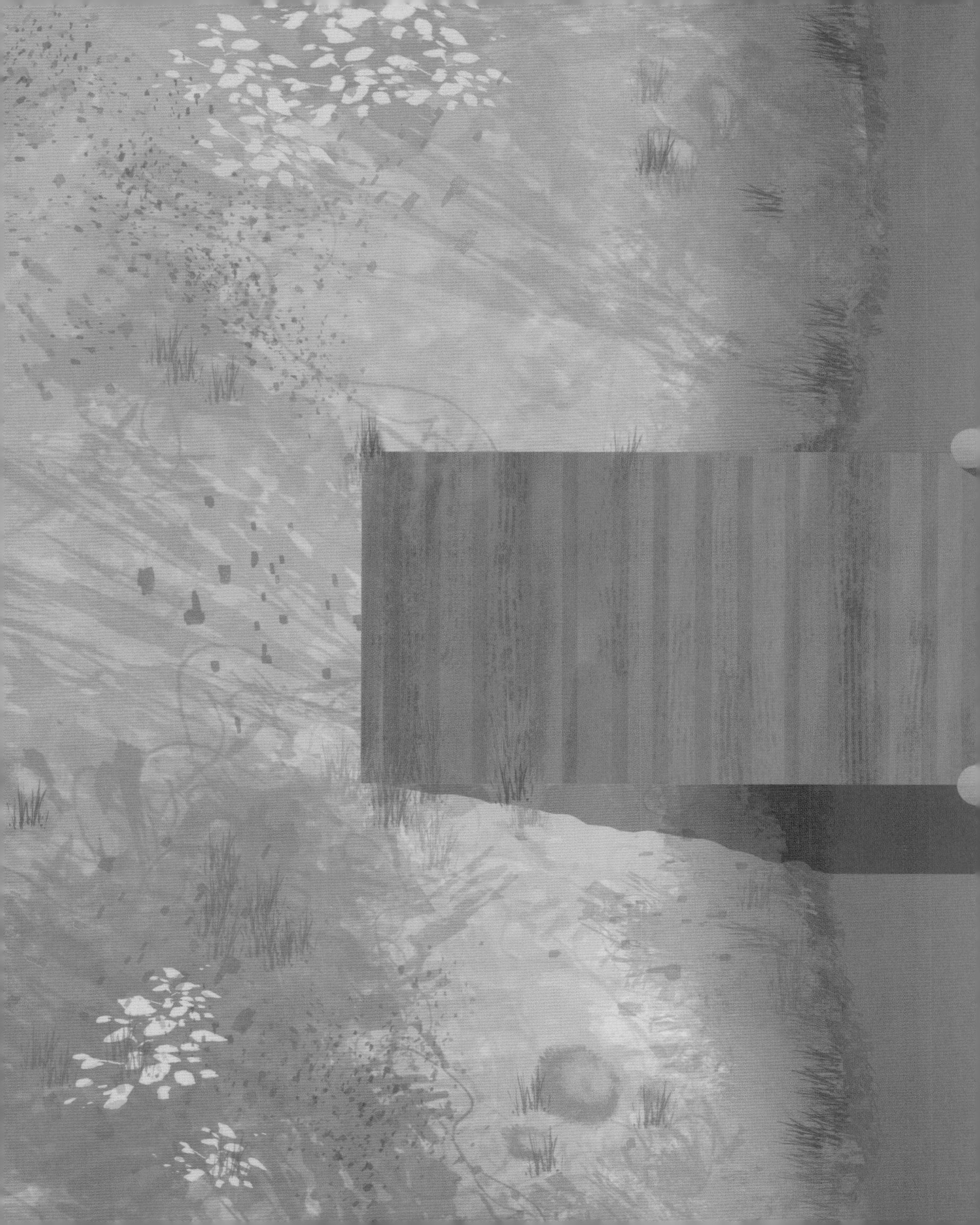

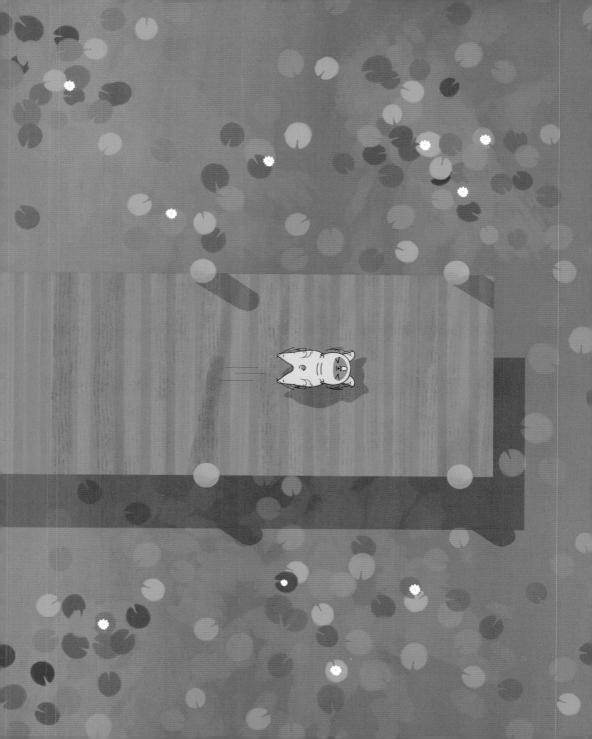

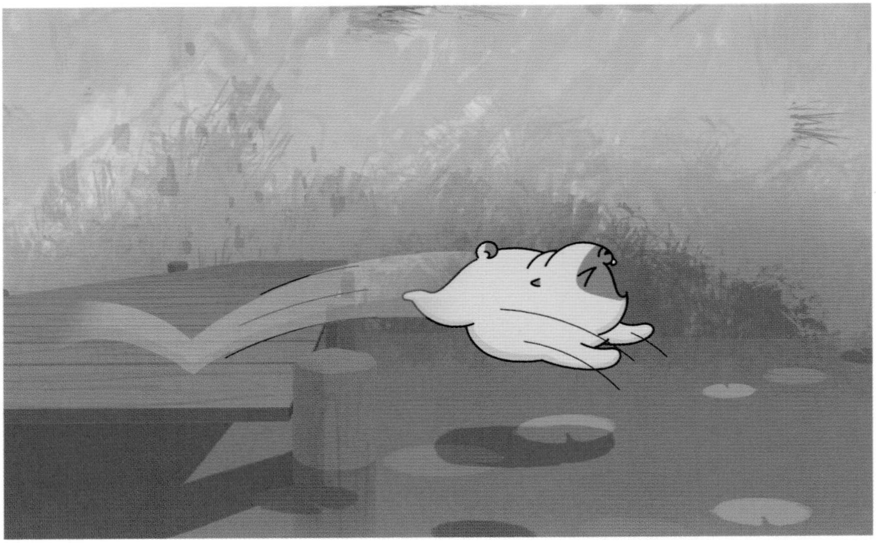

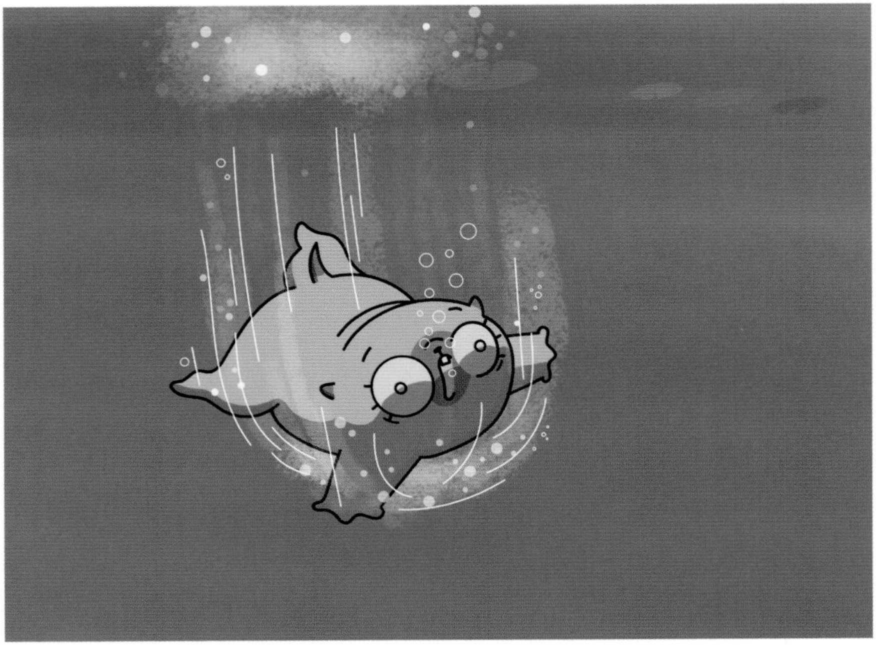

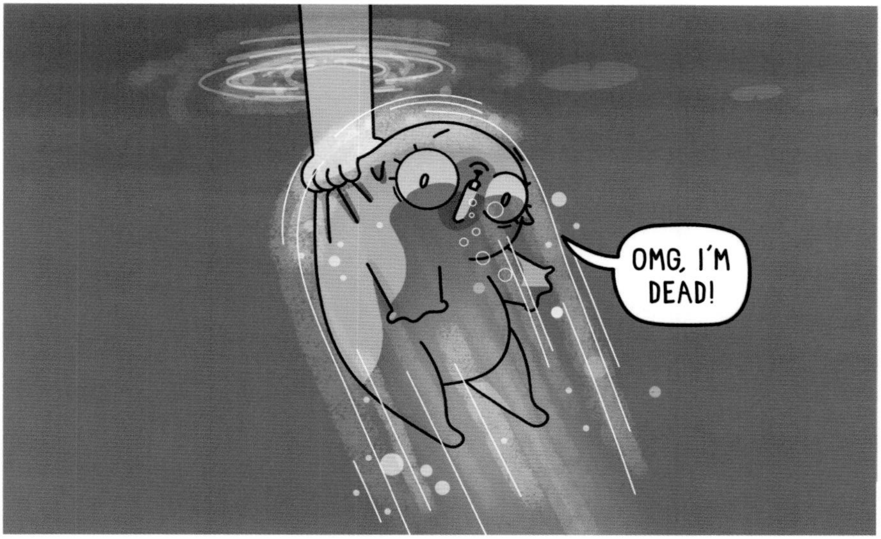
OMG, I'M
DEAD!

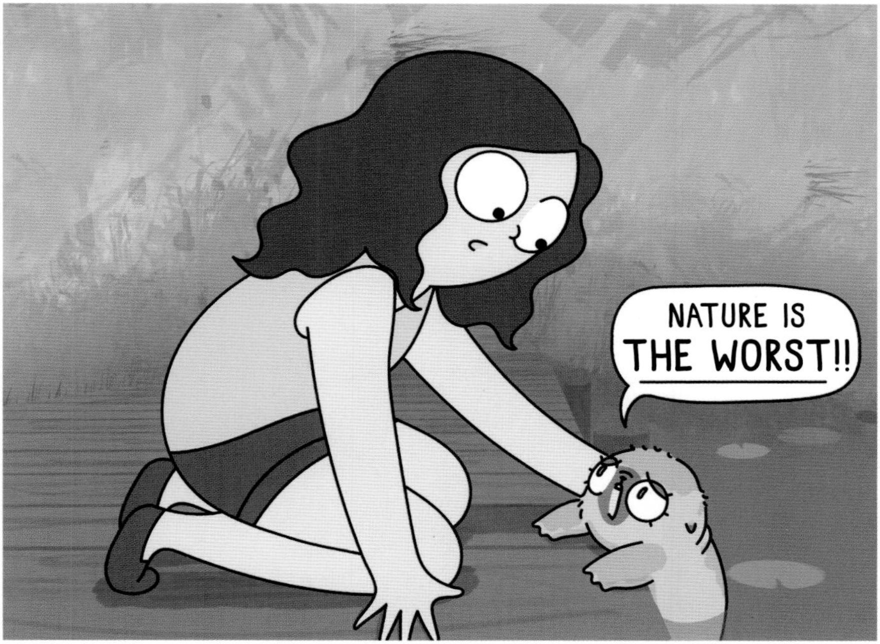
NATURE IS
THE WORST!!

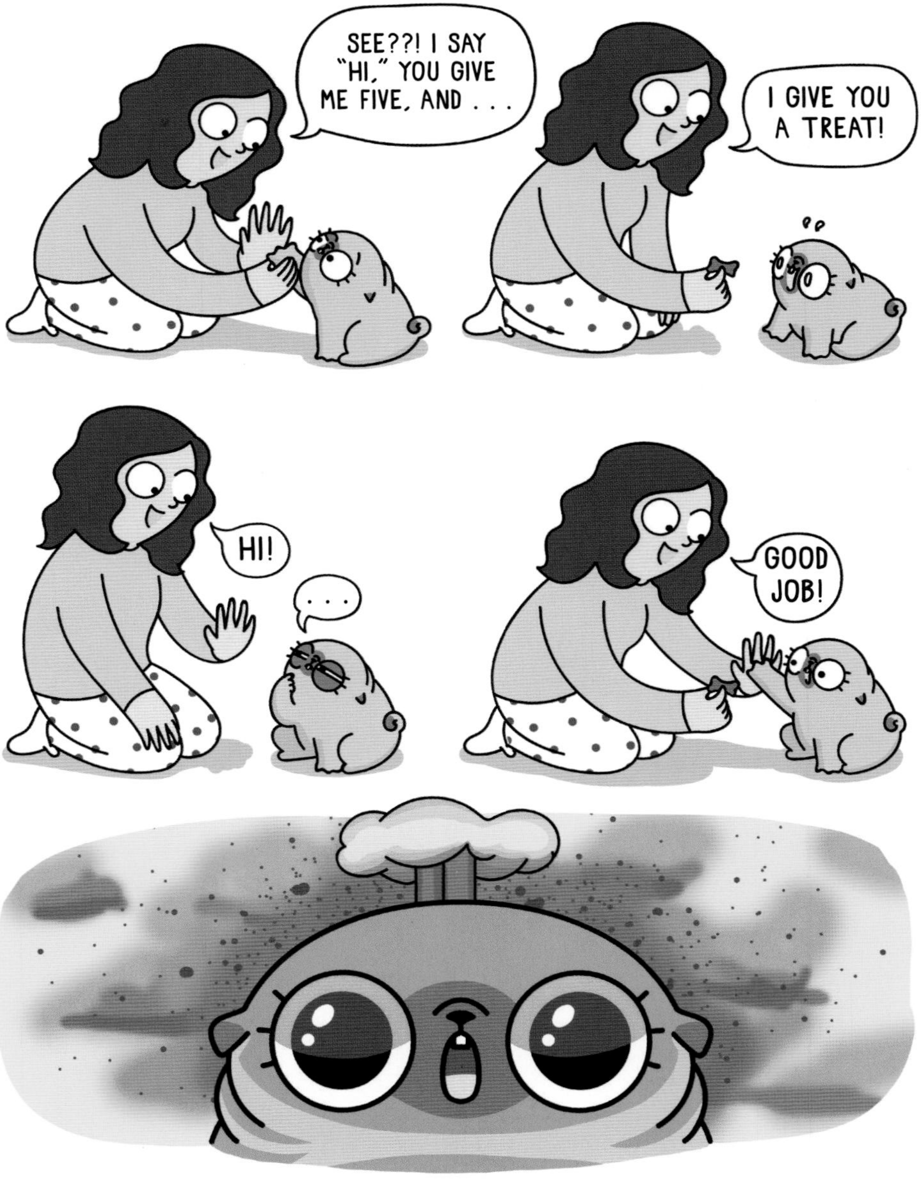
SEE??! I SAY "HI," YOU GIVE ME FIVE, AND . . .
I GIVE YOU A TREAT!
HI!
. . .
GOOD JOB!

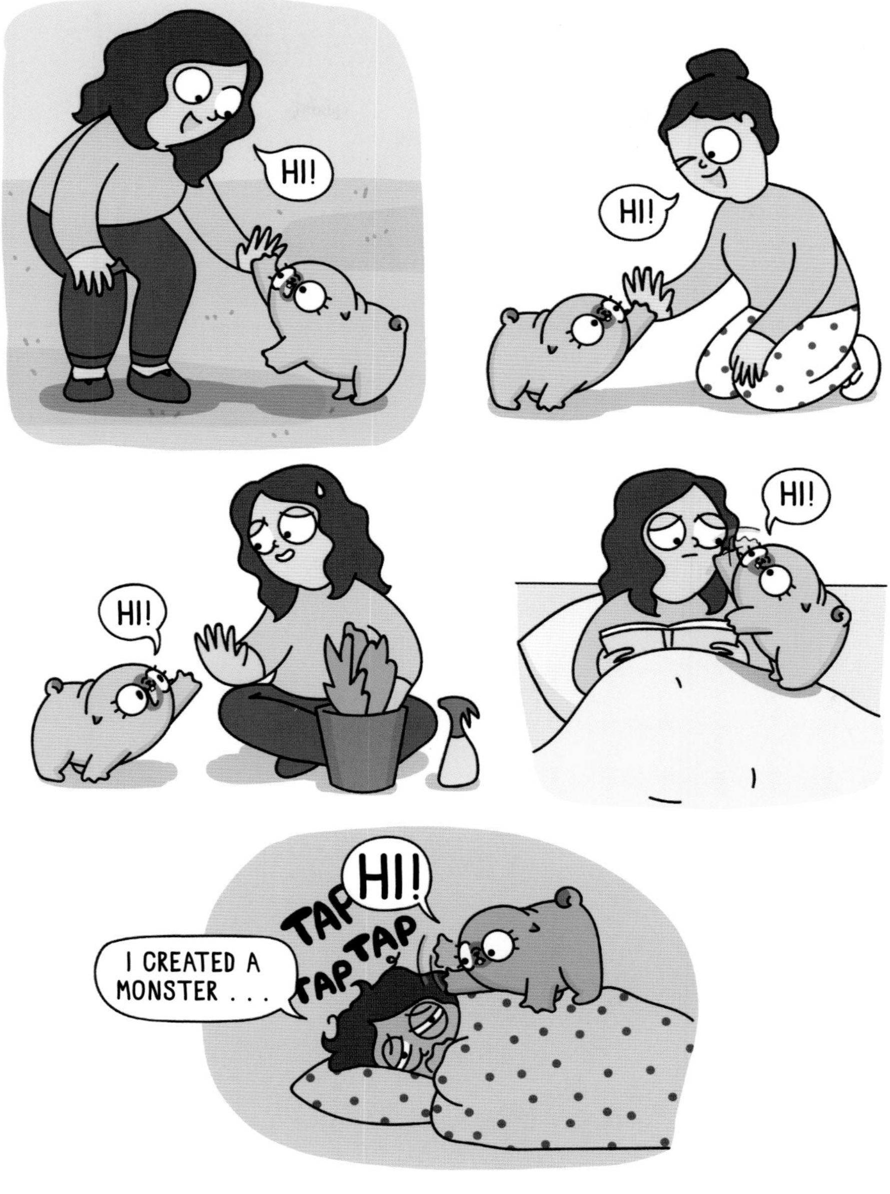
HI!
HI!
HI!
HI!
HI!
TAP
TAP TAP
I CREATED A MONSTER . . .

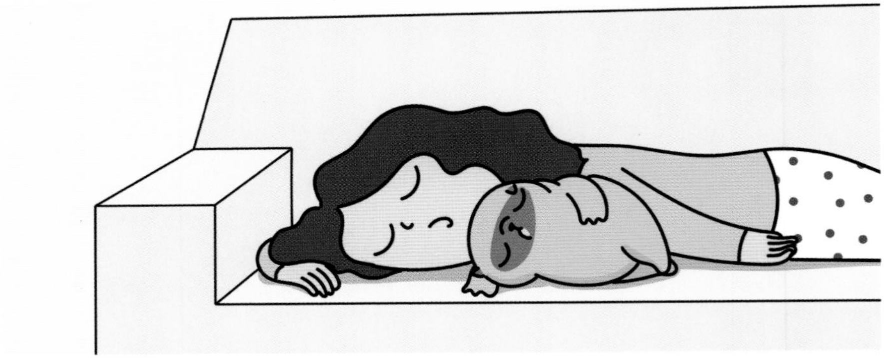

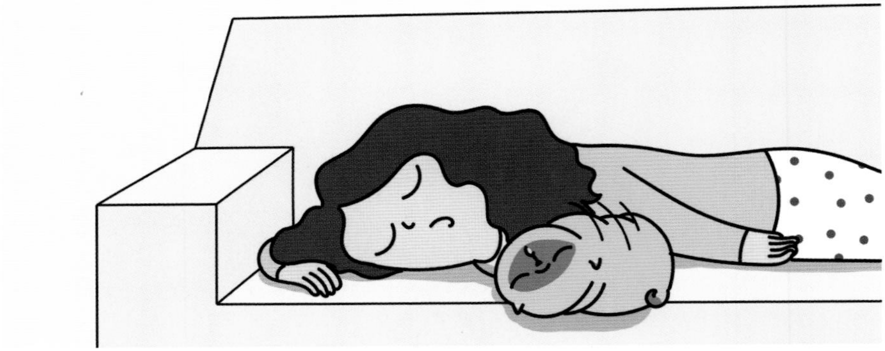

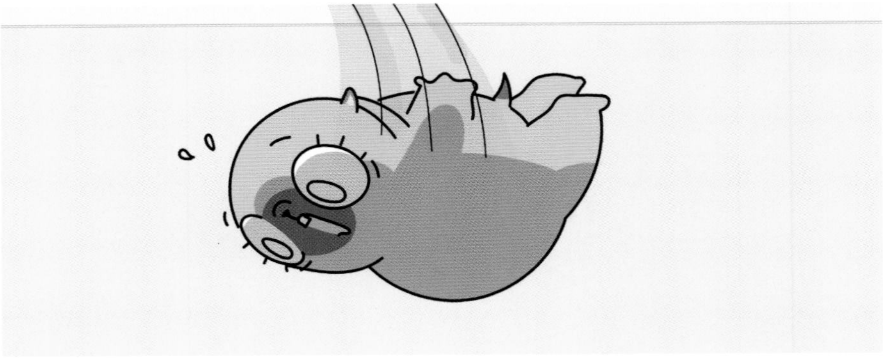

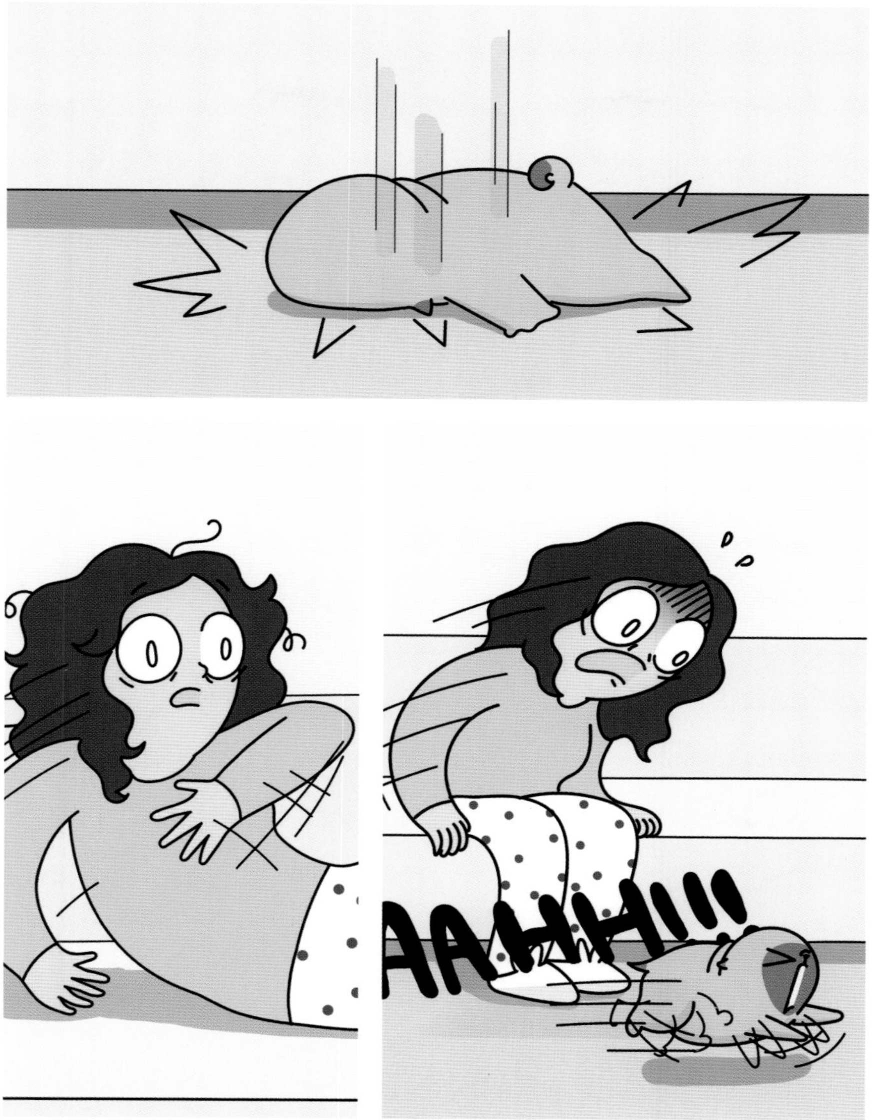
AAHHH!!!

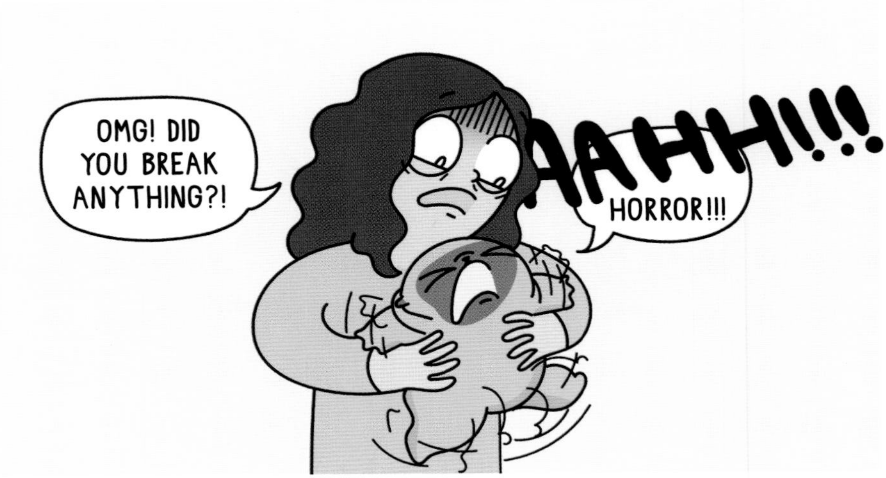
OMG! DID YOU BREAK ANYTHING?!
AAHH!!!
HORROR!!!

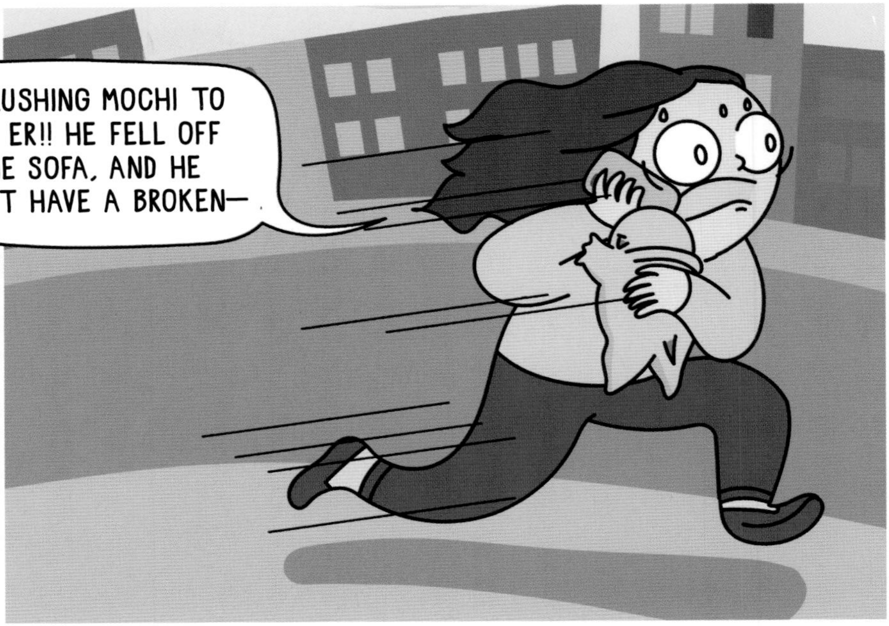
I'M RUSHING MOCHI TO THE ER!! HE FELL OFF THE SOFA, AND HE MIGHT HAVE A BROKEN—

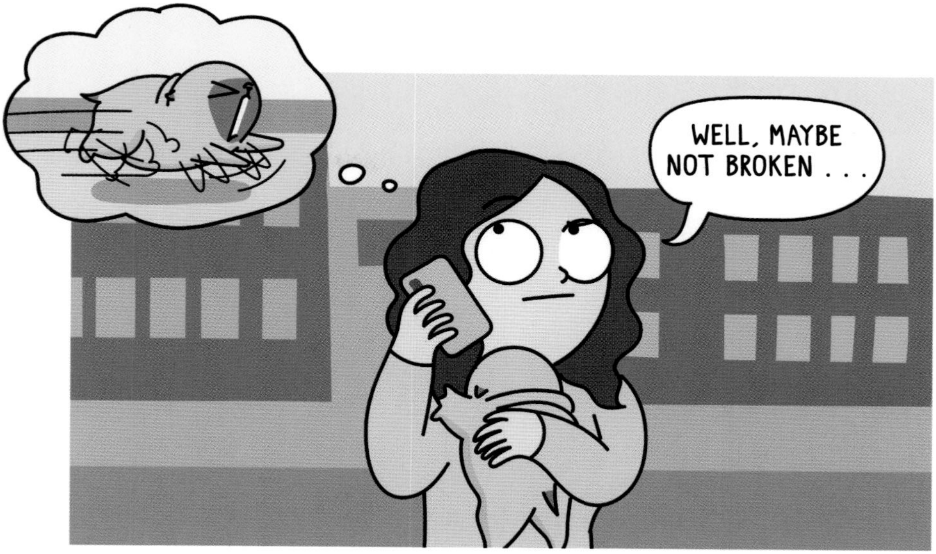
WELL, MAYBE NOT BROKEN . . .

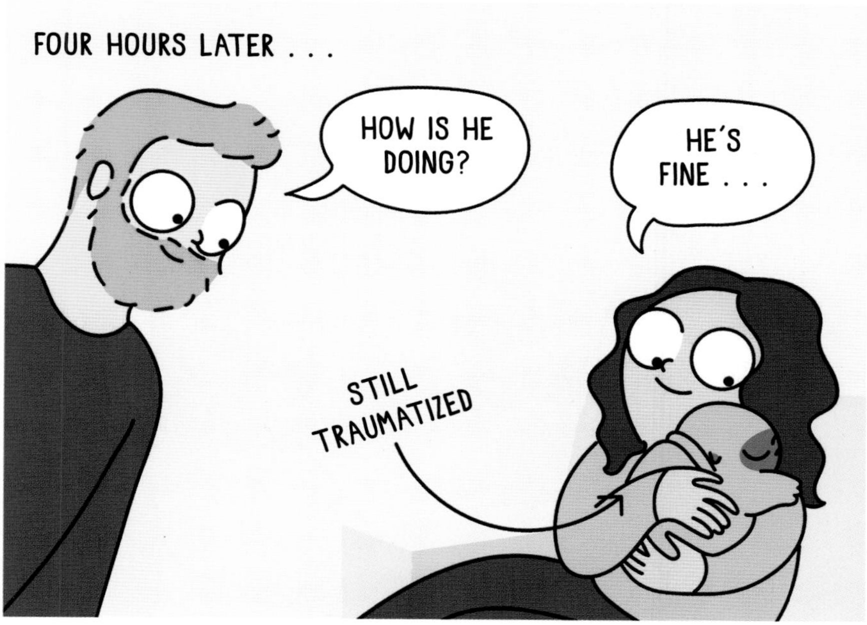
FOUR HOURS LATER . . .
HOW IS HE DOING?
HE'S FINE . . .
STILL TRAUMATIZED

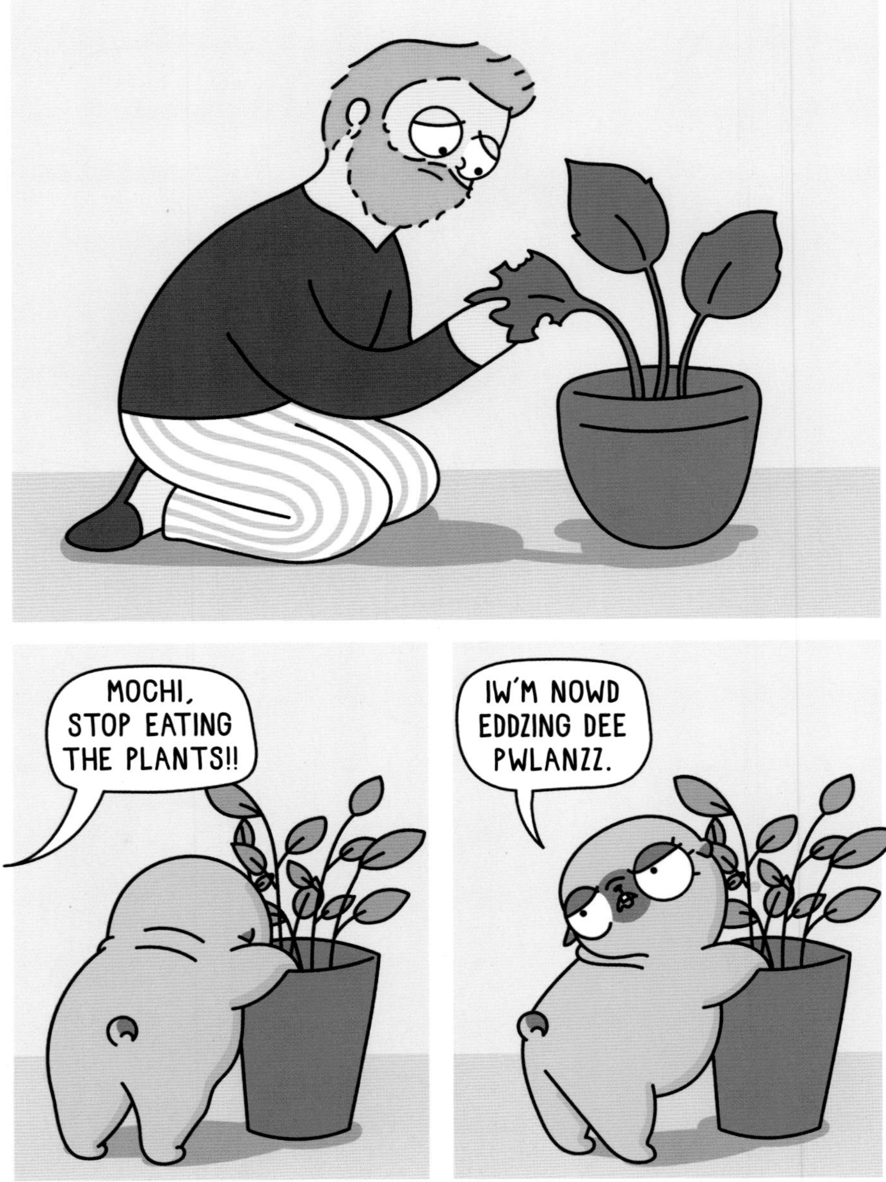
MOCHI, STOP EATING THE PLANTS!!
IW'M NOWD EDDZING DEE PWLANZZ.

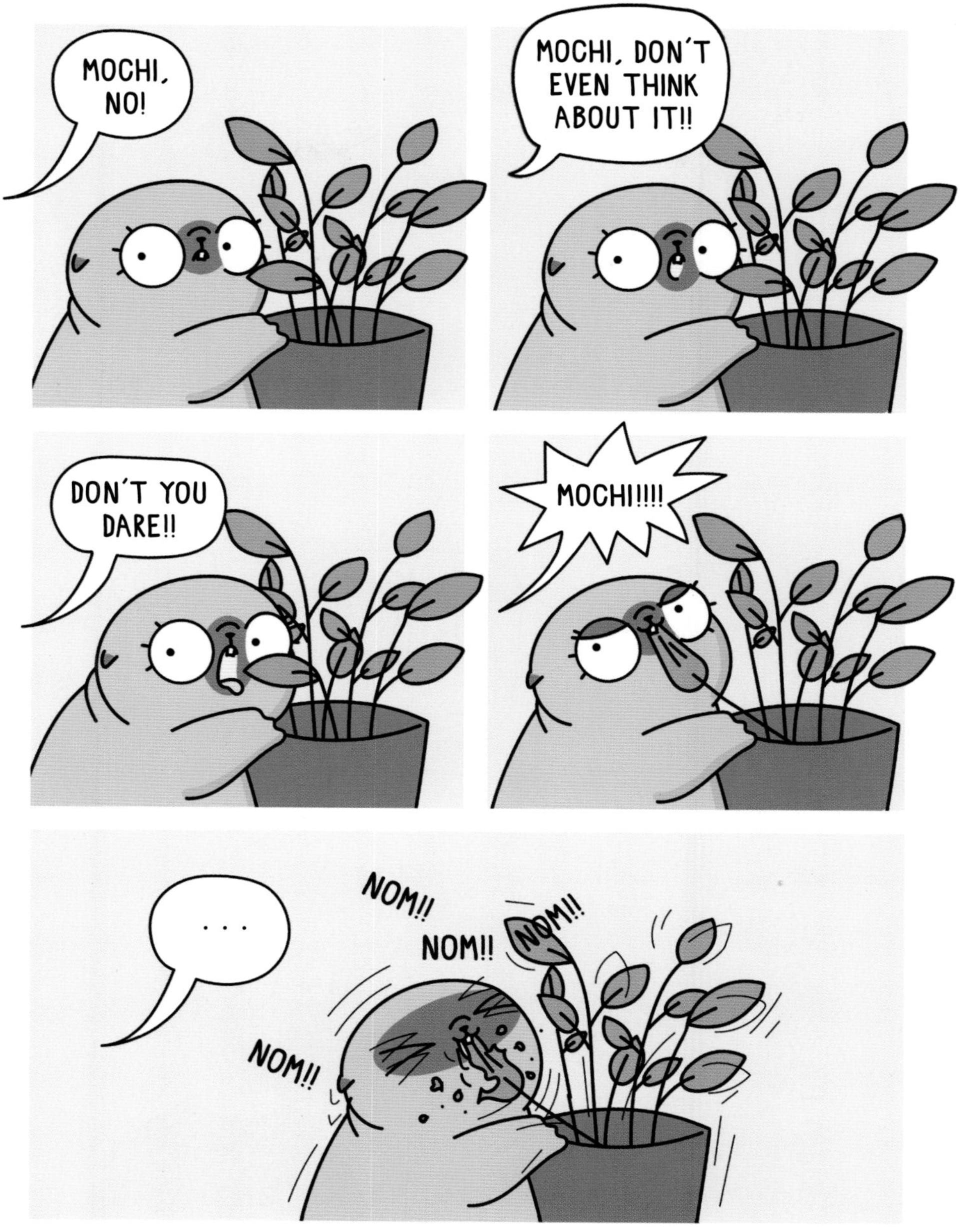
MOCHI, NO!
MOCHI, DON'T EVEN THINK ABOUT IT!!
DON'T YOU DARE!!
MOCHI!!!!!
. . .
NOM!!
NOM!!
NOM!!
NOM!!

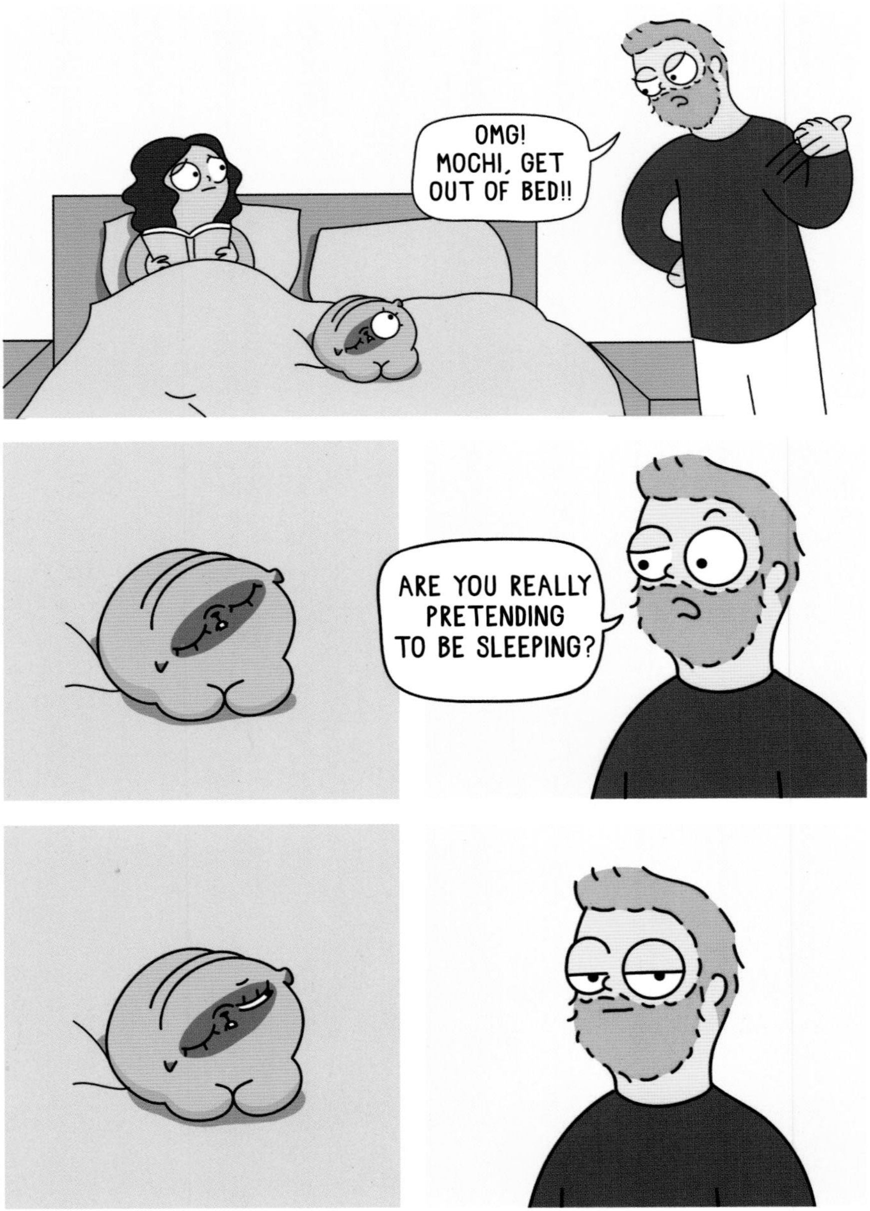
OMG!
MOCHI, GET
OUT OF BED!!
ARE YOU REALLY
PRETENDING
TO BE SLEEPING?

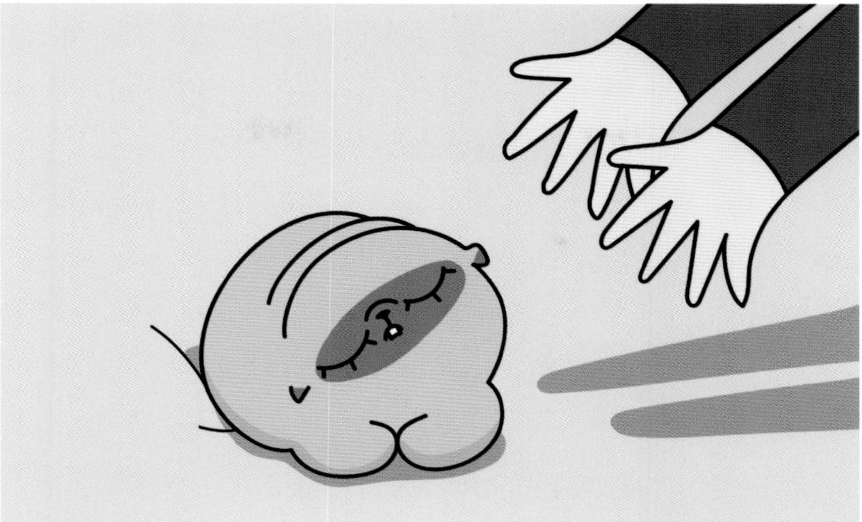

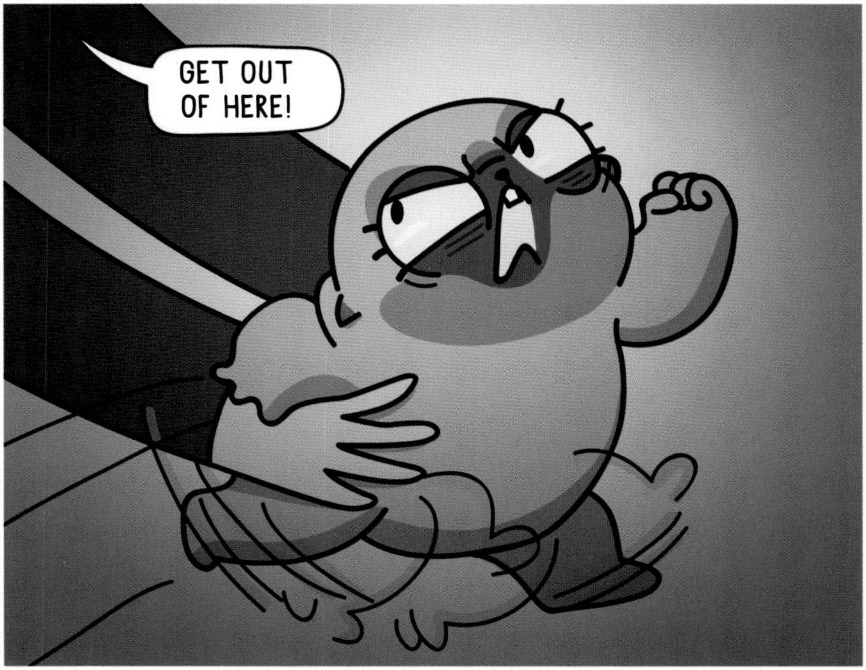
GET OUT OF HERE!

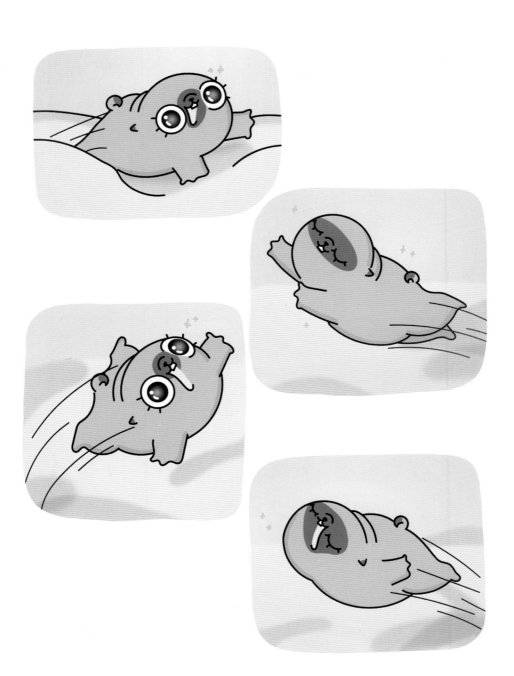

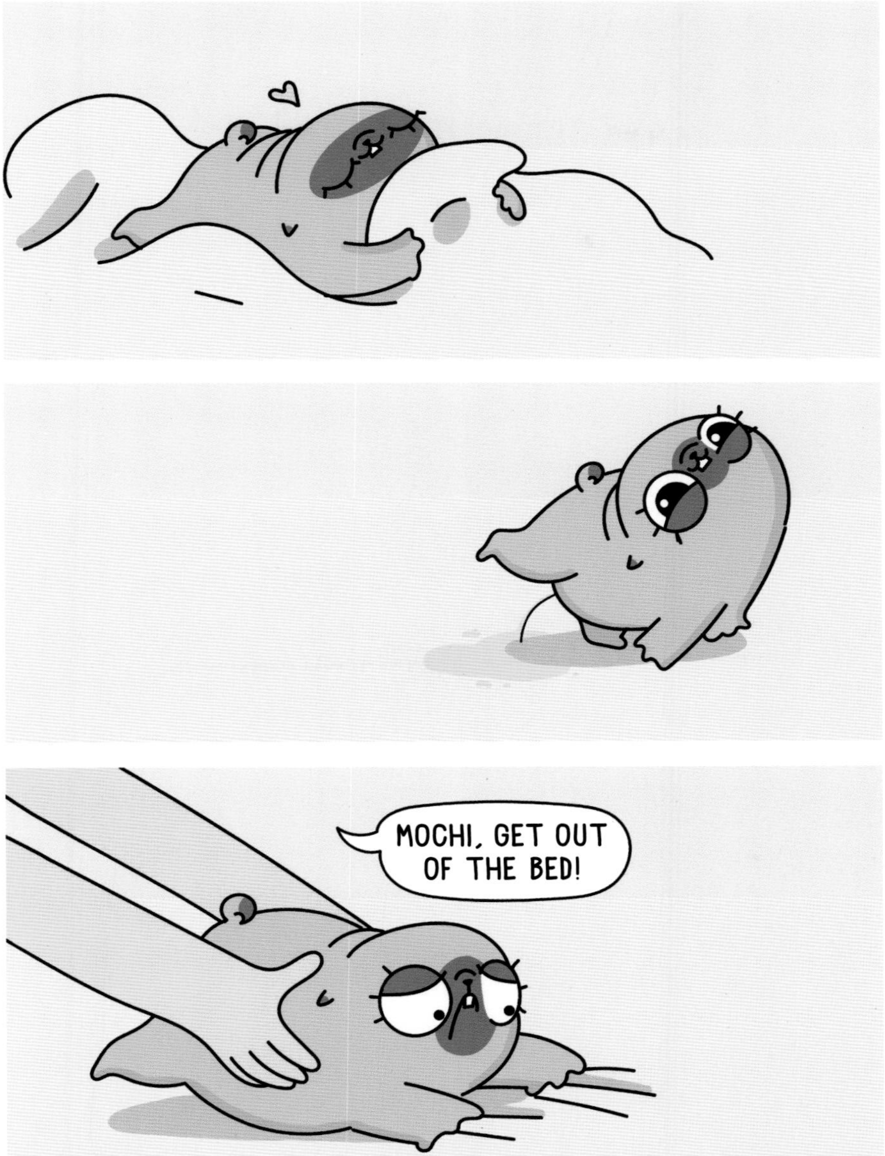
MOCHI, GET OUT OF THE BED!

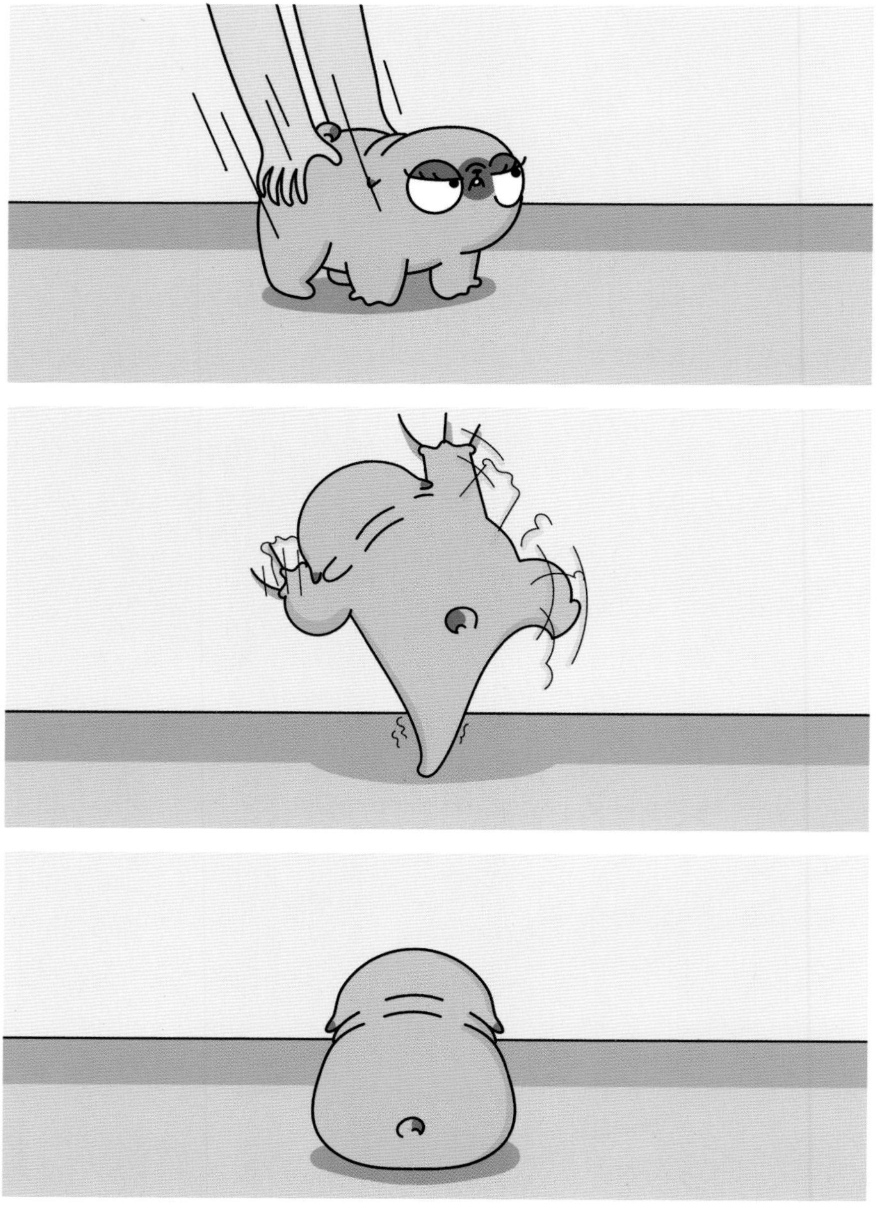

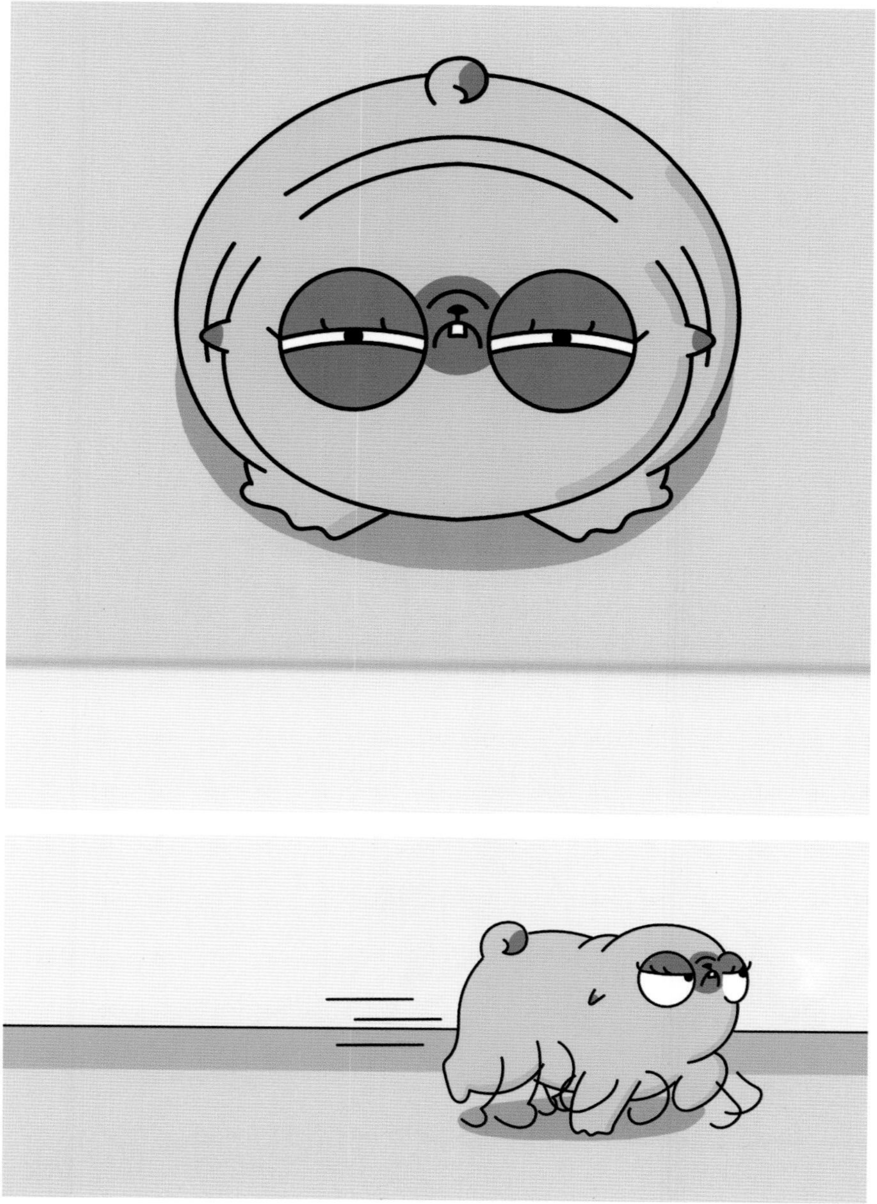

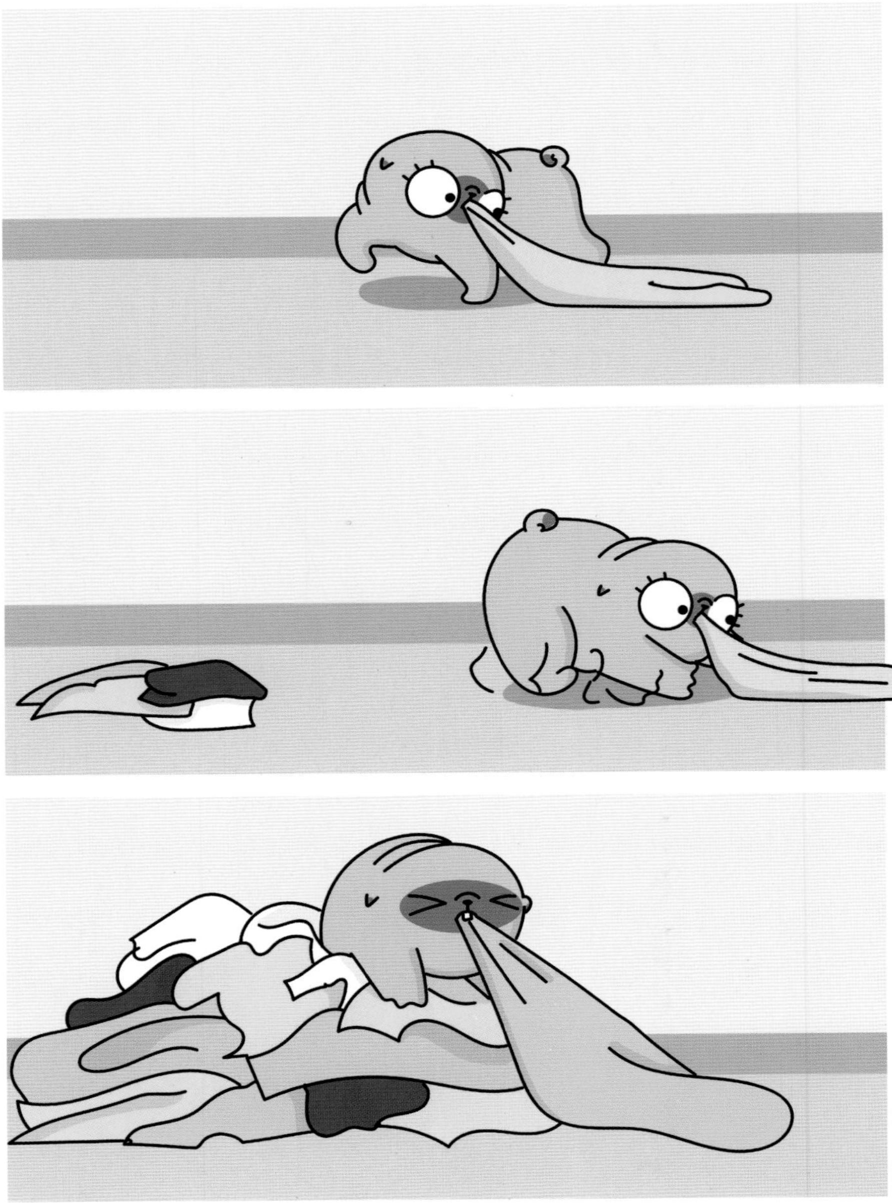

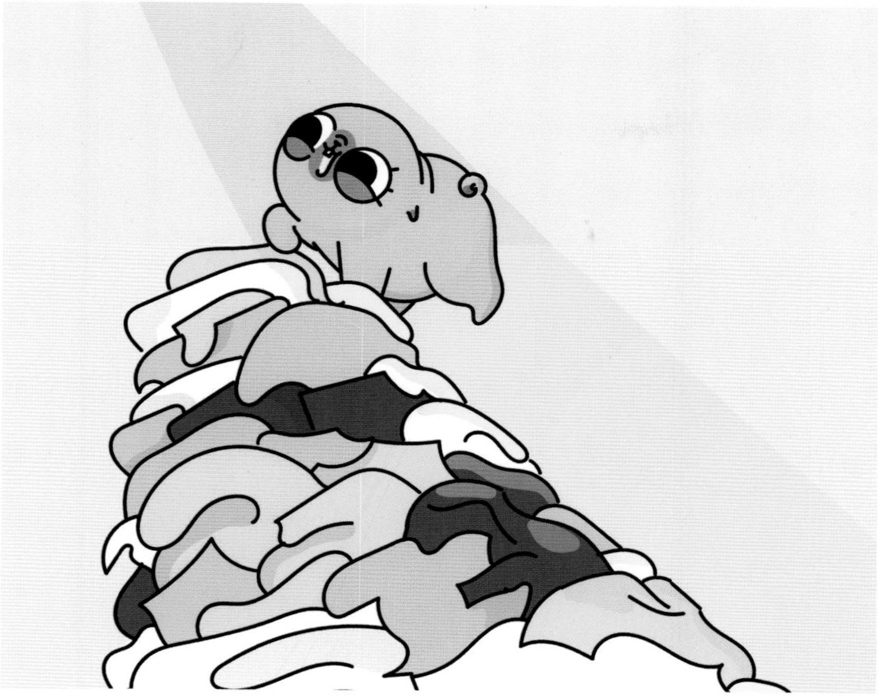

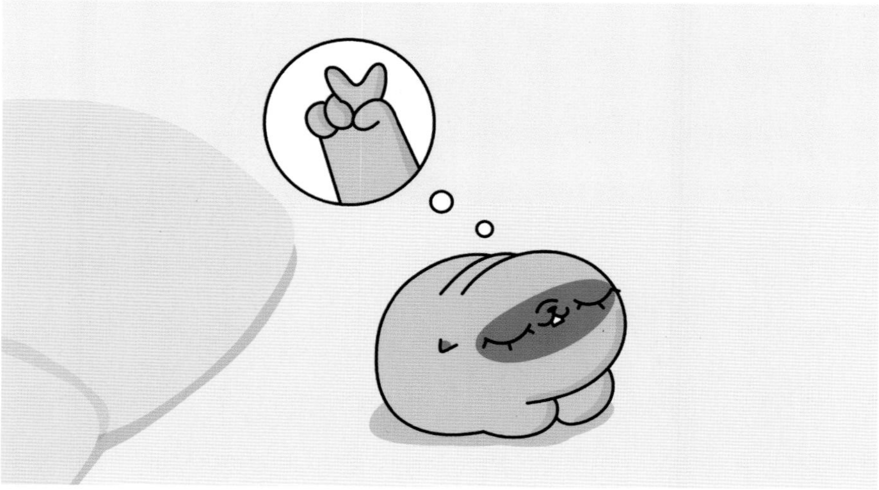

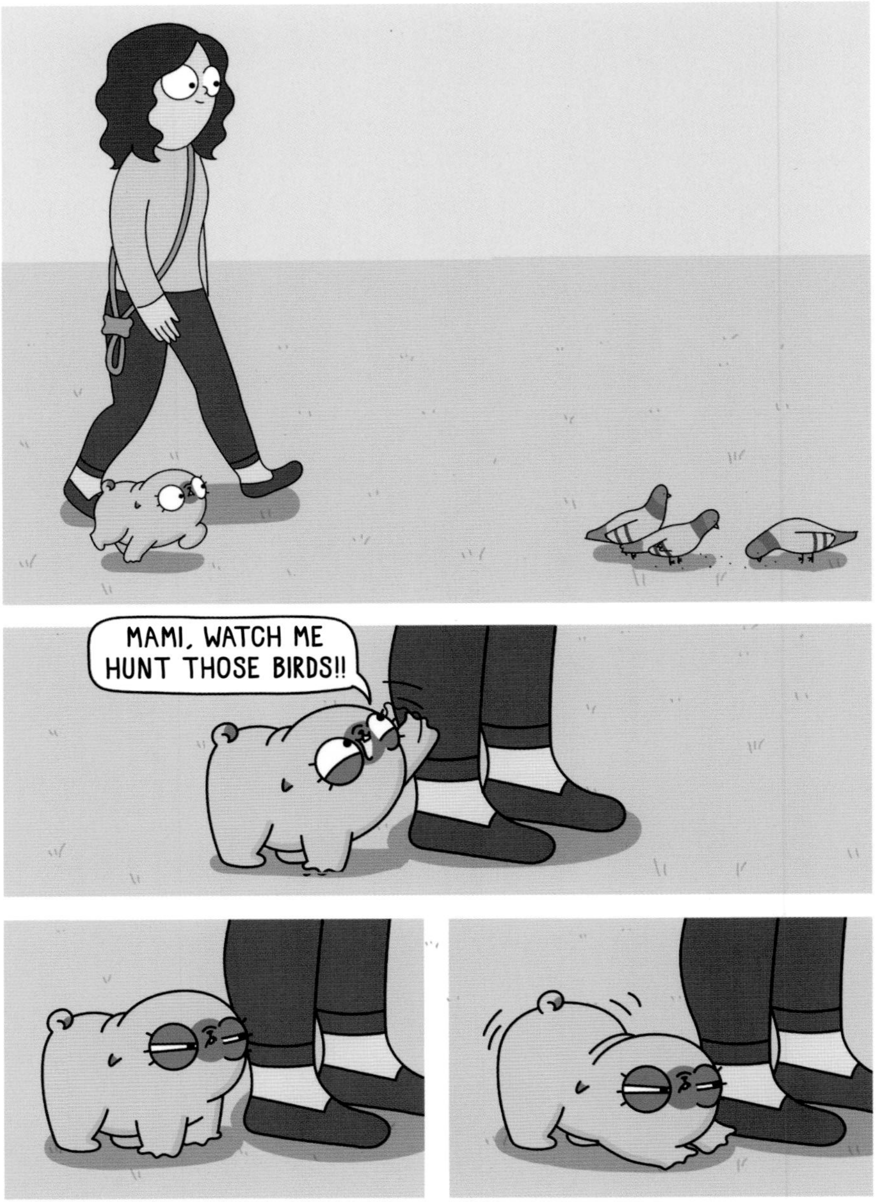
MAMI, WATCH ME HUNT THOSE BIRDS!!

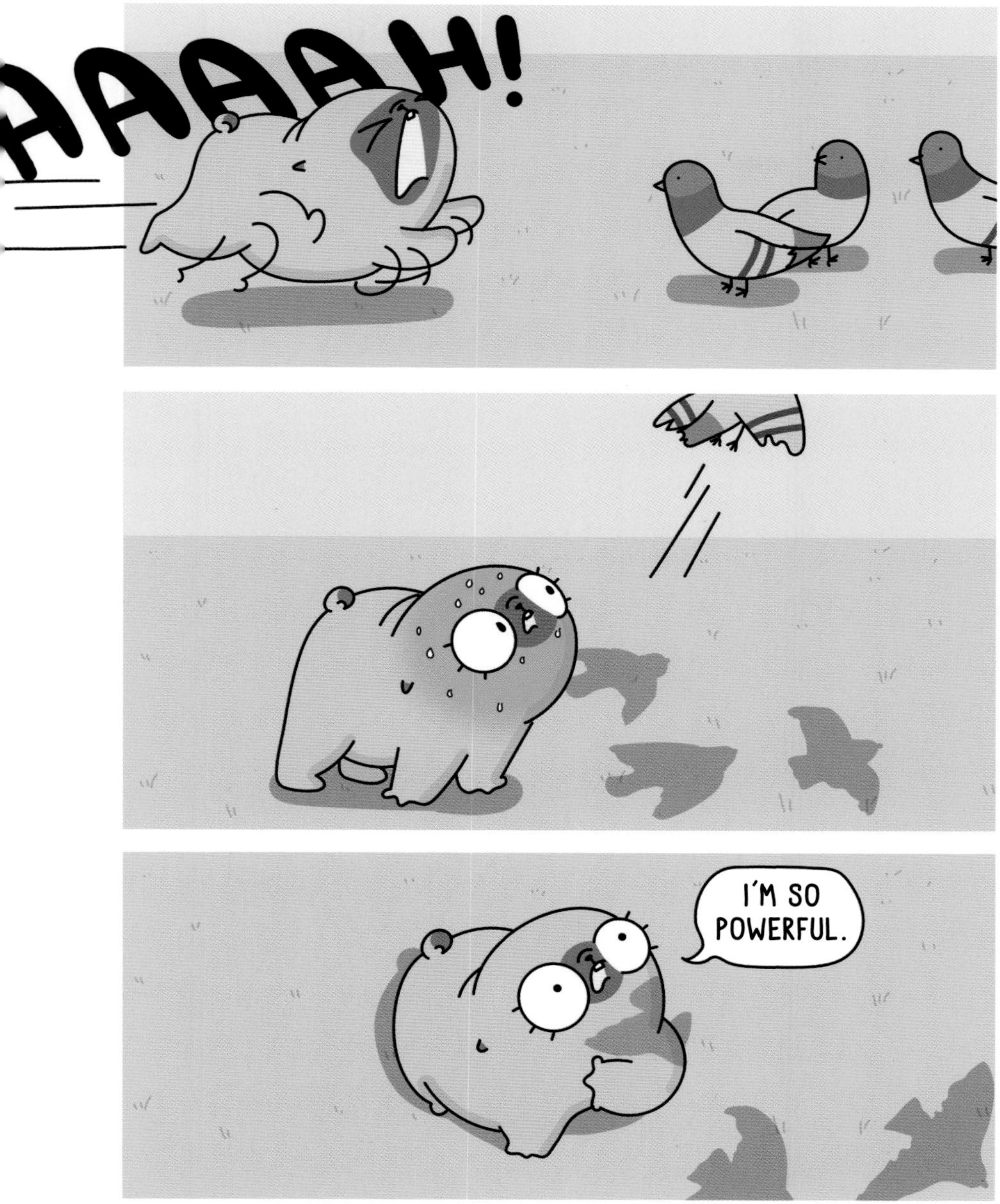
AAAAAH!
I'M SO POWERFUL.

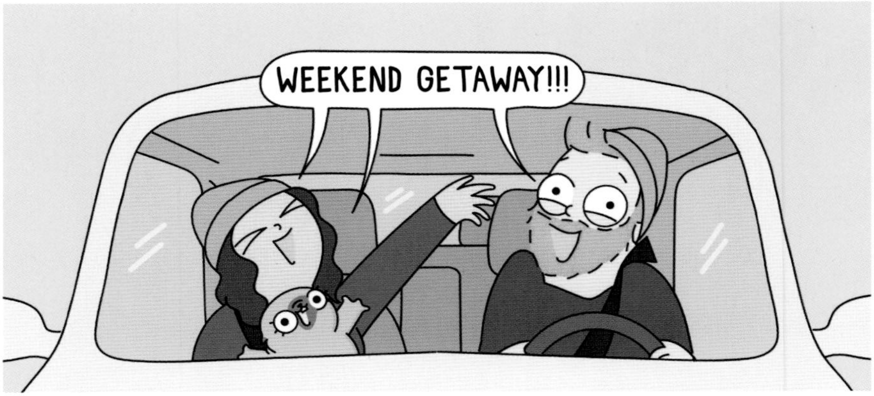
WEEKEND GETAWAY!!!

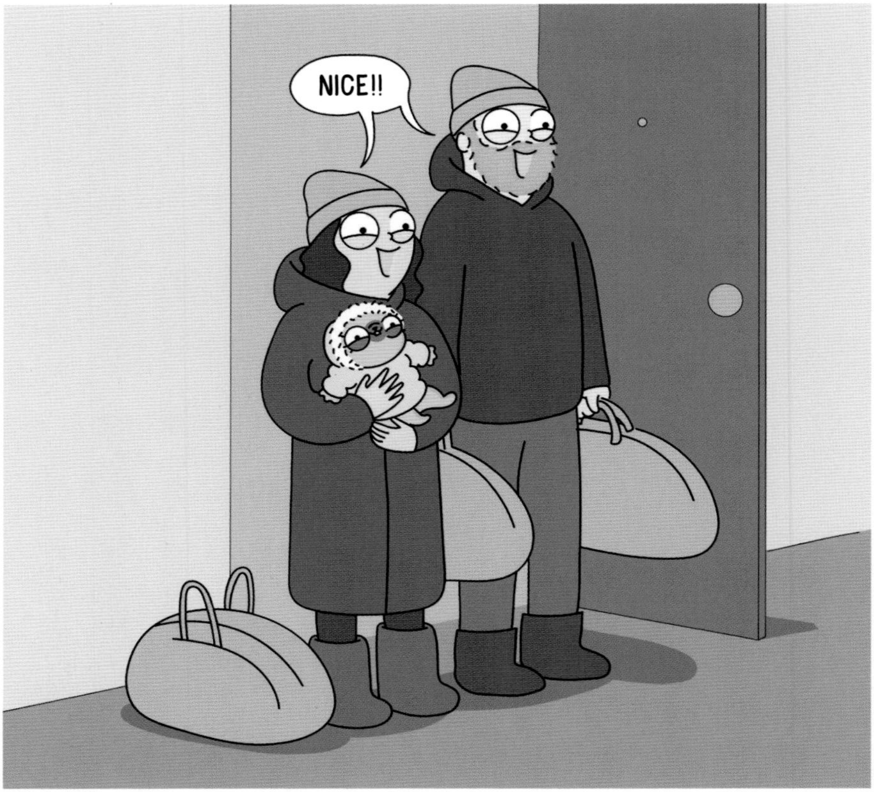
NICE!!

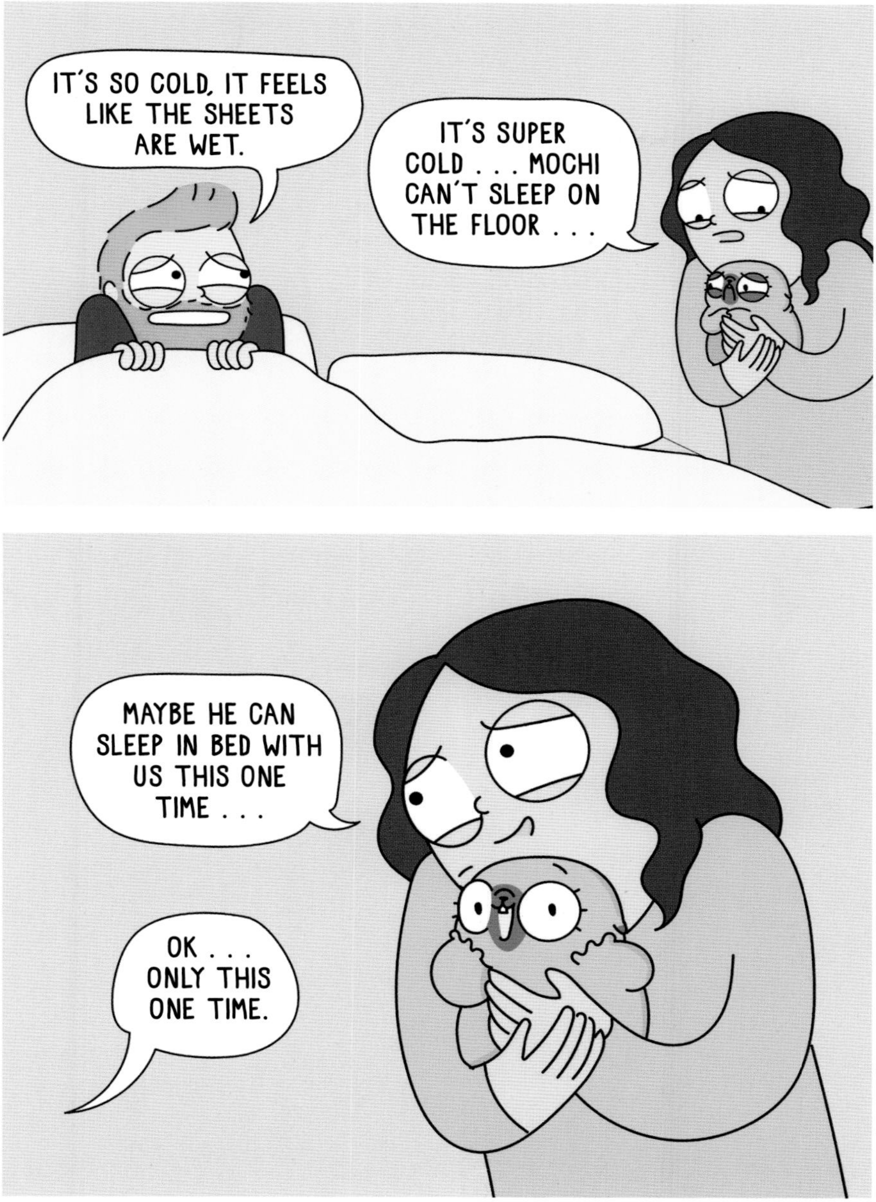
IT'S SO COLD, IT FEELS LIKE THE SHEETS ARE WET.
IT'S SUPER COLD . . . MOCHI CAN'T SLEEP ON THE FLOOR . . .
MAYBE HE CAN SLEEP IN BED WITH US THIS ONE TIME . . .
OK . . . ONLY THIS ONE TIME.

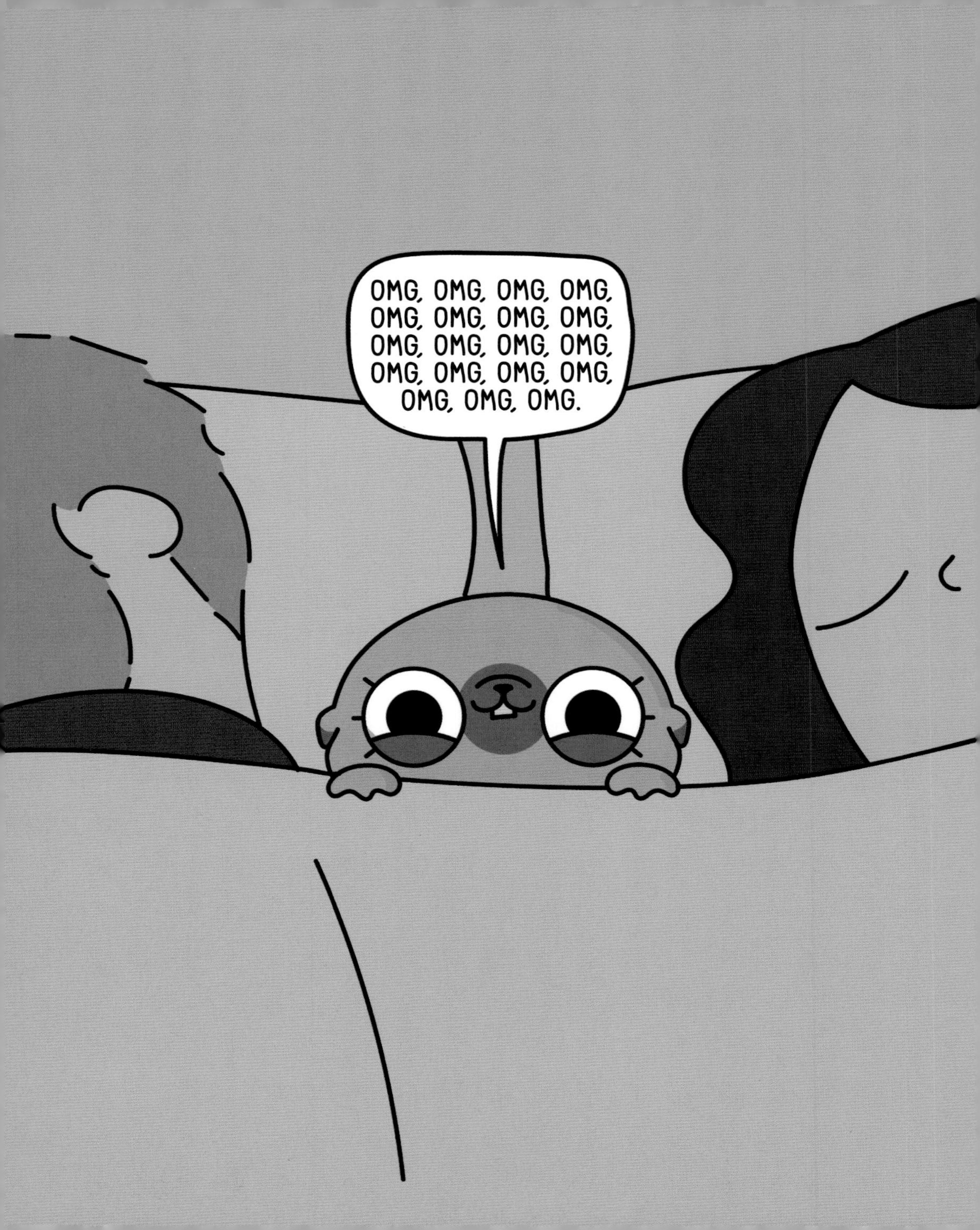
OMG, OMG, OMG, OMG, OMG, OMG, OMG, OMG, OMG, OMG, OMG, OMG, OMG, OMG, OMG, OMG, OMG, OMG, OMG.

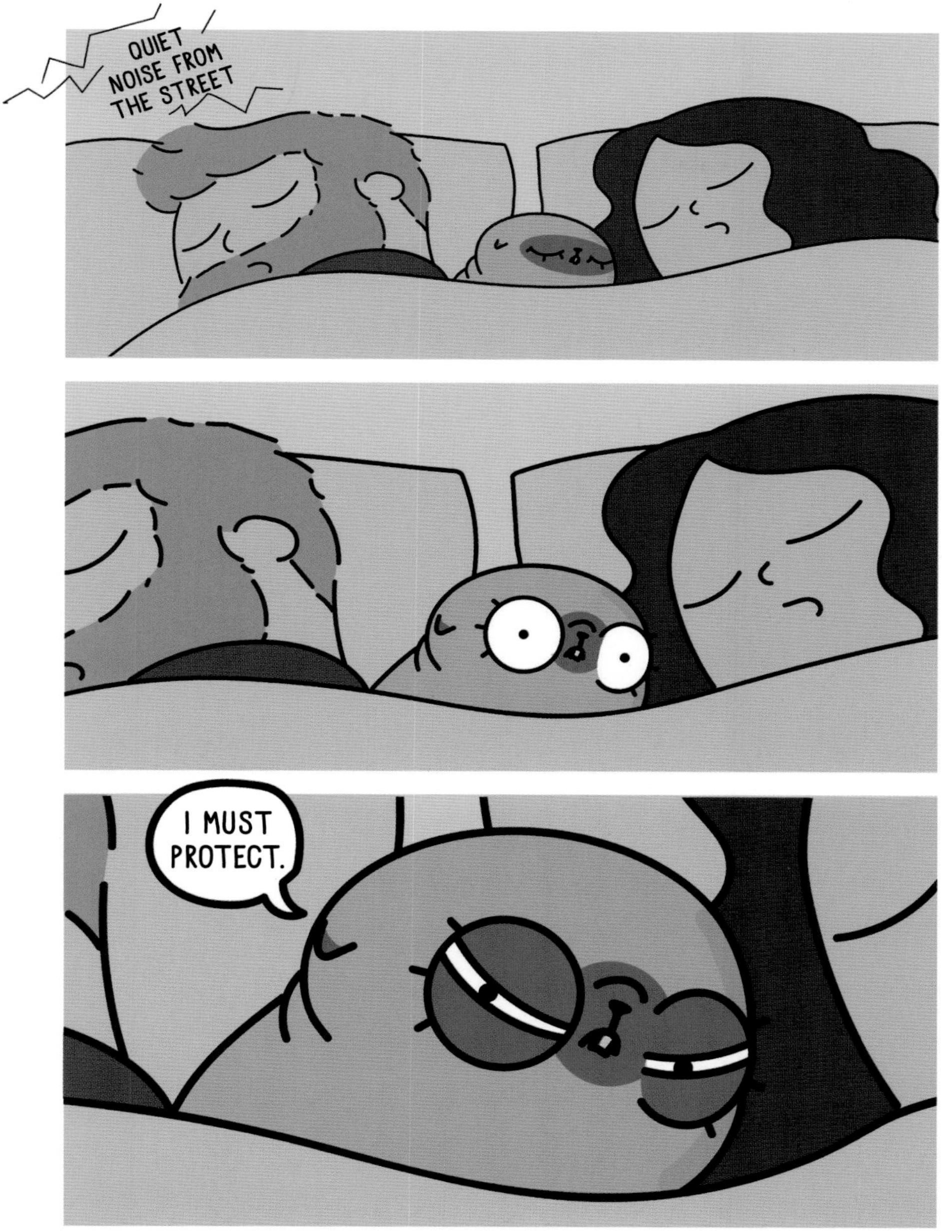
QUIET NOISE FROM THE STREET
I MUST PROTECT.

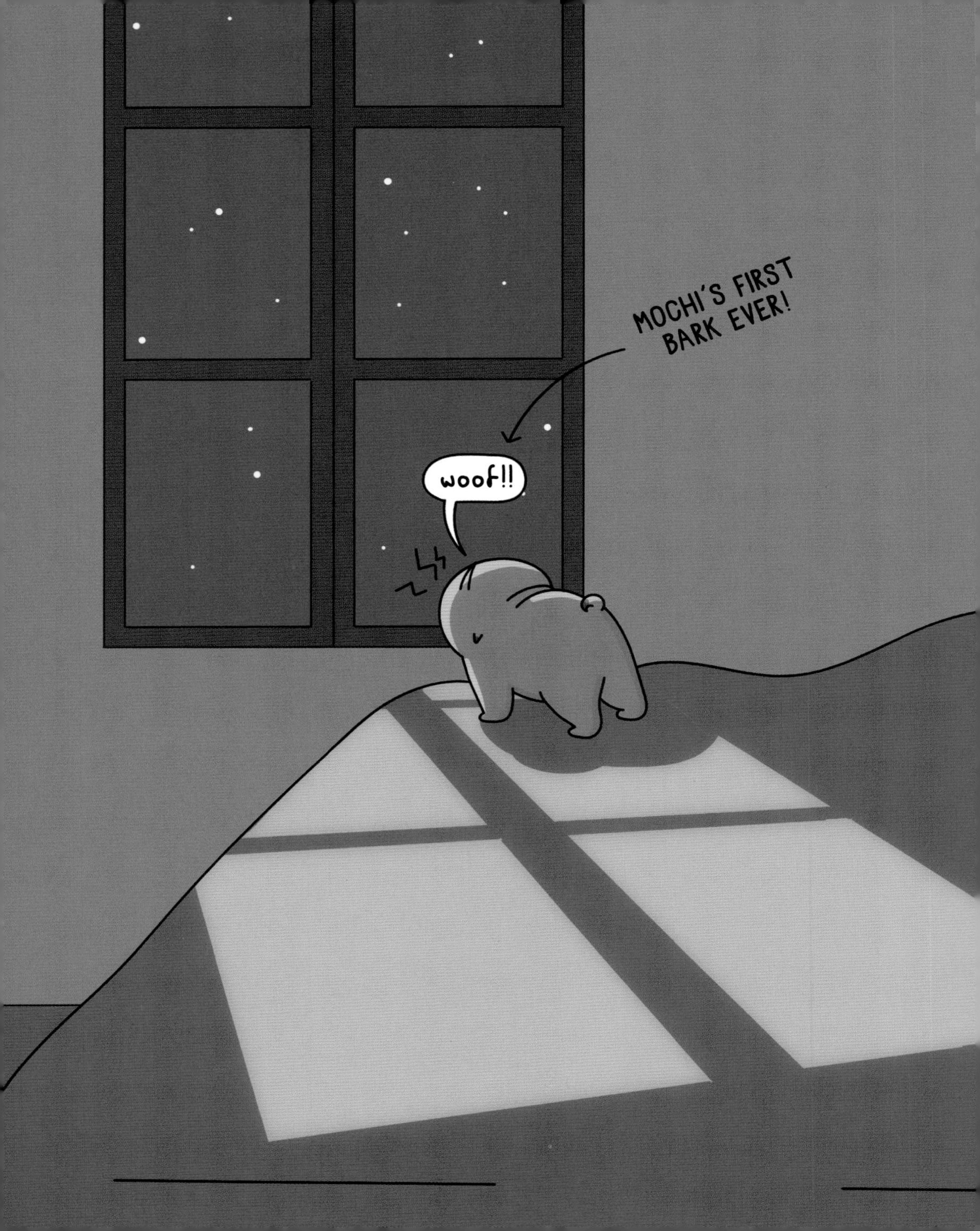
MOCHI'S FIRST BARK EVER!
woof!!

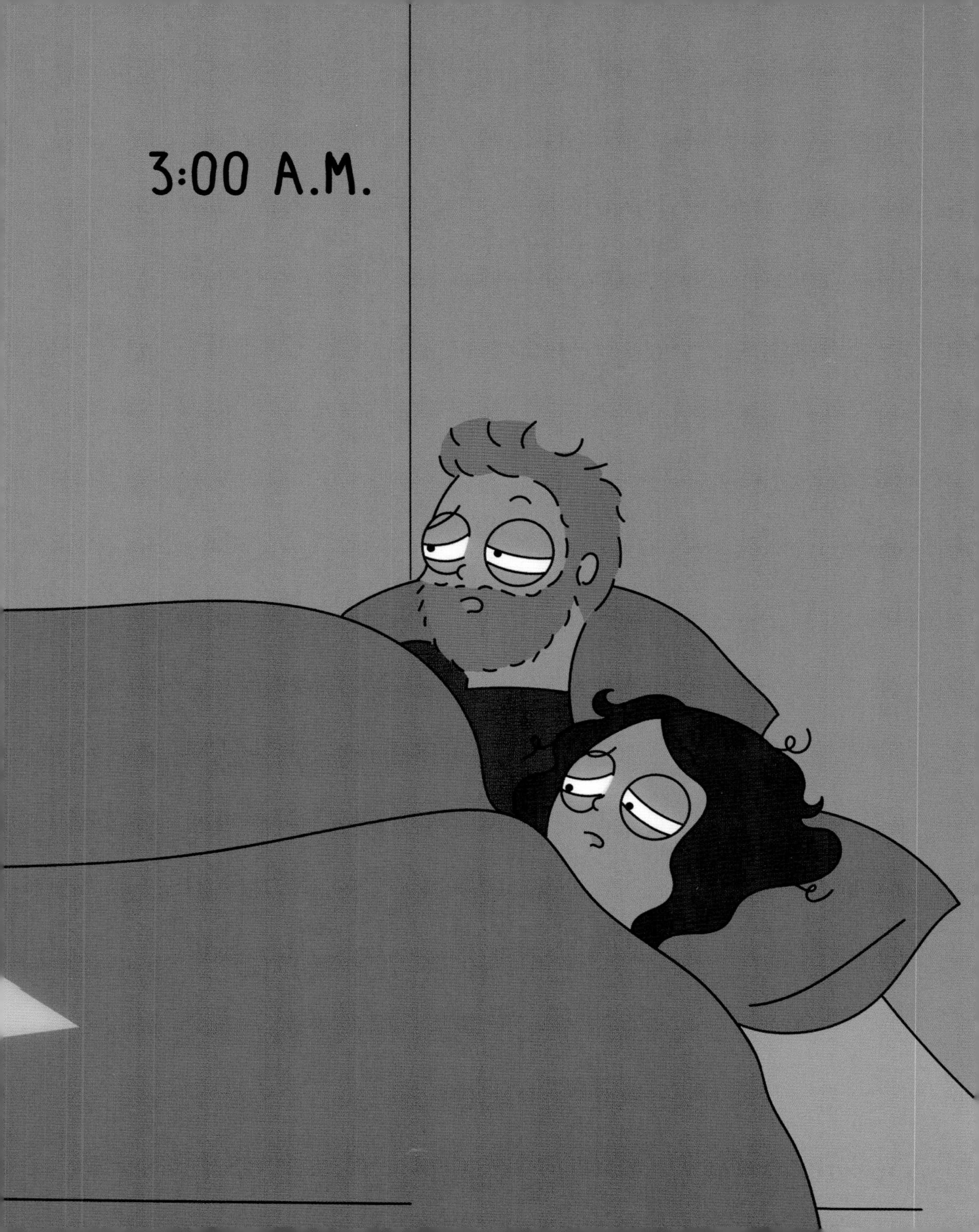
3:00 A.M.

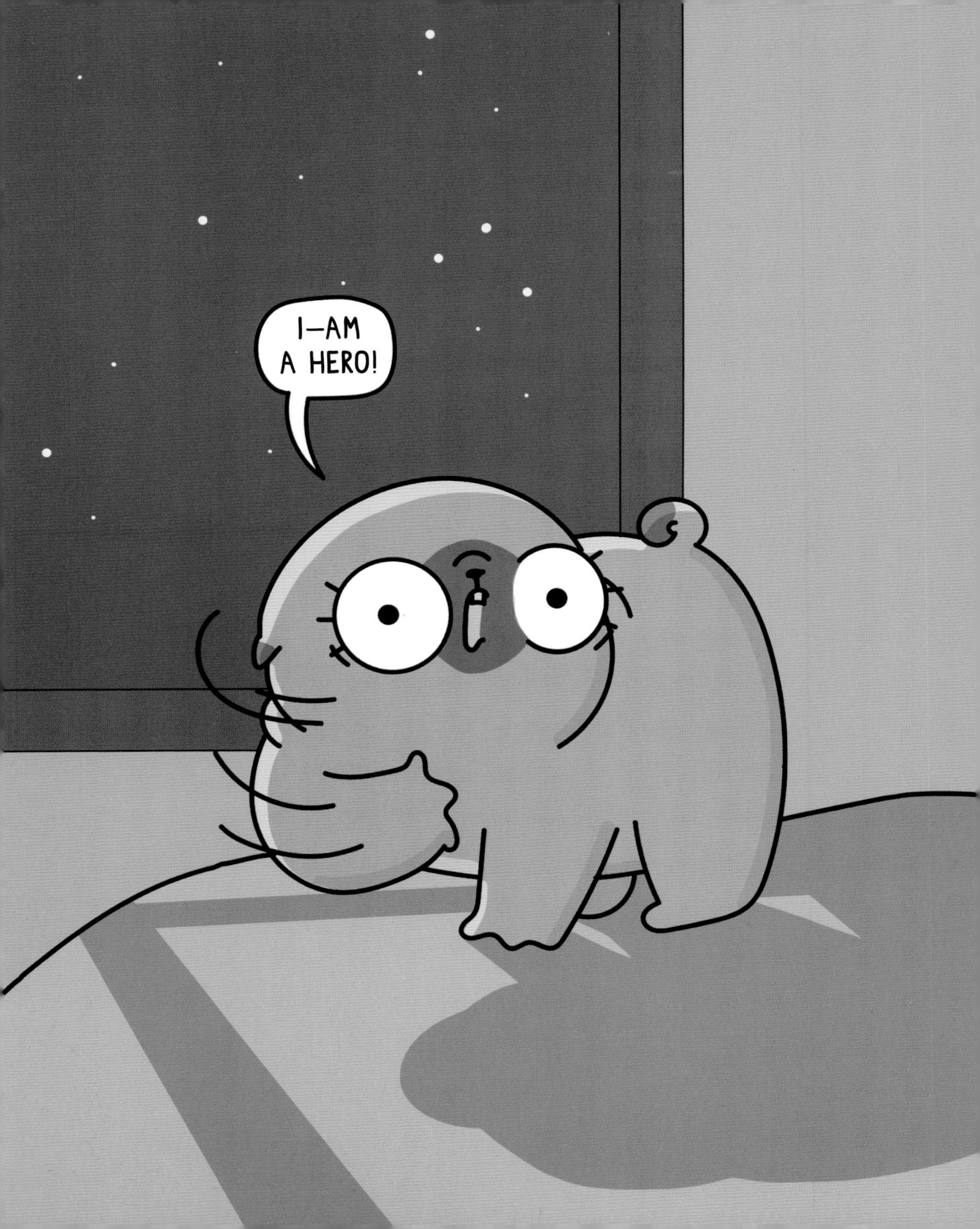
I—AM
A HERO!

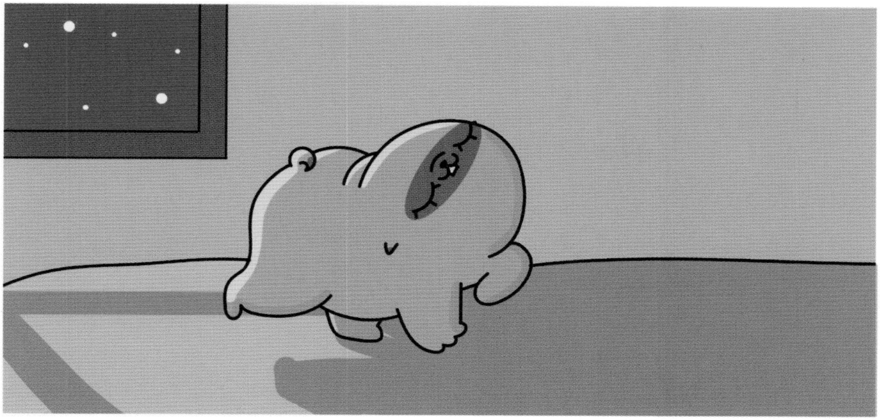

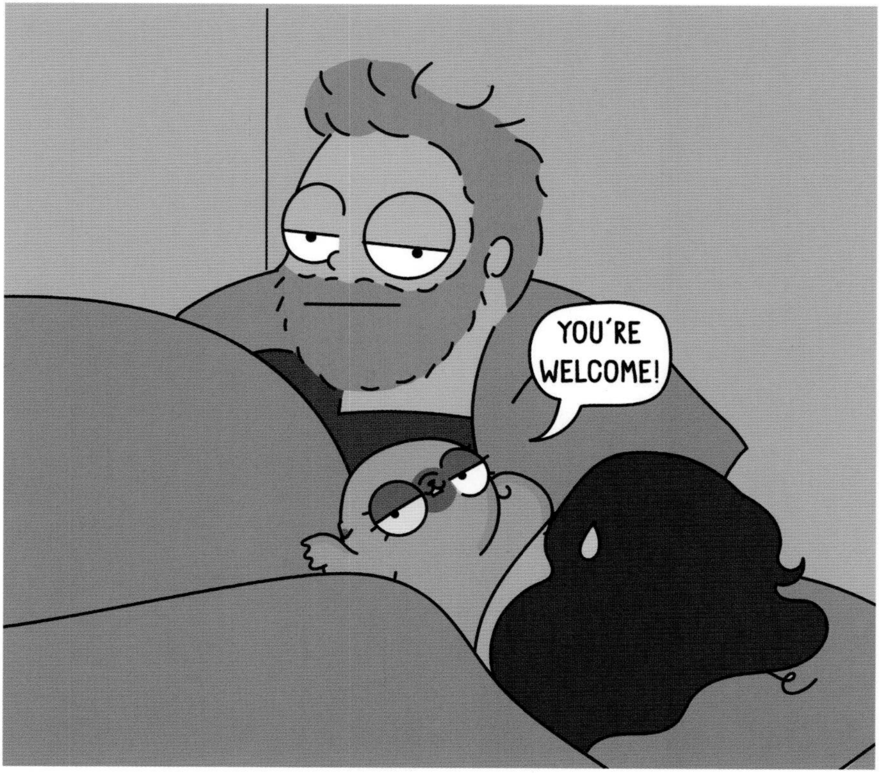
YOU'RE WELCOME!

AND HE HAS SLEPT IN OUR BED EVER SINCE. WE, OF COURSE, NEEDED THE PROTECTION.

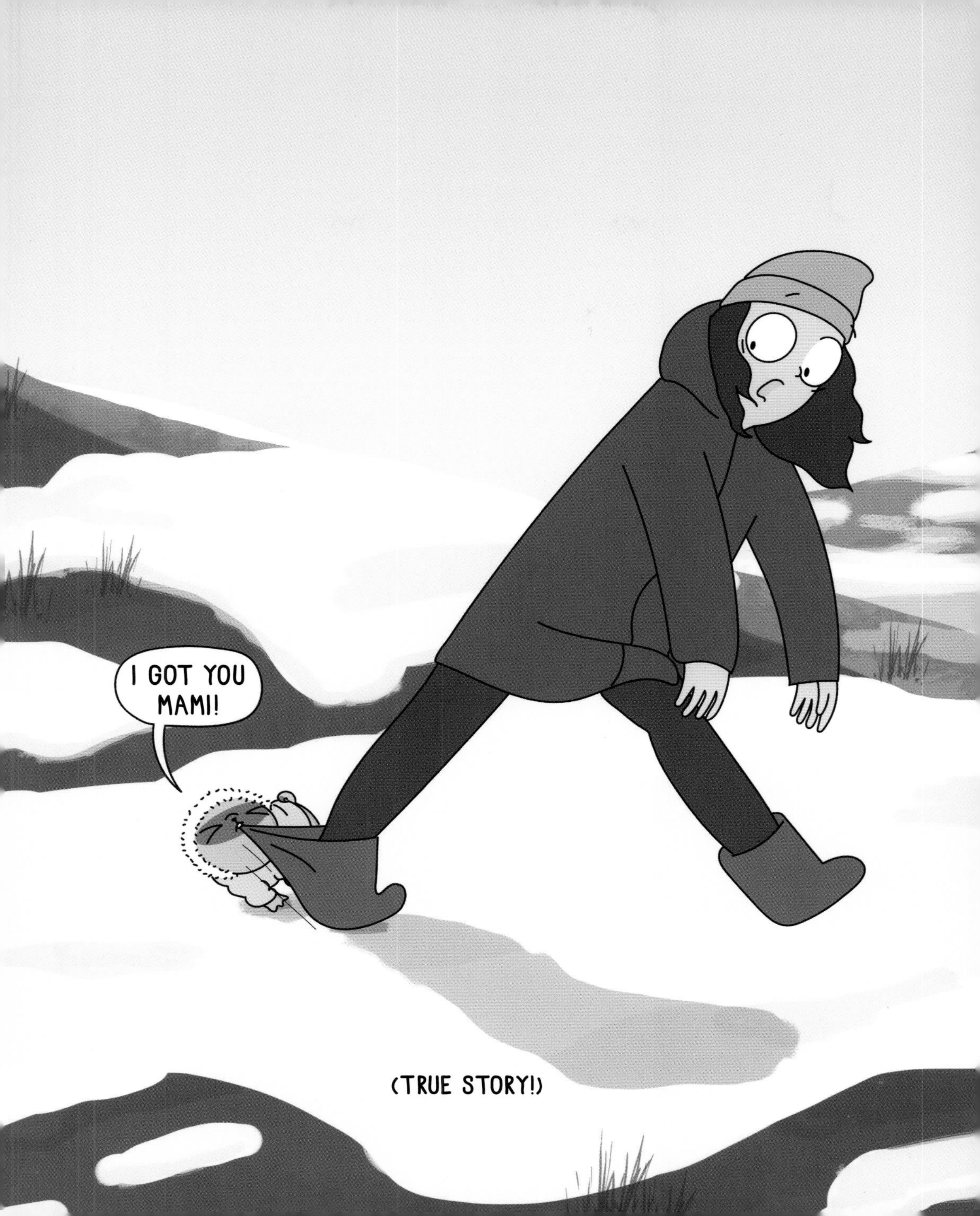
I GOT YOU MAMI!
(TRUE STORY!)

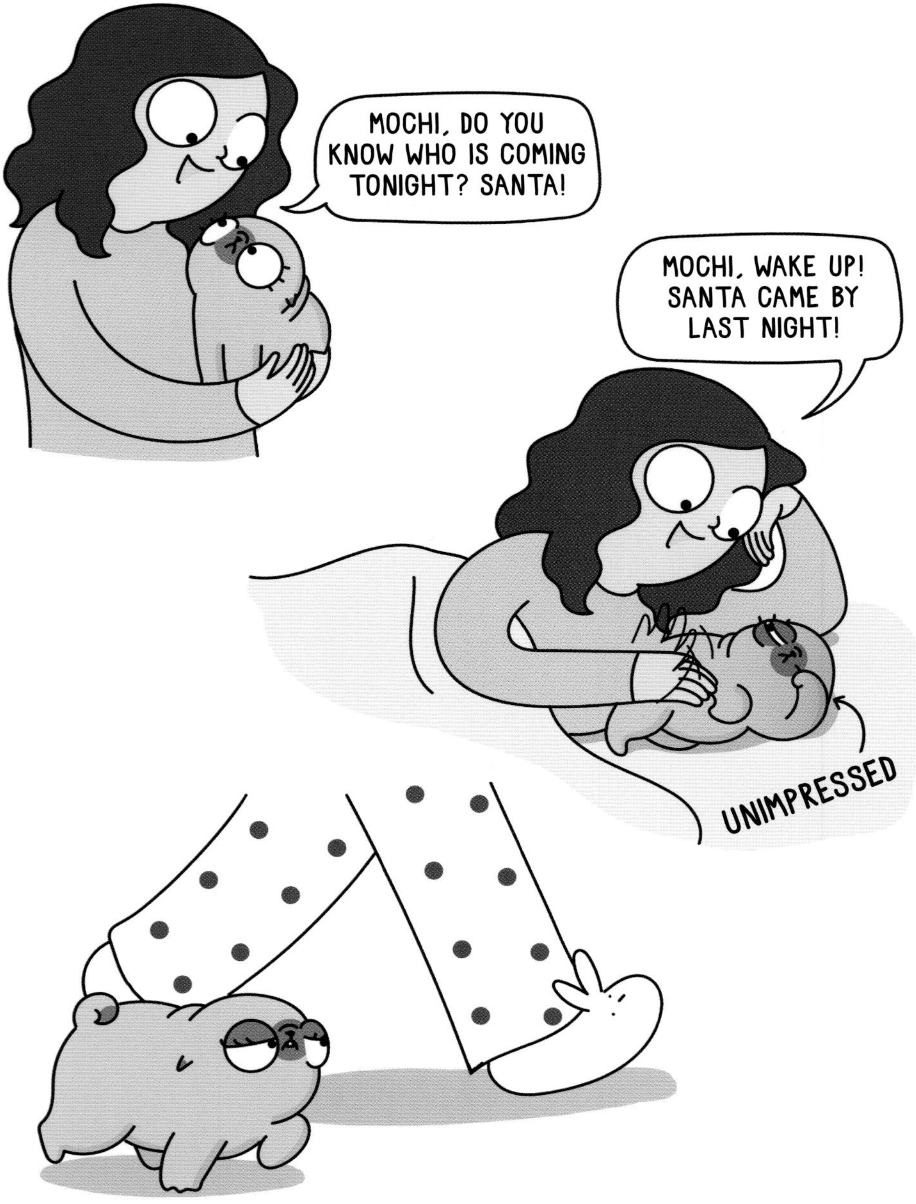
MOCHI, DO YOU KNOW WHO IS COMING TONIGHT? SANTA!
MOCHI, WAKE UP! SANTA CAME BY LAST NIGHT!
UNIMPRESSED

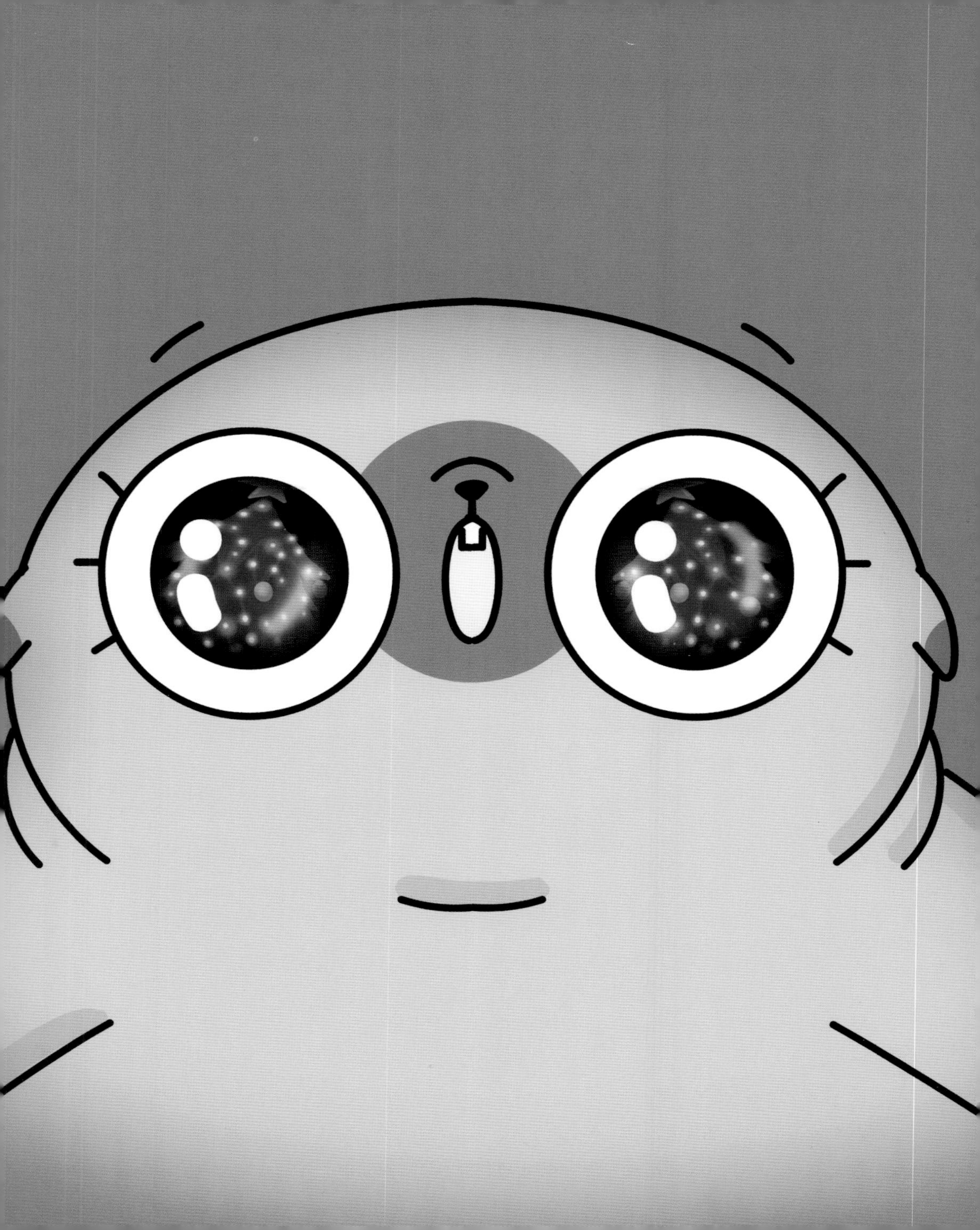

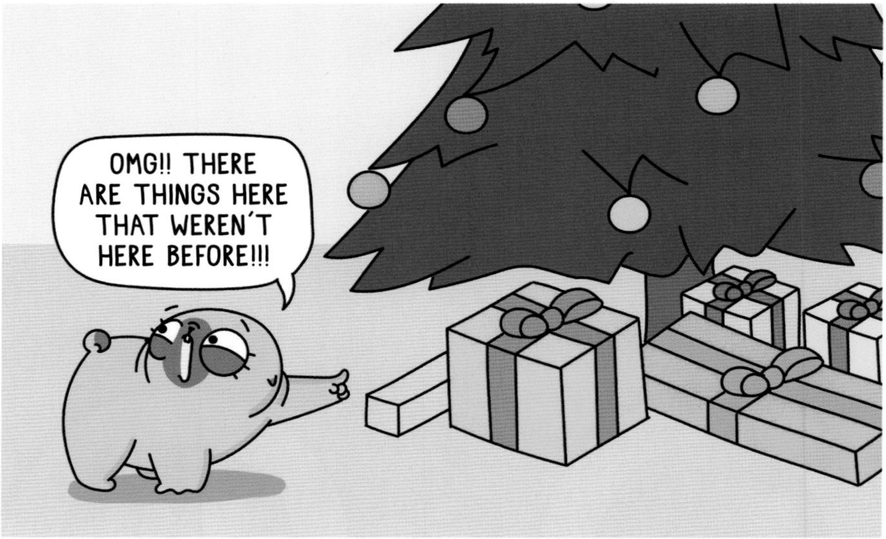
OMG!! THERE ARE THINGS HERE THAT WEREN'T HERE BEFORE!!!

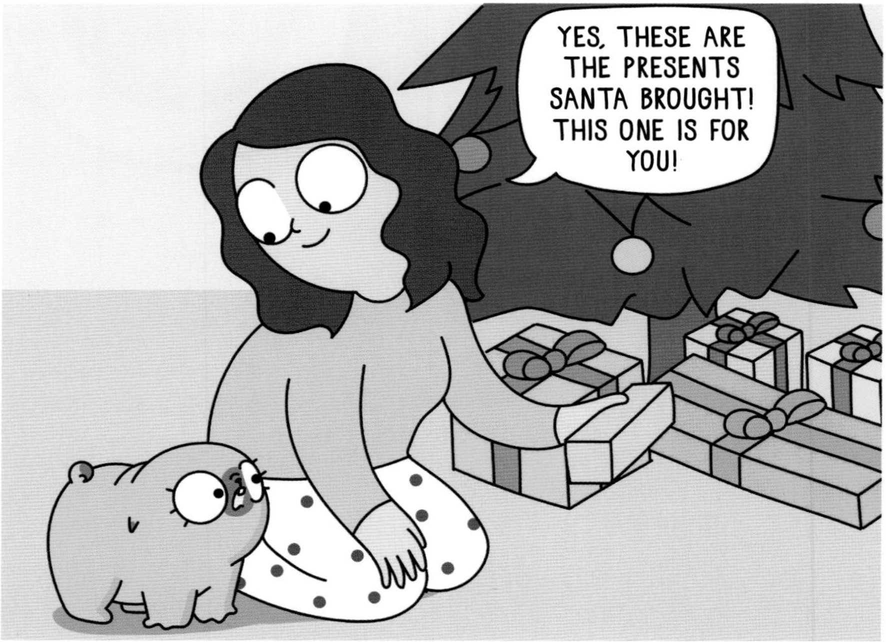
YES, THESE ARE THE PRESENTS SANTA BROUGHT! THIS ONE IS FOR YOU!

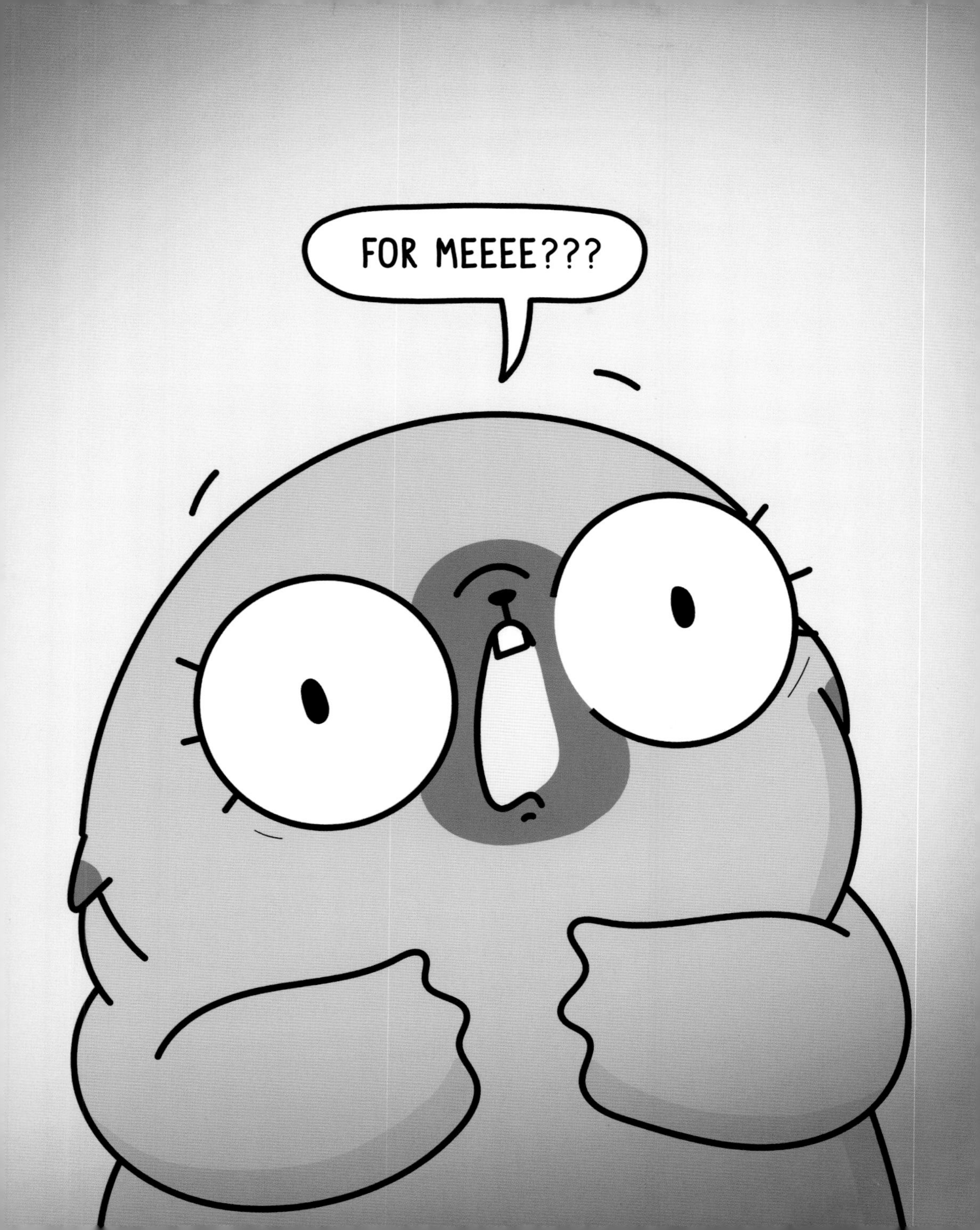
FOR MEEEE???

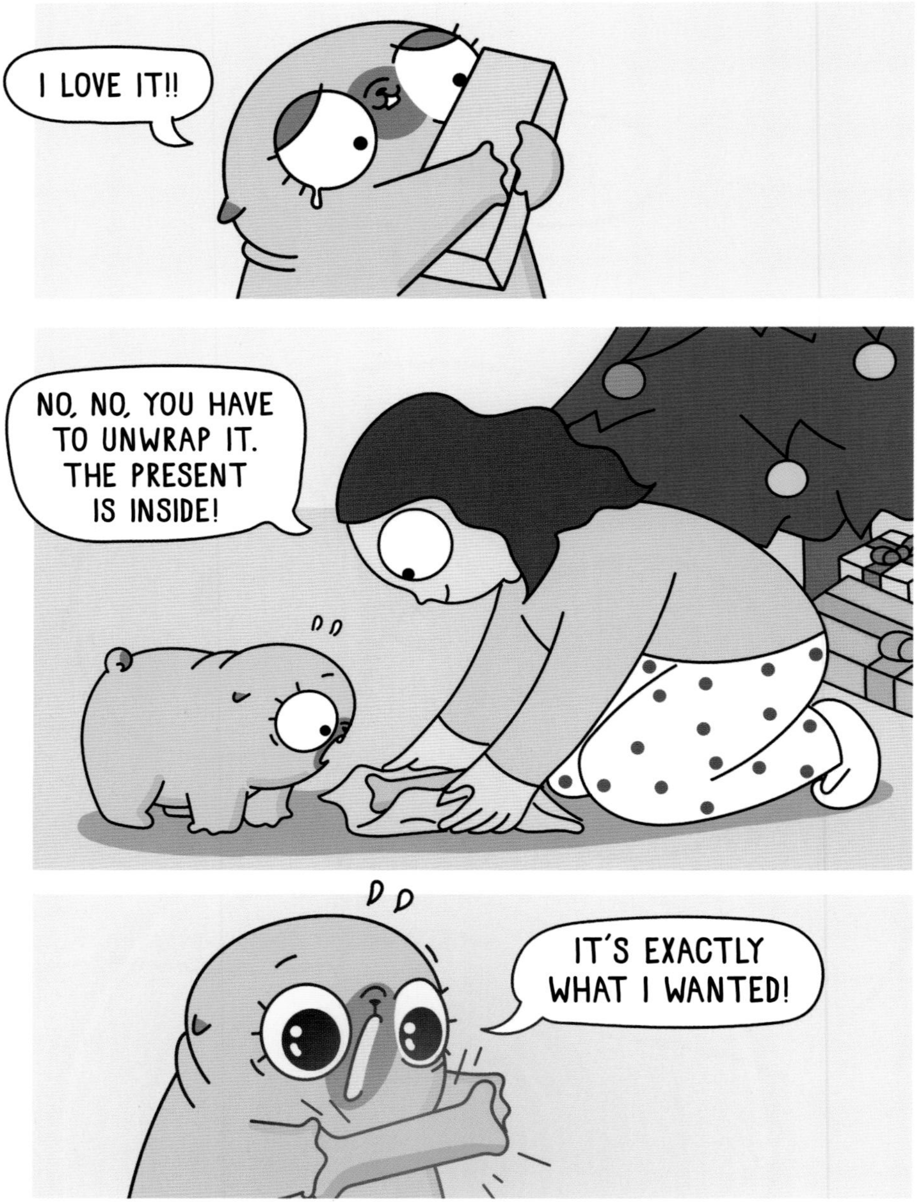
I LOVE IT!!
NO, NO, YOU HAVE TO UNWRAP IT. THE PRESENT IS INSIDE!
IT'S EXACTLY WHAT I WANTED!

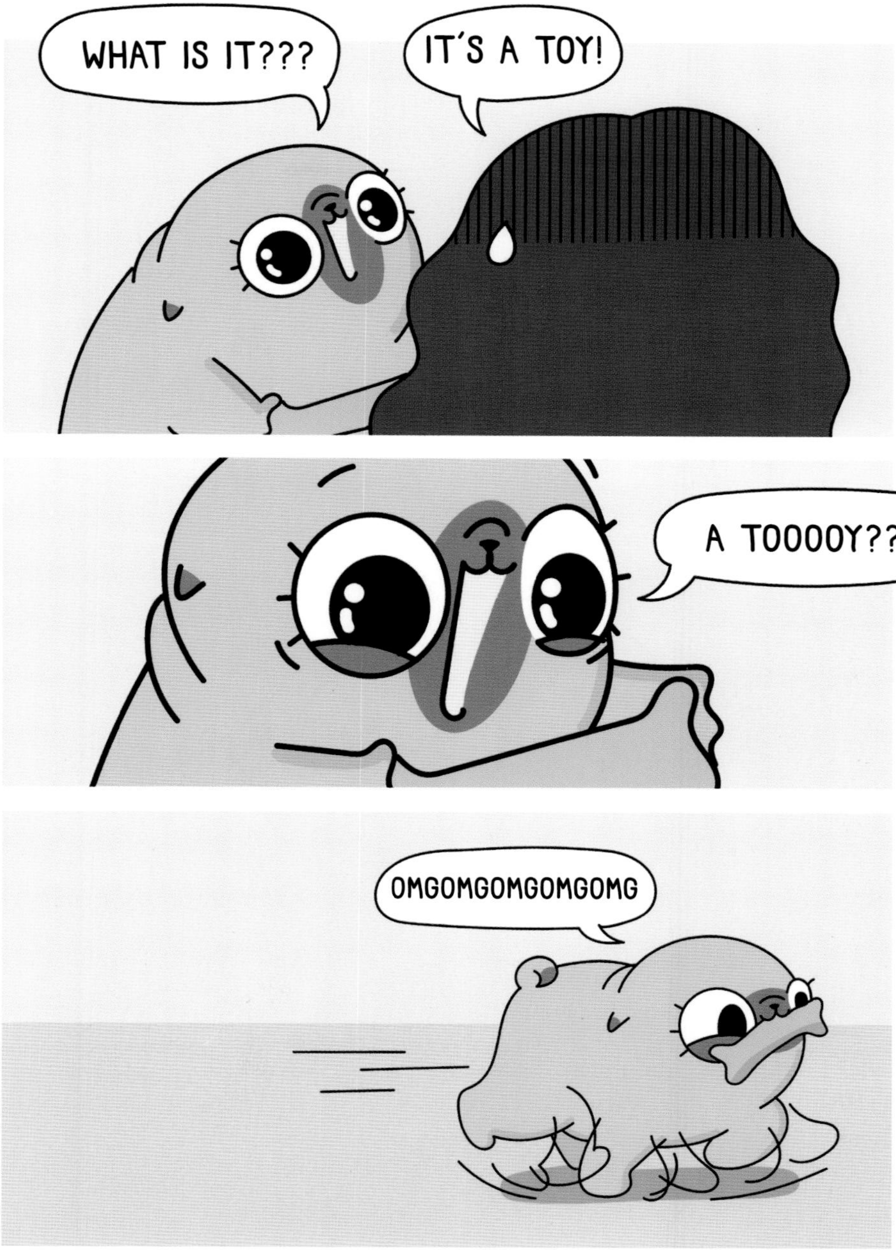
WHAT IS IT???
IT'S A TOY!
A TOOOOY???
OMGOMGOMGOMGOMG

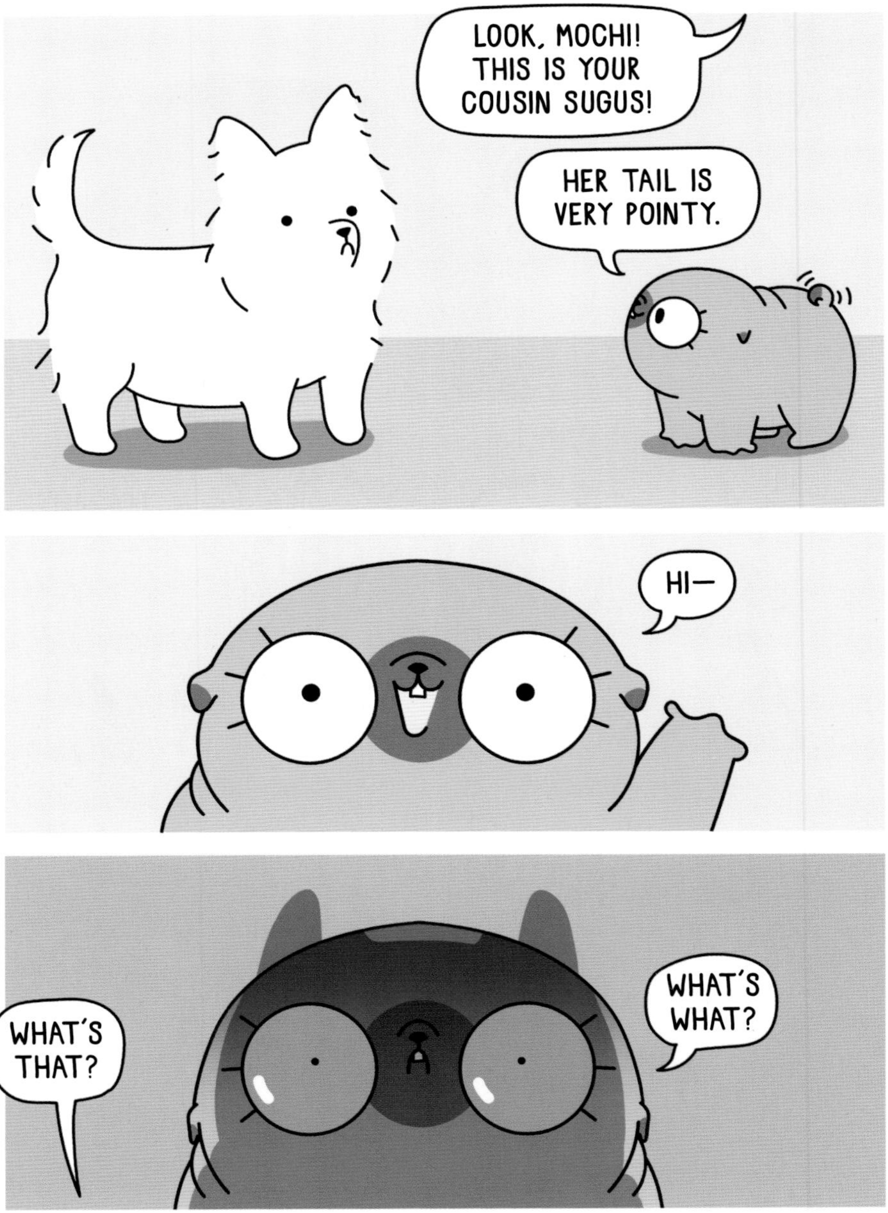
LOOK, MOCHI! THIS IS YOUR COUSIN SUGUS!
HER TAIL IS VERY POINTY.
HI—
WHAT'S THAT?
WHAT'S WHAT?

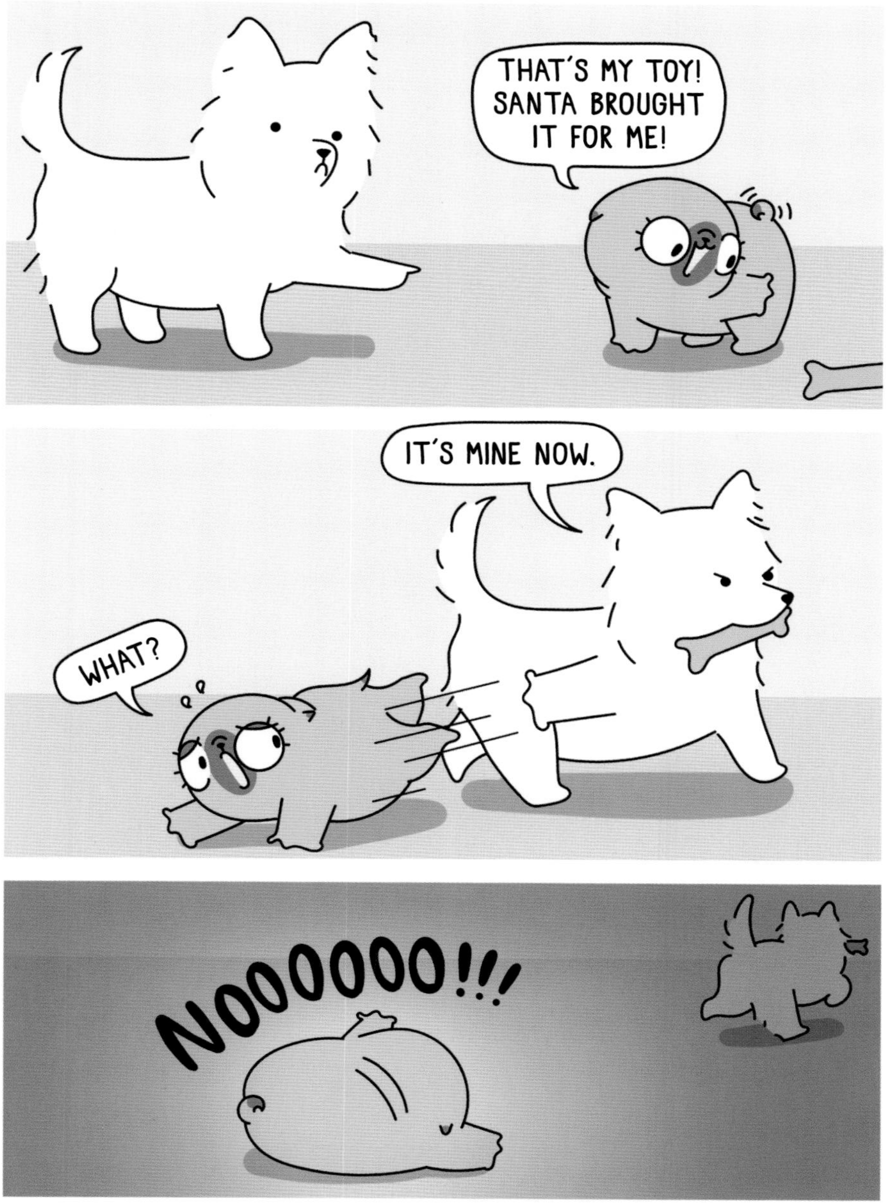
THAT'S MY TOY! SANTA BROUGHT IT FOR ME!
IT'S MINE NOW.
WHAT?
NOOOOOO!!!

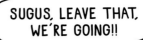

SUGUS, LEAVE THAT, WE'RE GOING!!

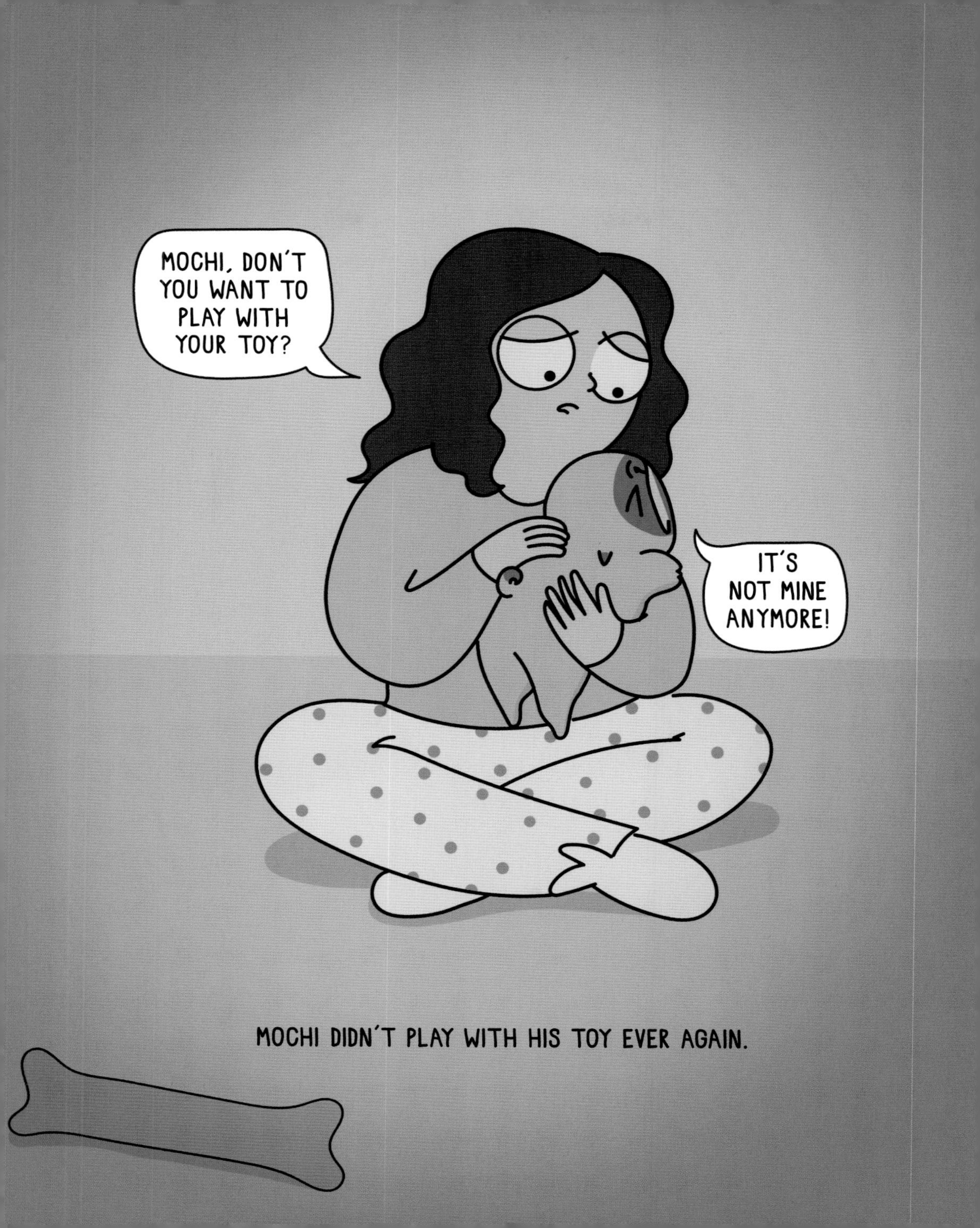
MOCHI, DON'T YOU WANT TO PLAY WITH YOUR TOY?
IT'S NOT MINE ANYMORE!
MOCHI DIDN'T PLAY WITH HIS TOY EVER AGAIN.

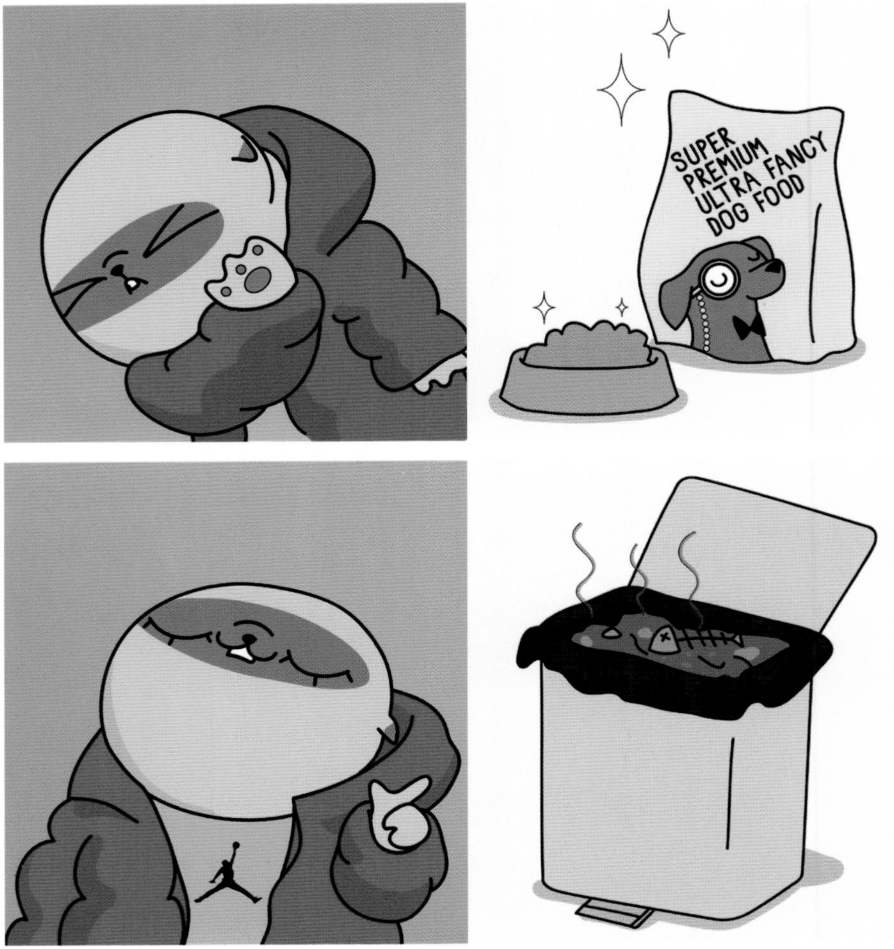
SUPER
PREMIUM
ULTRA FANCY
DOG FOOD

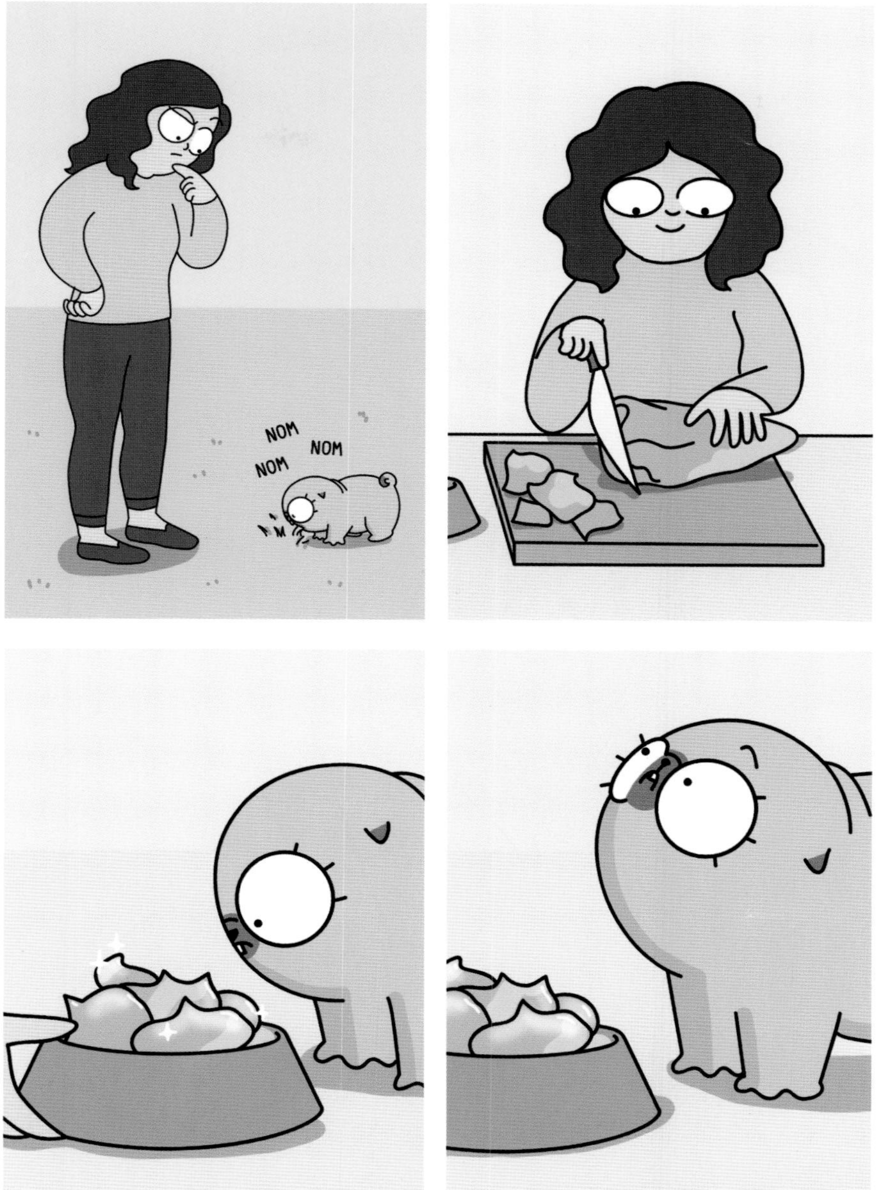
NOM
NOM
NOM

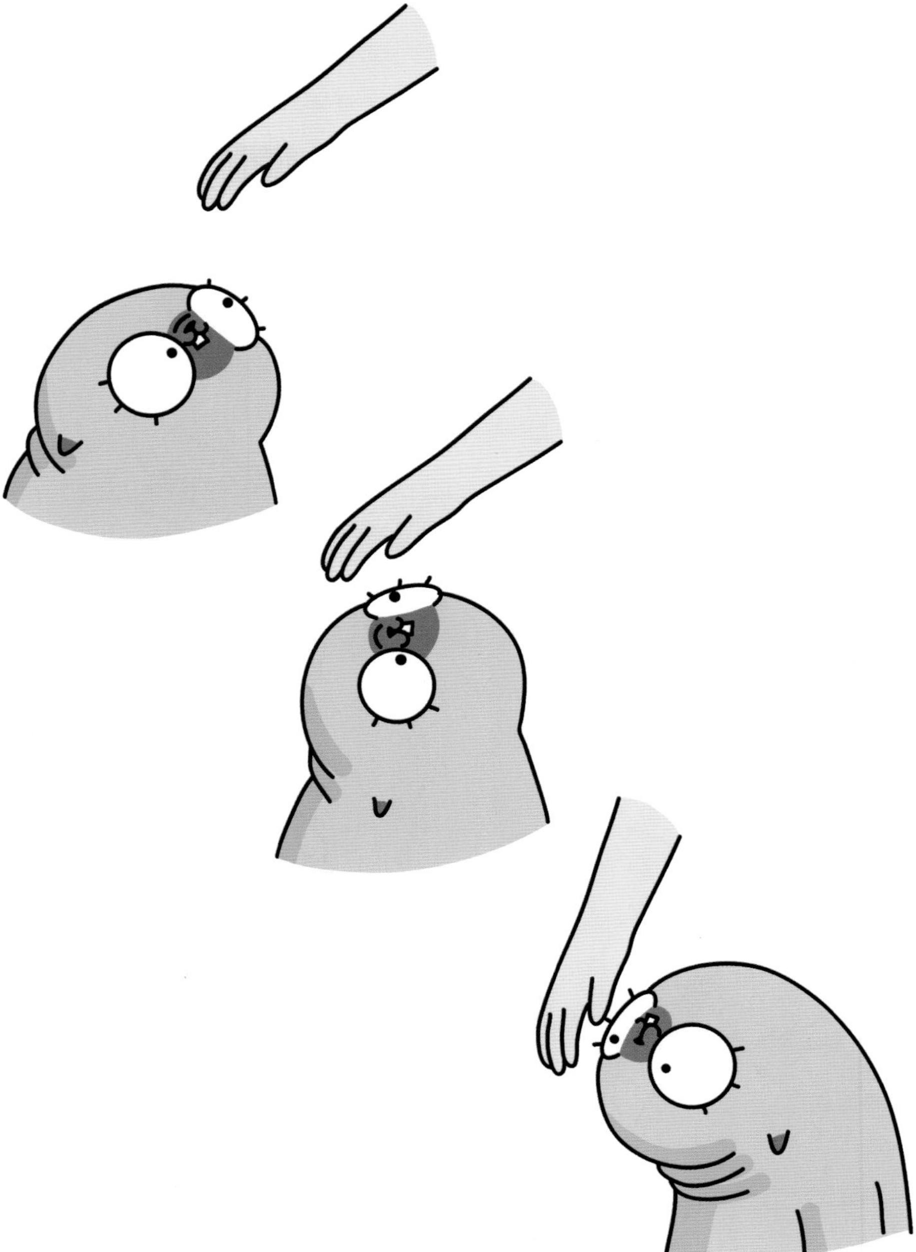

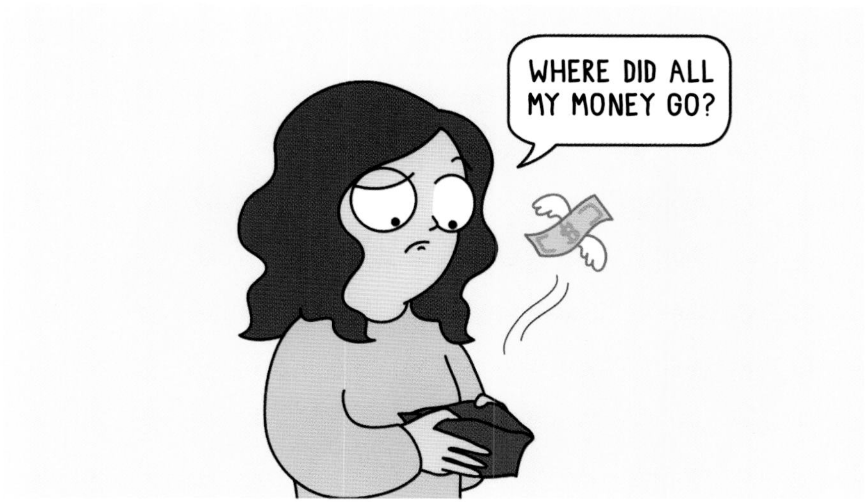
WHERE DID ALL MY MONEY GO?

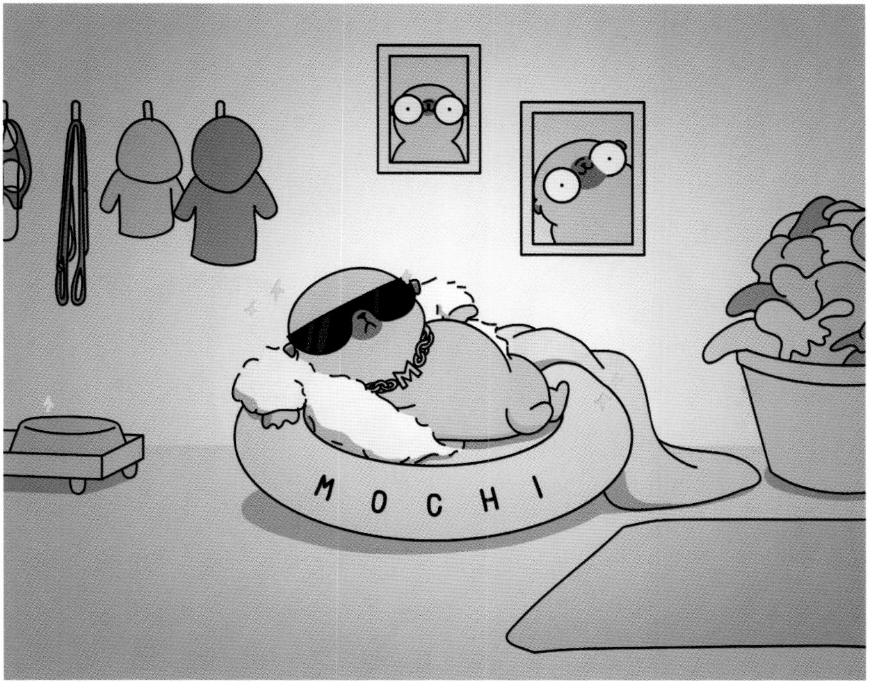
MOCHI

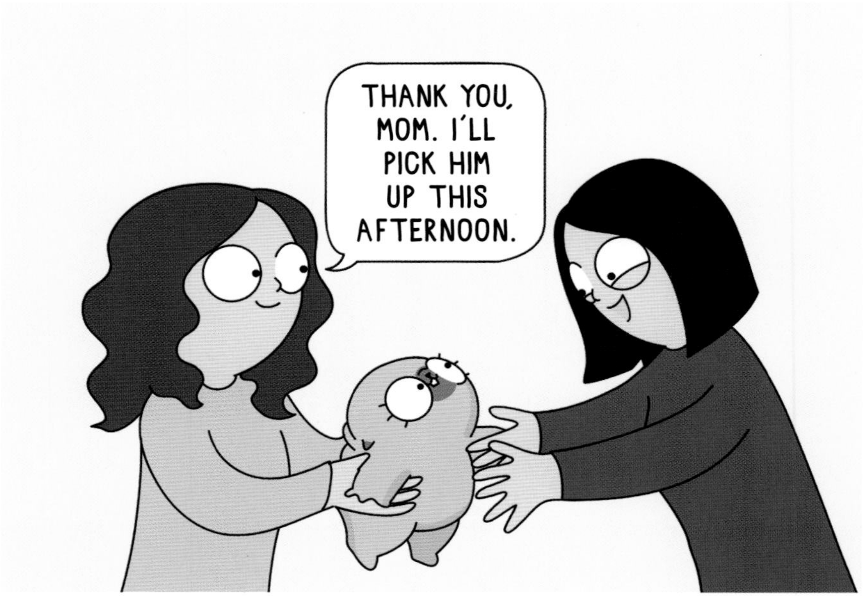
THANK YOU, MOM. I'LL PICK HIM UP THIS AFTERNOON.

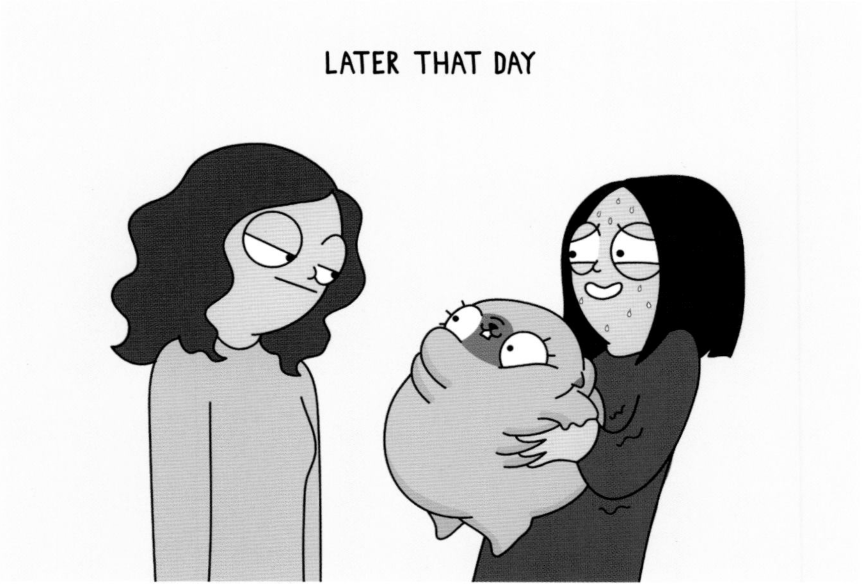
LATER THAT DAY

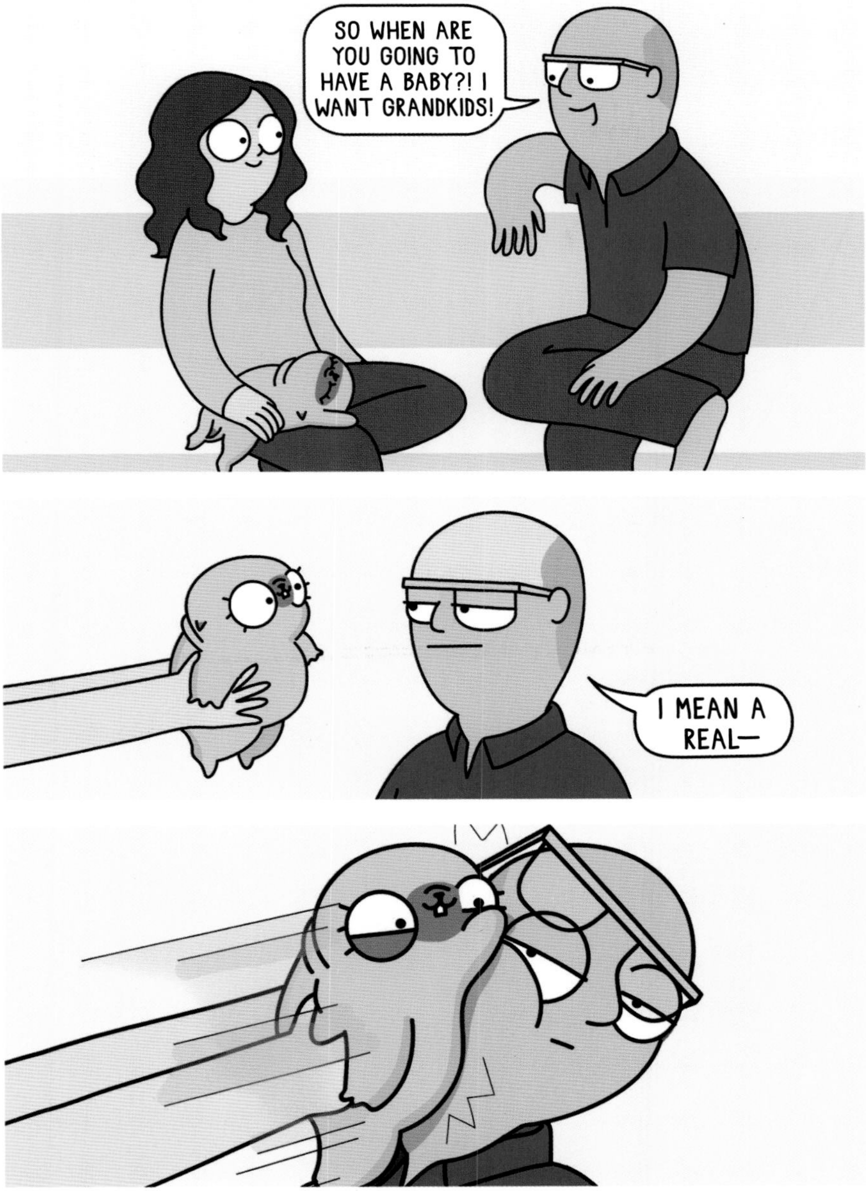
SO WHEN ARE YOU GOING TO HAVE A BABY?! I WANT GRANDKIDS!
I MEAN A REAL—

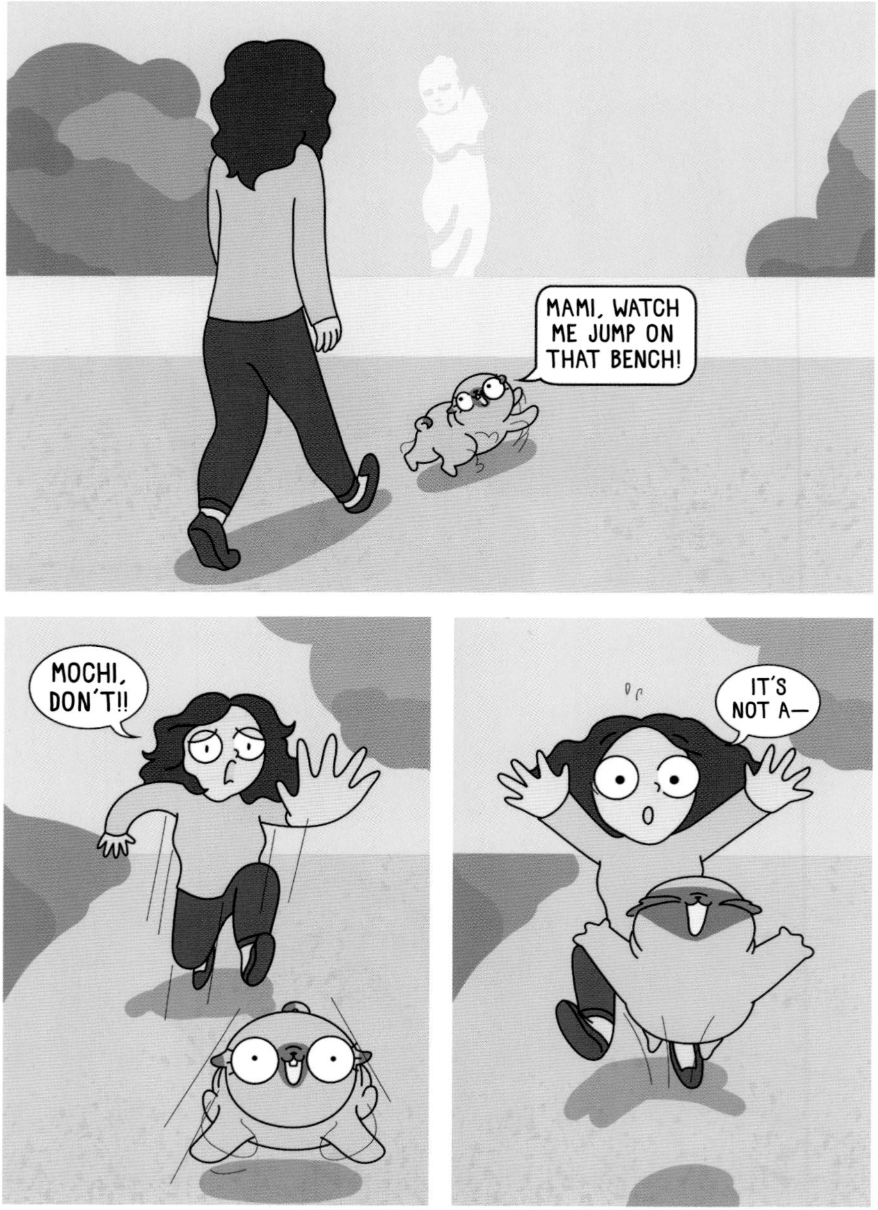
MAMI, WATCH ME JUMP ON THAT BENCH!
MOCHI, DON'T!!
IT'S NOT A—

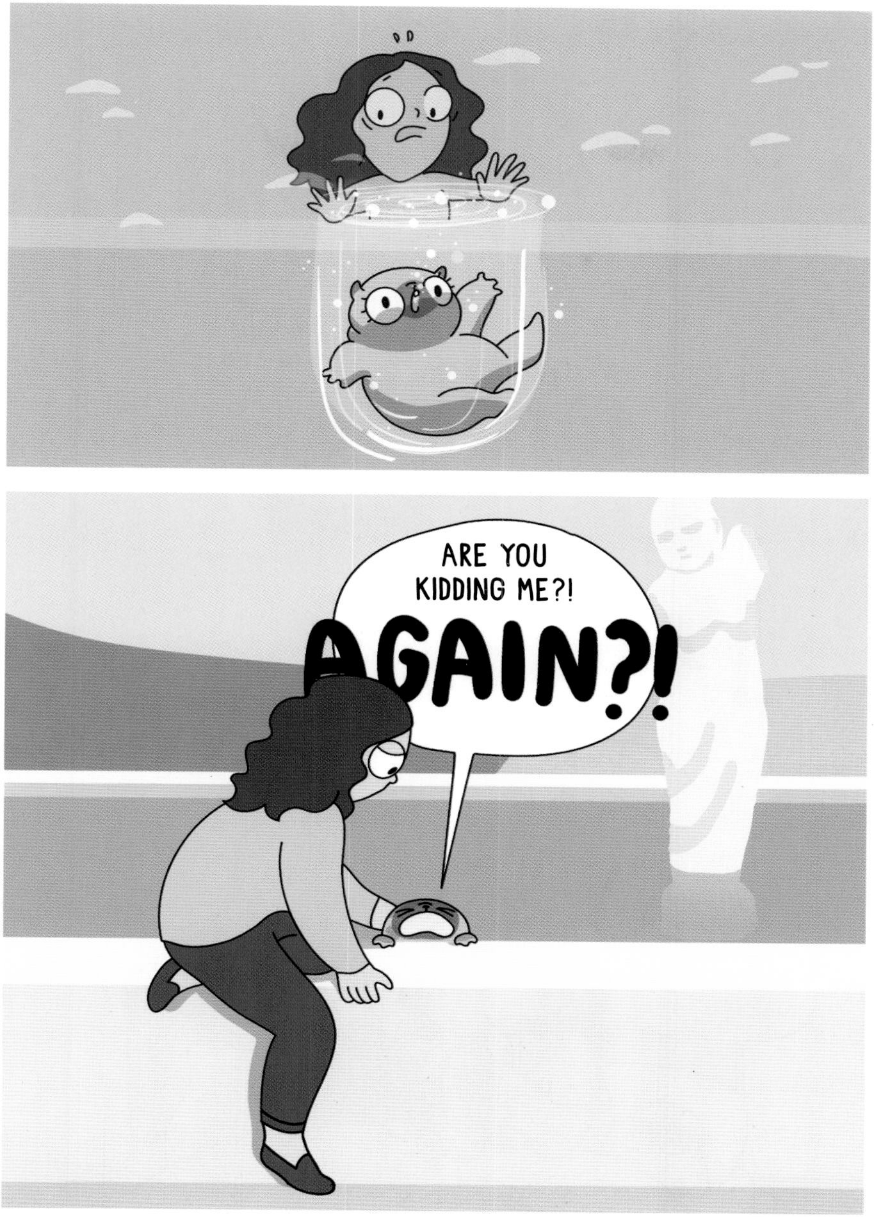
ARE YOU KIDDING ME?!
AGAIN?!

ONE DAY EVERYTHING CHANGED . . .

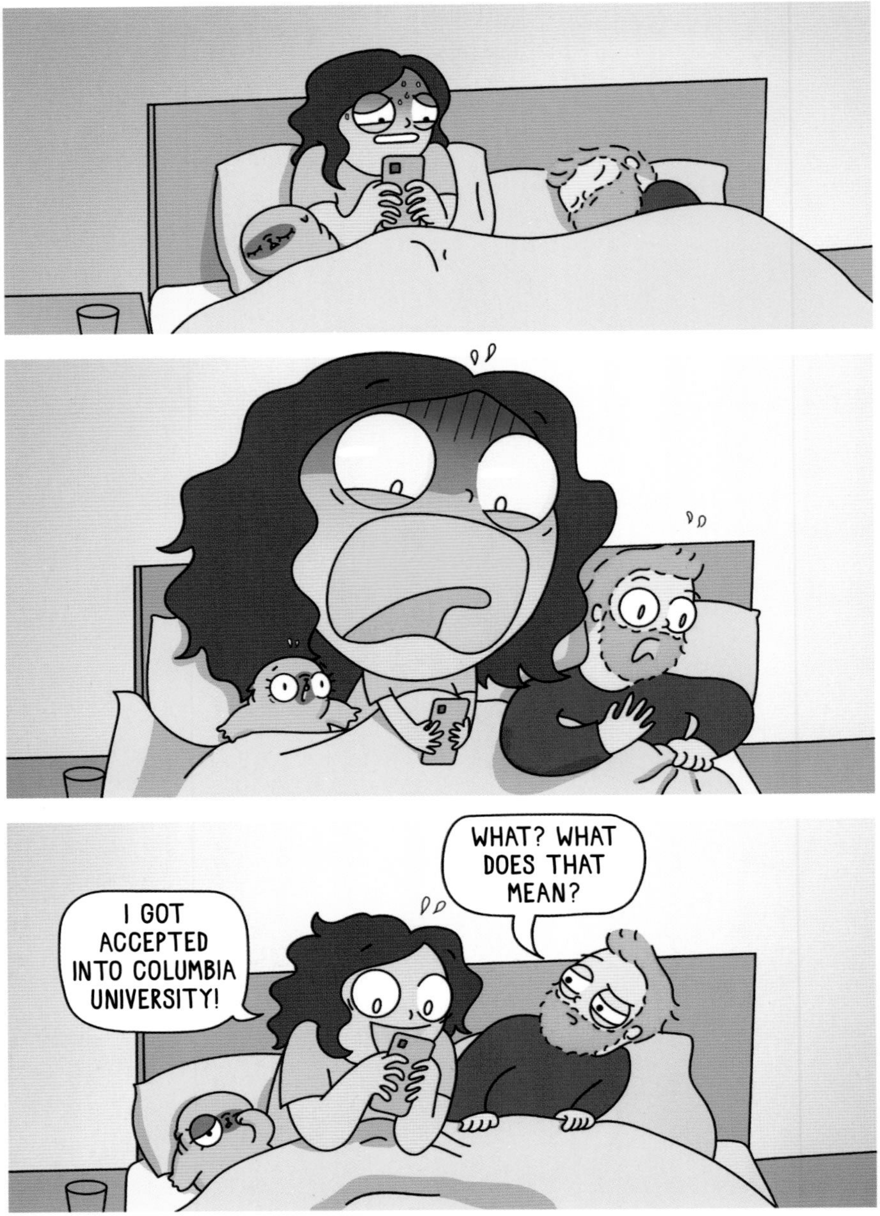
I GOT ACCEPTED INTO COLUMBIA UNIVERSITY!
WHAT? WHAT DOES THAT MEAN?

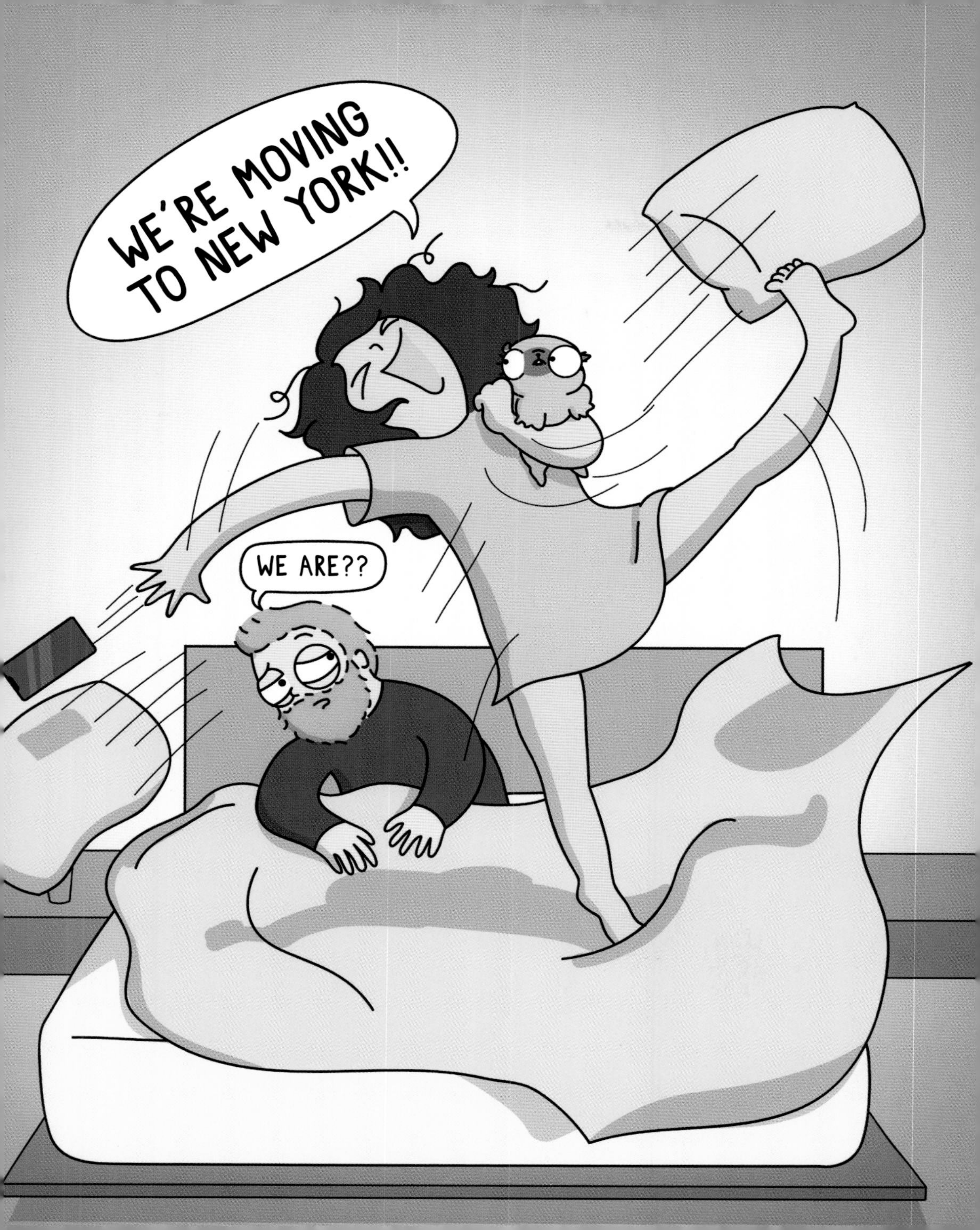
WE'RE MOVING TO NEW YORK!!
WE ARE??

PELI HAD TO FINISH SOME WORK BEFORE HE COULD JOIN US IN NEW YORK, SO MOCHI AND I SPENT A SUMMER ALONE.

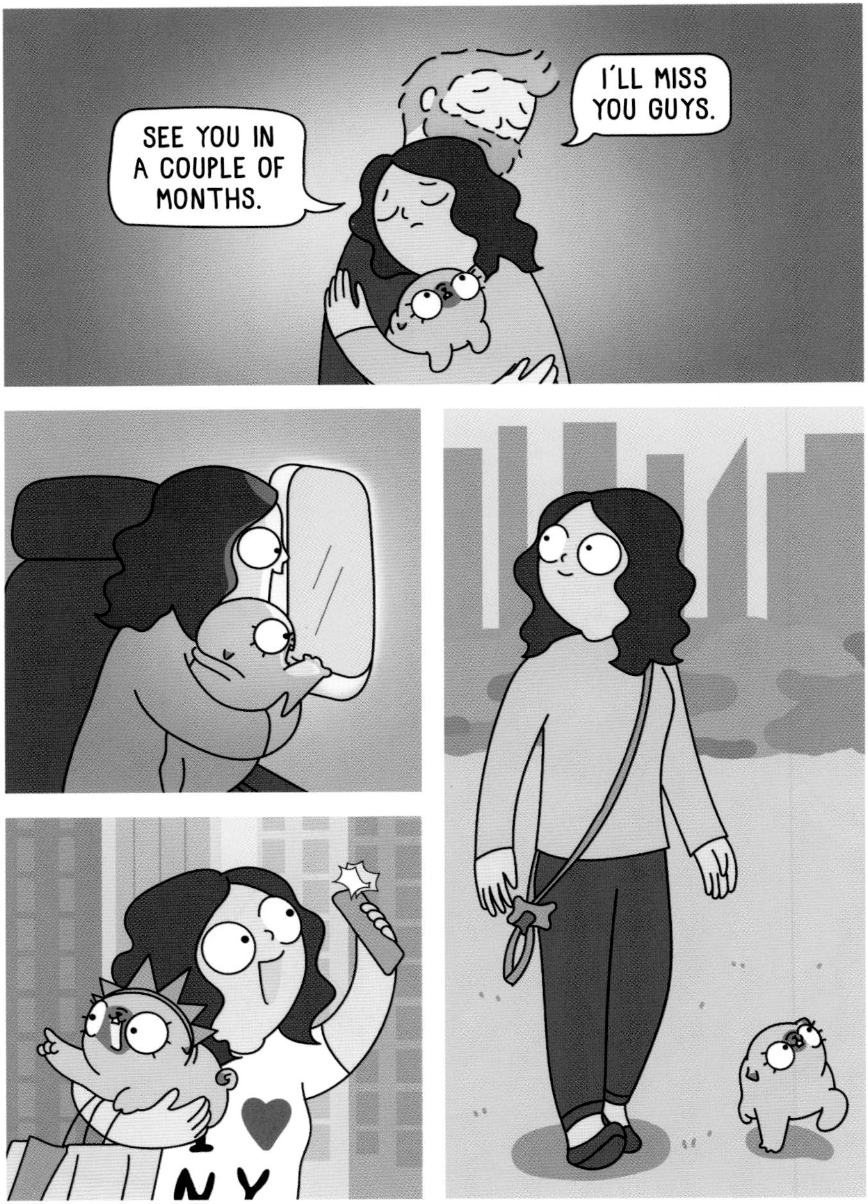
I'LL MISS YOU GUYS.
SEE YOU IN A COUPLE OF MONTHS.
I ♥ NY

WE HAD A MOUSE PROBLEM FOR TWO DAYS. WE WERE SCARED OF GOING INTO THE KITCHEN, AND MOCHI GOT SICK BECAUSE ALL WE ATE WAS TAKEOUT.

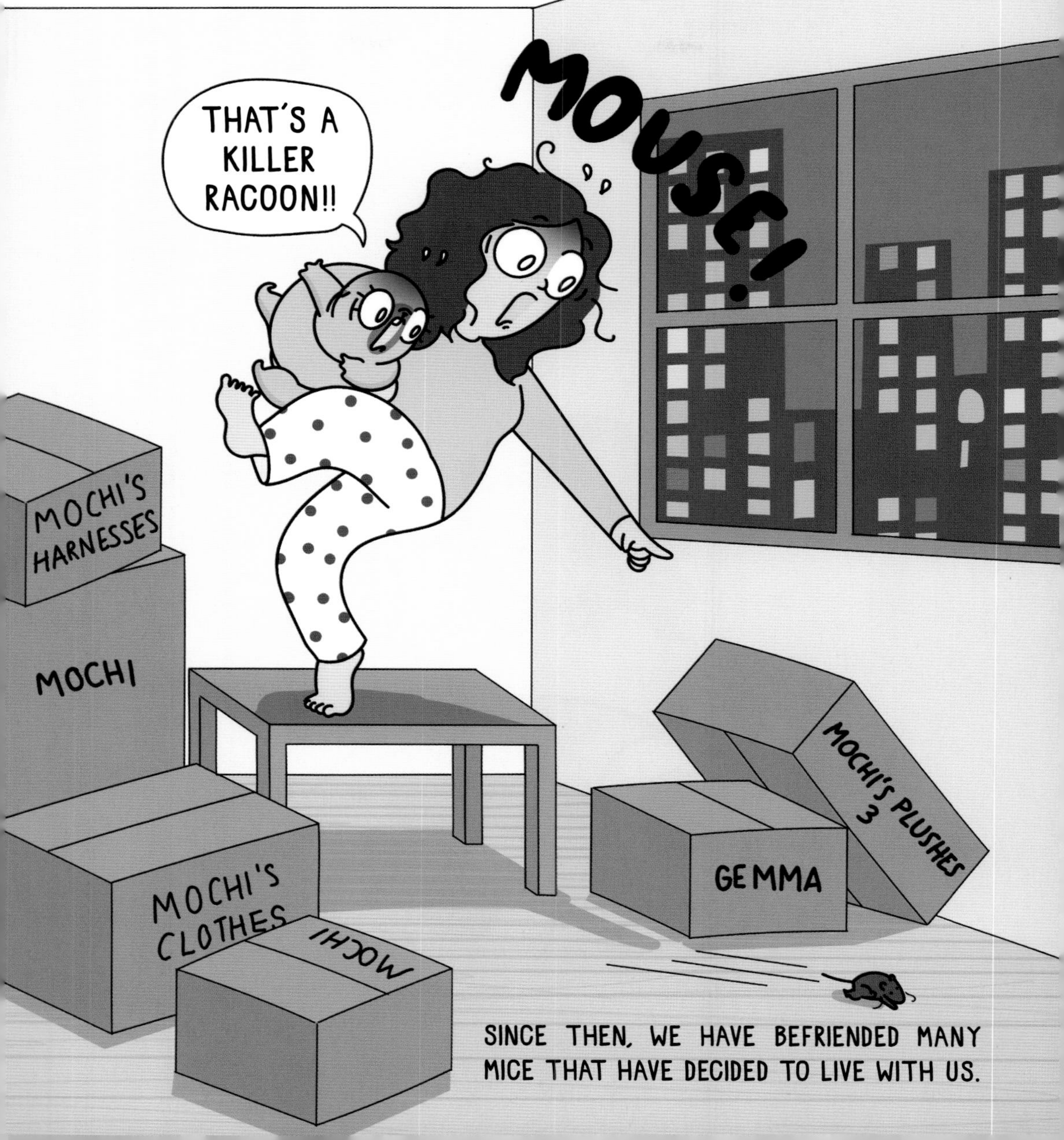

THAT'S A KILLER RACOON!!
MOUSE!
MOCHI'S HARNESSES
MOCHI
MOCHI'S CLOTHES
MOCHI
GEMMA
MOCHI'S PLUSHES 3
SINCE THEN, WE HAVE BEFRIENDED MANY MICE THAT HAVE DECIDED TO LIVE WITH US.

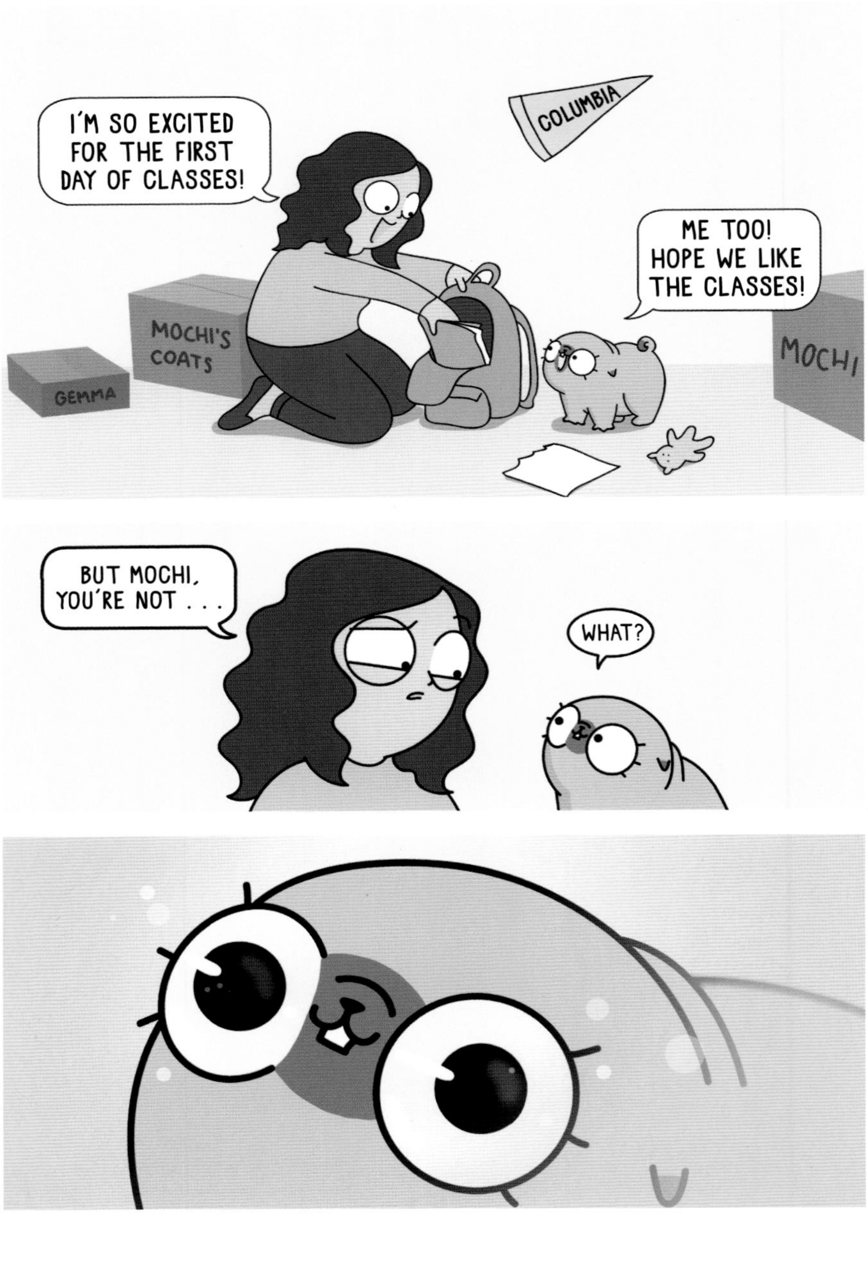
I'M SO EXCITED FOR THE FIRST DAY OF CLASSES!
COLUMBIA
ME TOO! HOPE WE LIKE THE CLASSES!
MOCHI'S COATS
GEMMA
MOCHI
BUT MOCHI, YOU'RE NOT . . .
WHAT?

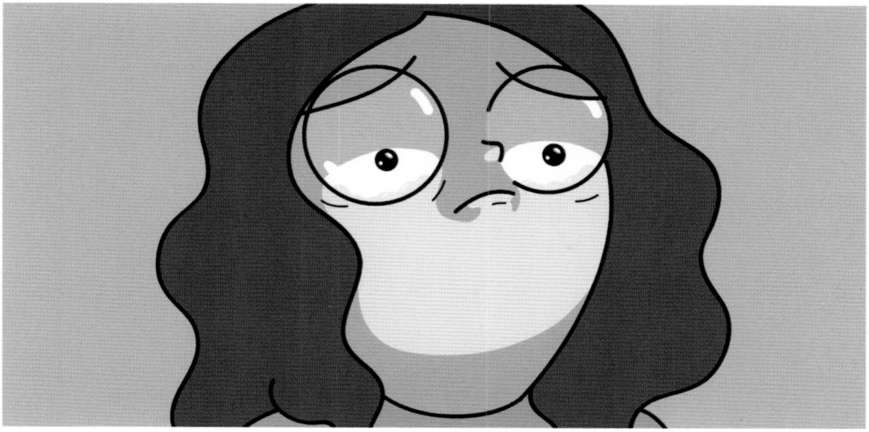

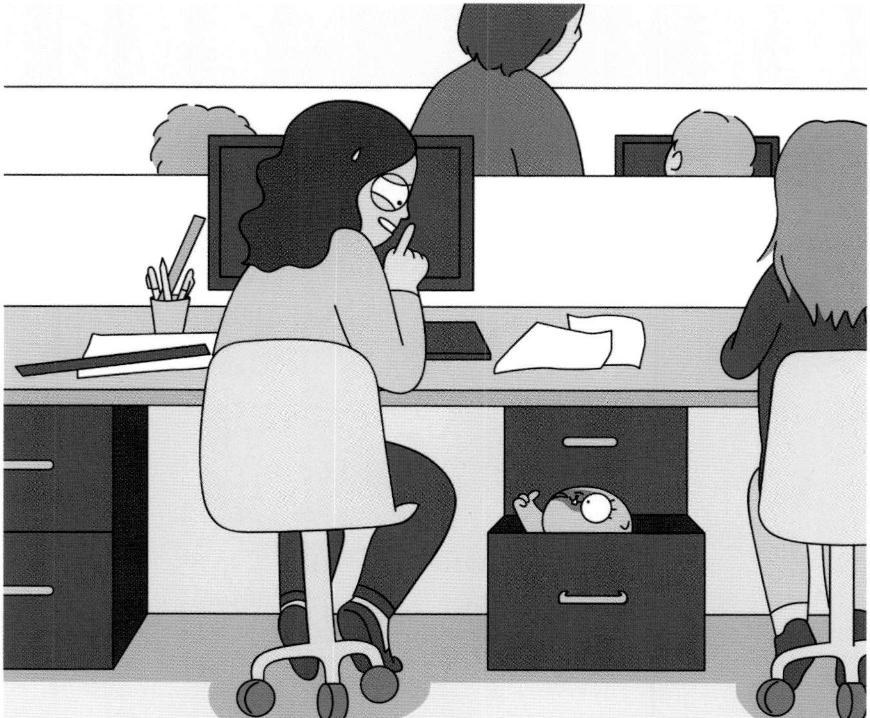

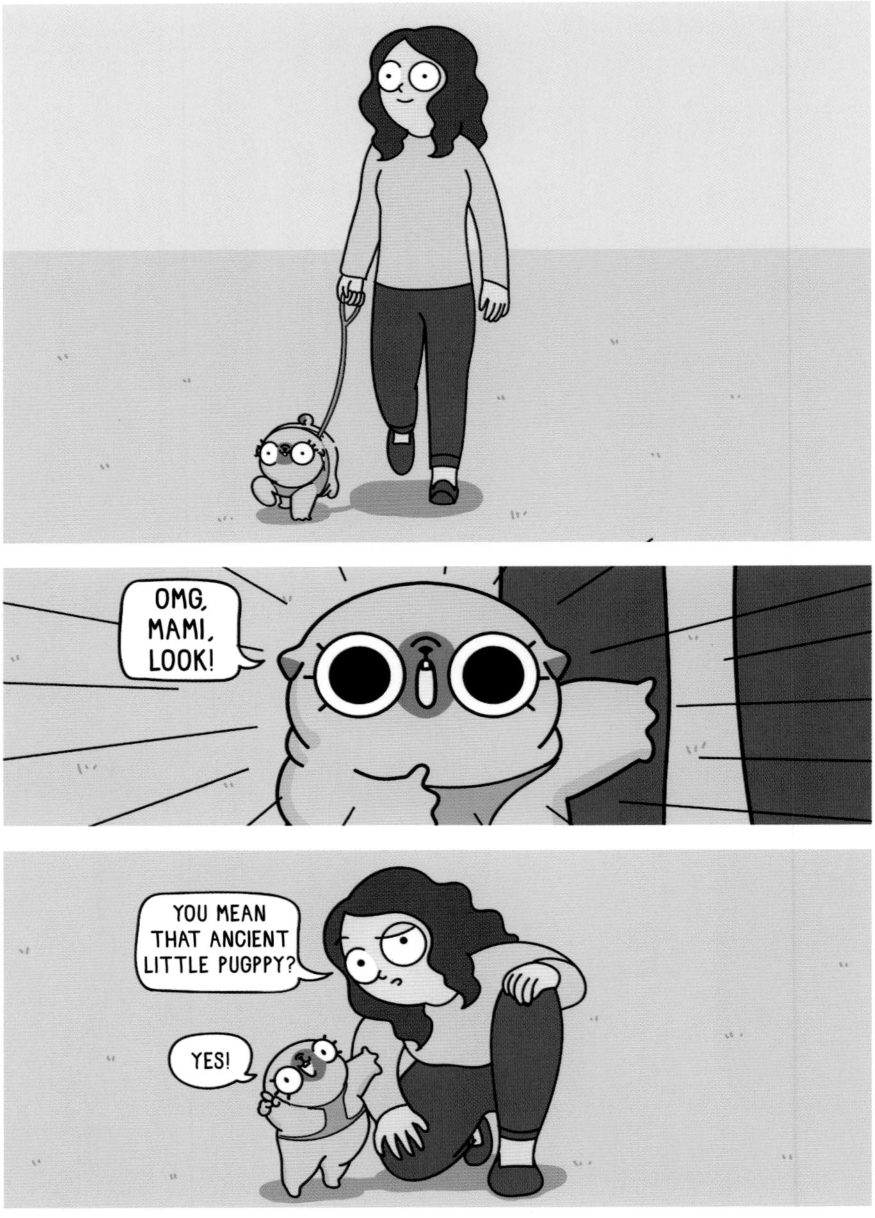
OMG, MAMI, LOOK!
YOU MEAN THAT ANCIENT LITTLE PUGPPY?
YES!

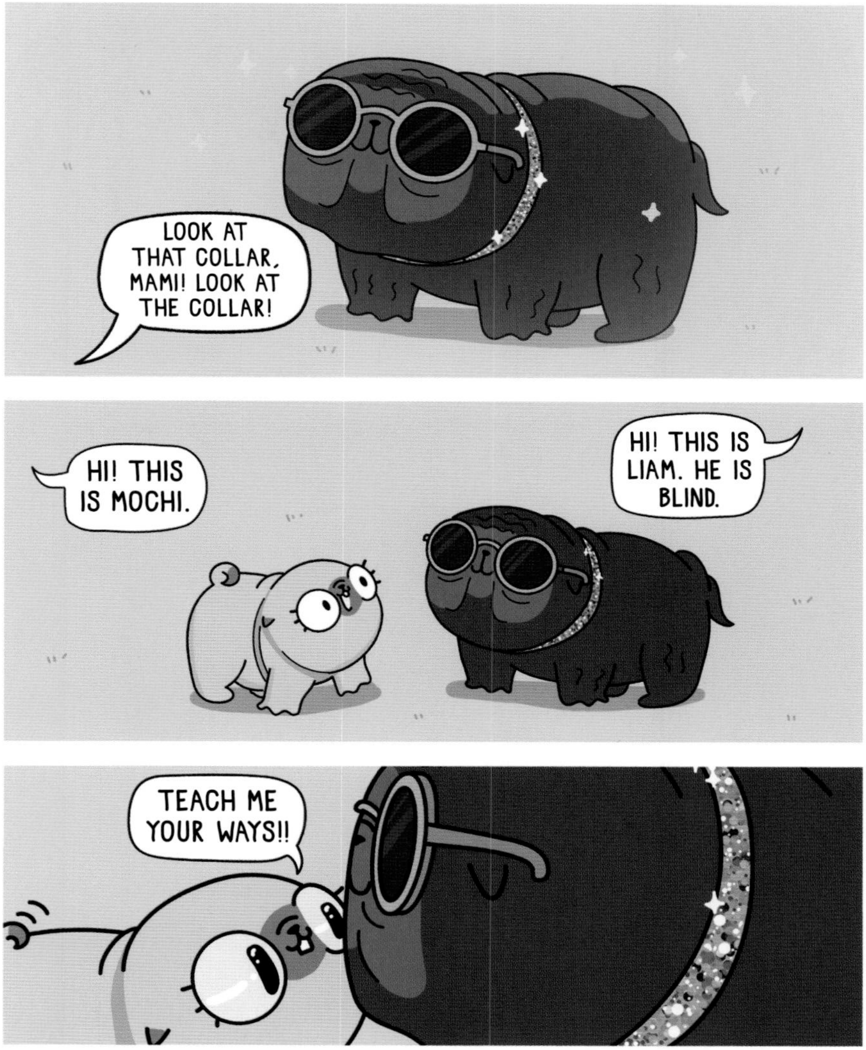
LOOK AT THAT COLLAR, MAMI! LOOK AT THE COLLAR!
HI! THIS IS MOCHI.
HI! THIS IS LIAM. HE IS BLIND.
TEACH ME YOUR WAYS!!

FOR SOME REASON, MOCHI HAS ALWAYS LOVED SENIOR DOGS. LIAM WAS THE FIRST DOG WE MET IN NEW YORK AND MOCHI WAS OBSESSED. I THINK MOCHI WAS BEGINNING TO COLLECT THE SASS AND PERSONALITY OF OLDER DOGS THAT HE ASPIRED TO BE LIKE LATER IN LIFE.

COME ON, MOCHI! IT'S SUPER LATE!
WAAAIT!!
OH, SORRY, MOCHI! I DIDN'T REALIZE YOU WERE DOING YOUR BUSINESS.

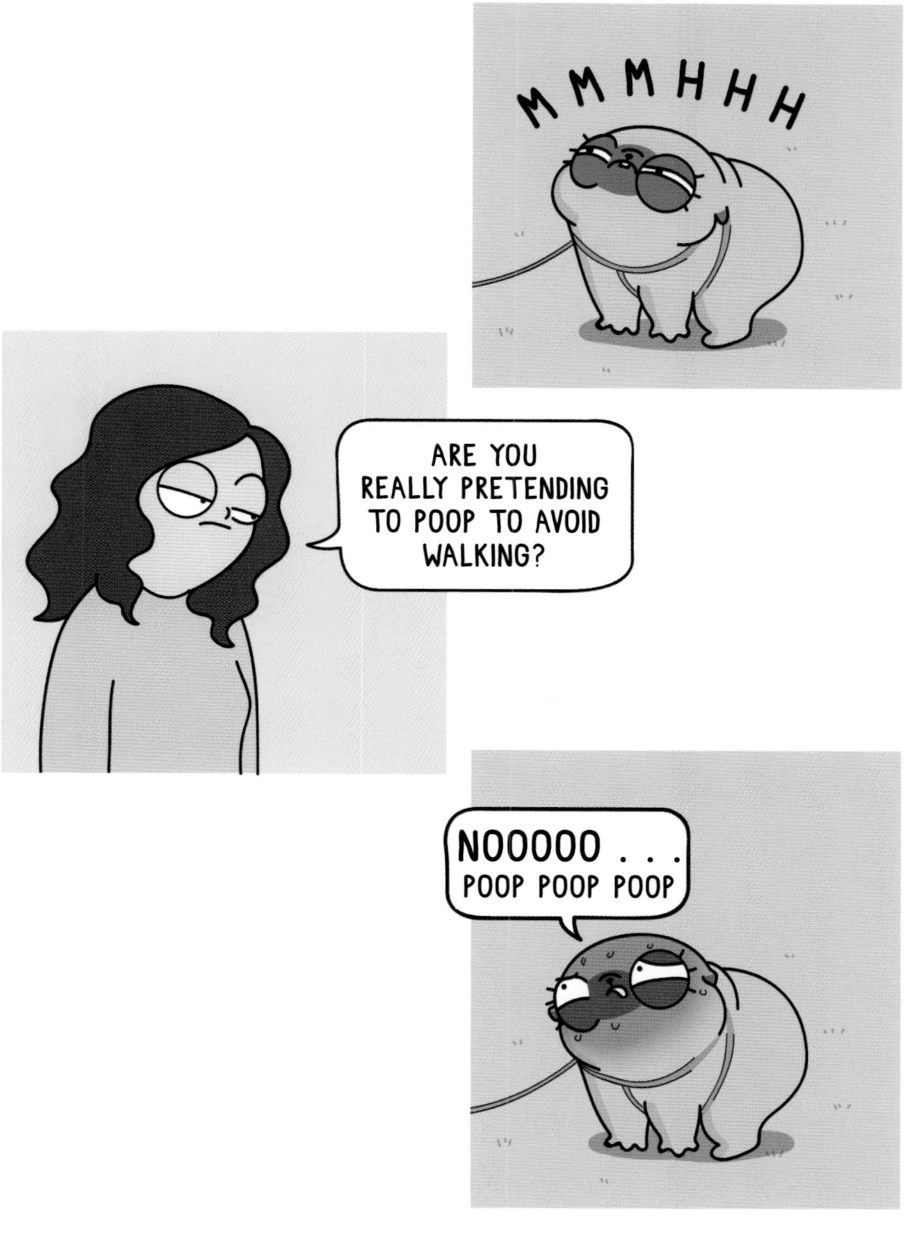
MMMHHH
ARE YOU REALLY PRETENDING TO POOP TO AVOID WALKING?
NOOOOO . . . POOP POOP POOP

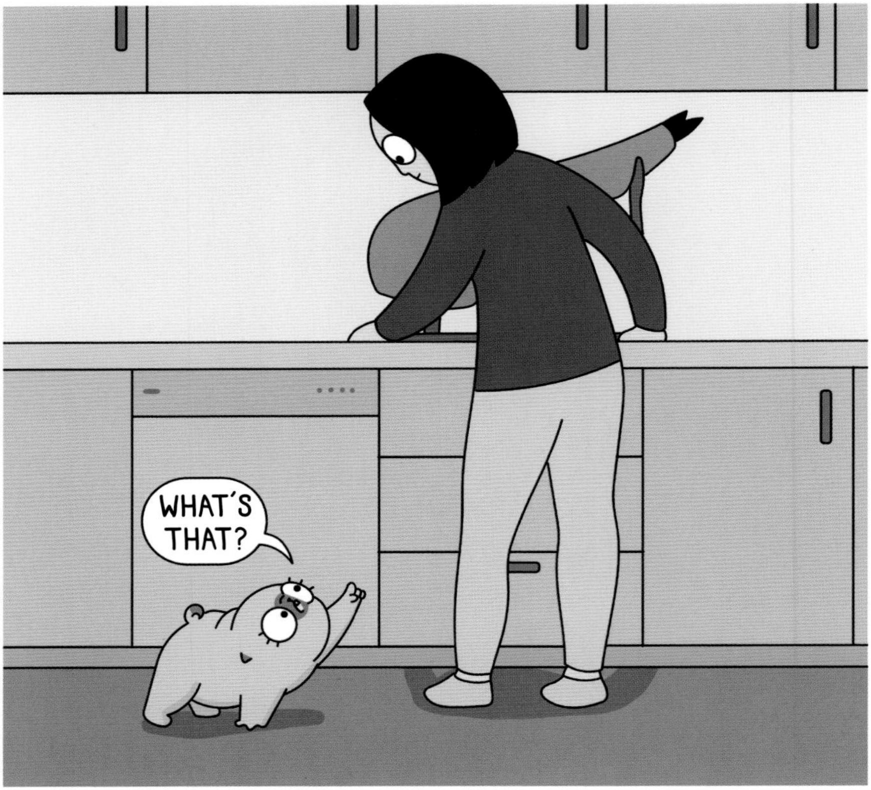
WHAT'S THAT?

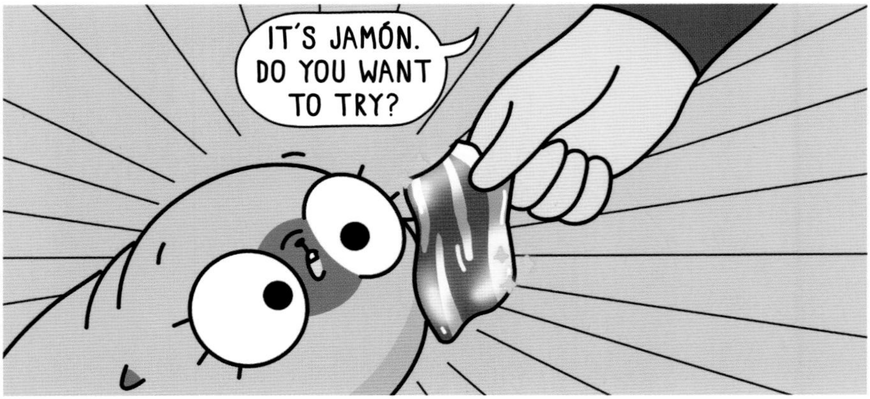
IT'S JAMÓN. DO YOU WANT TO TRY?

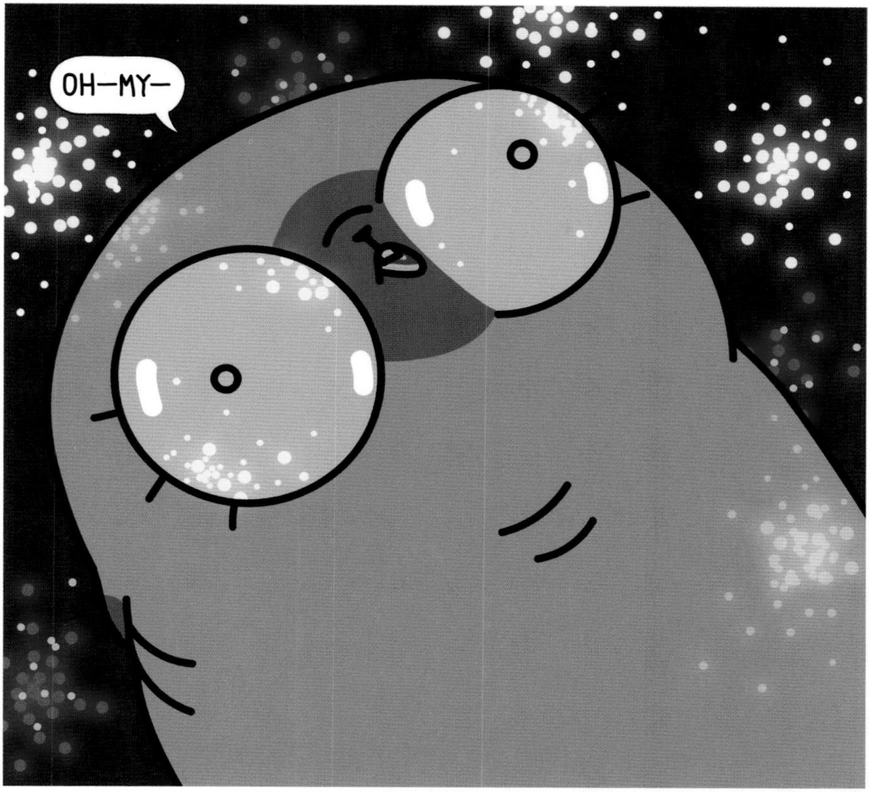
OH—MY—

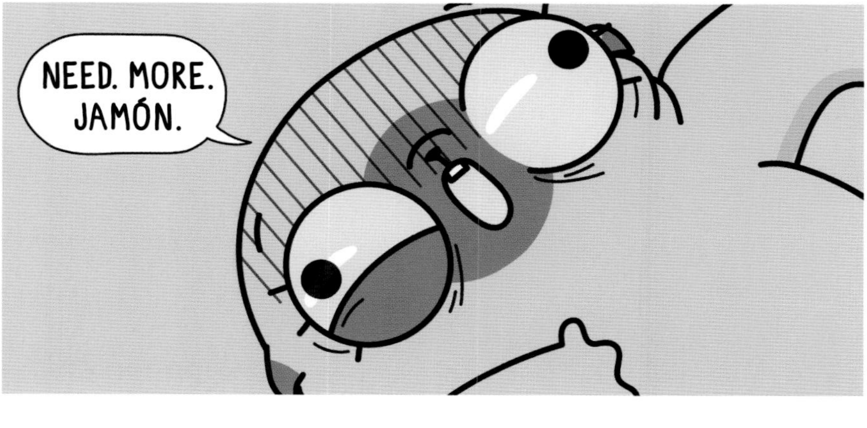
NEED. MORE. JAMÓN.

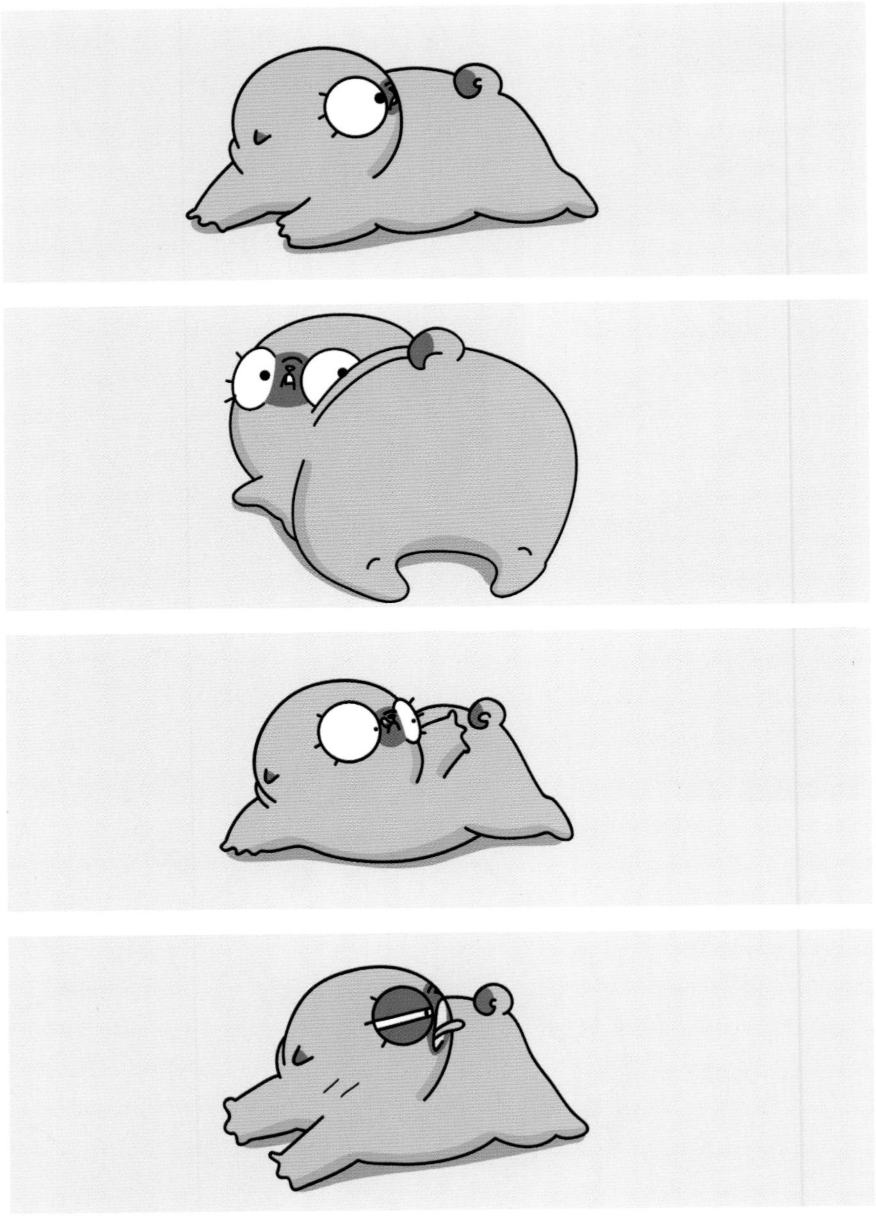

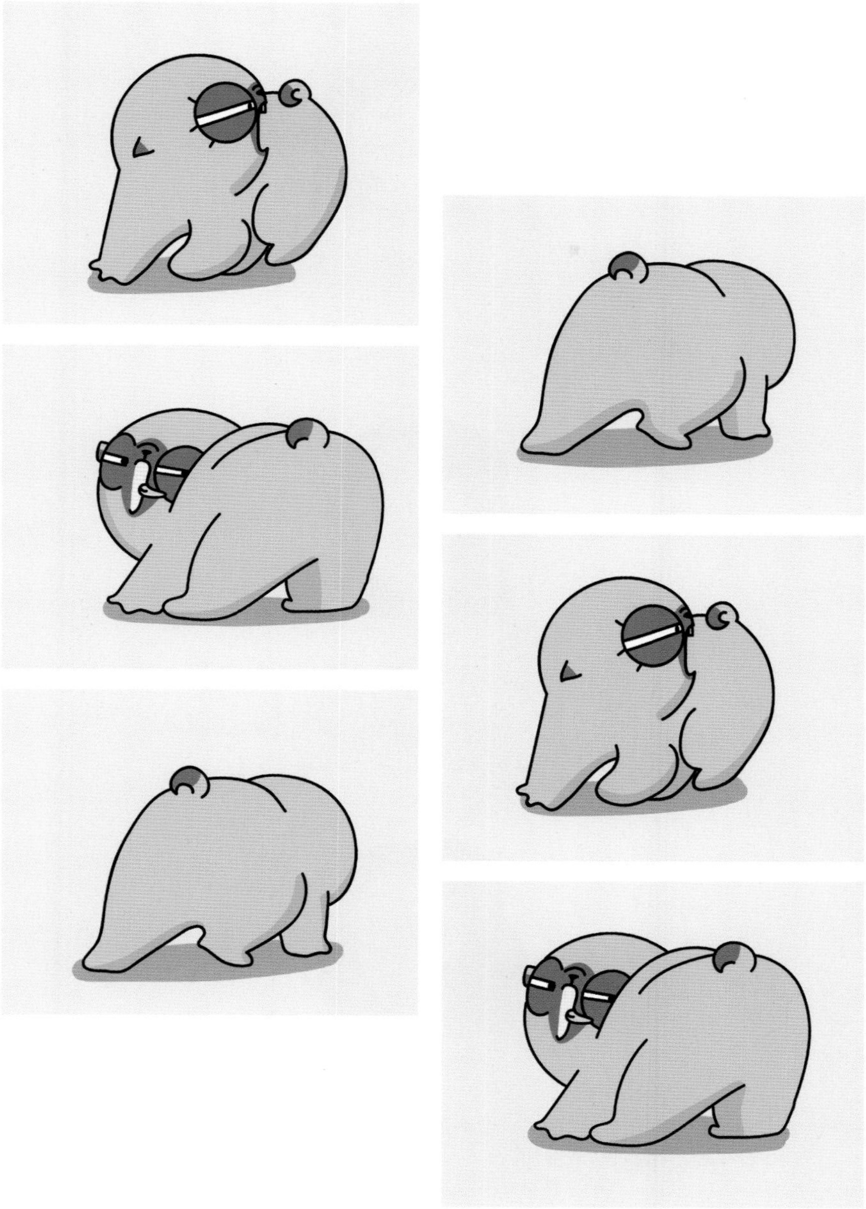

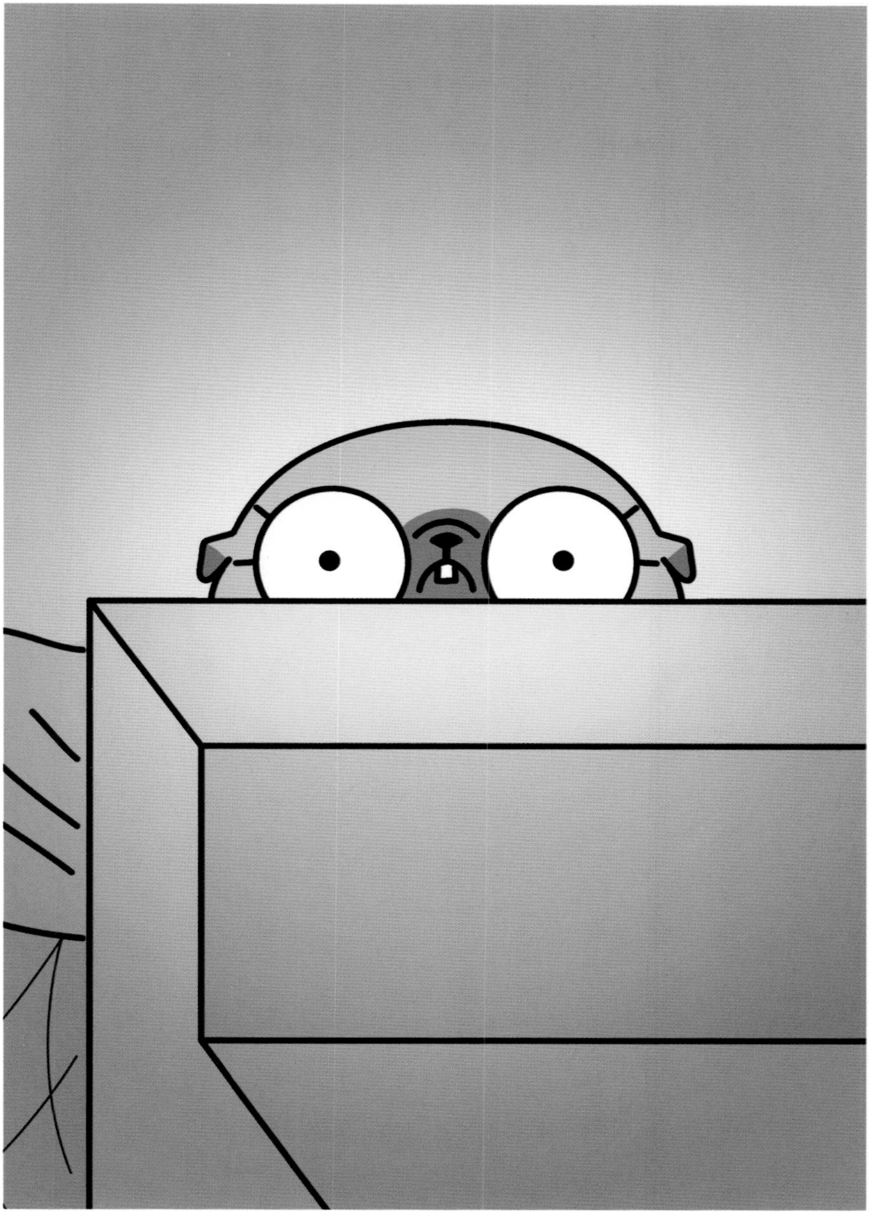

I'VE COME TO ACCEPT I'LL FOREVER BE COVERED IN FUR

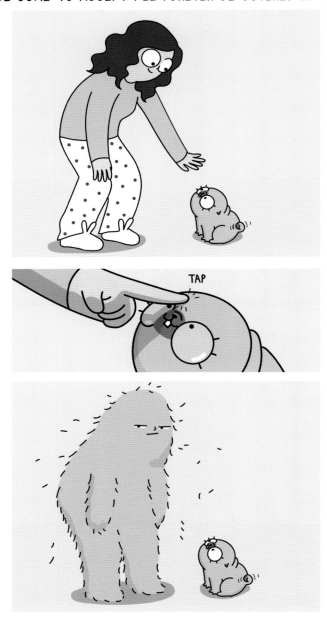

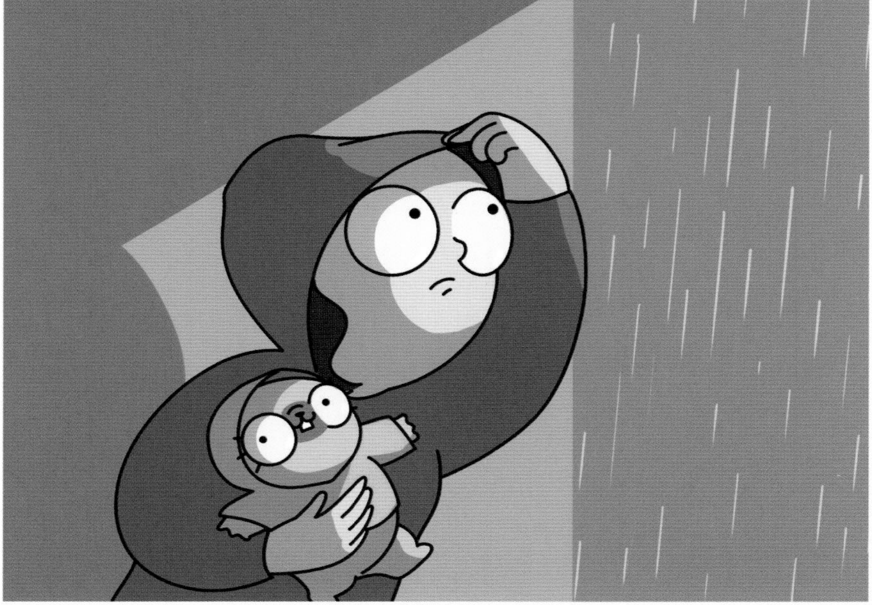

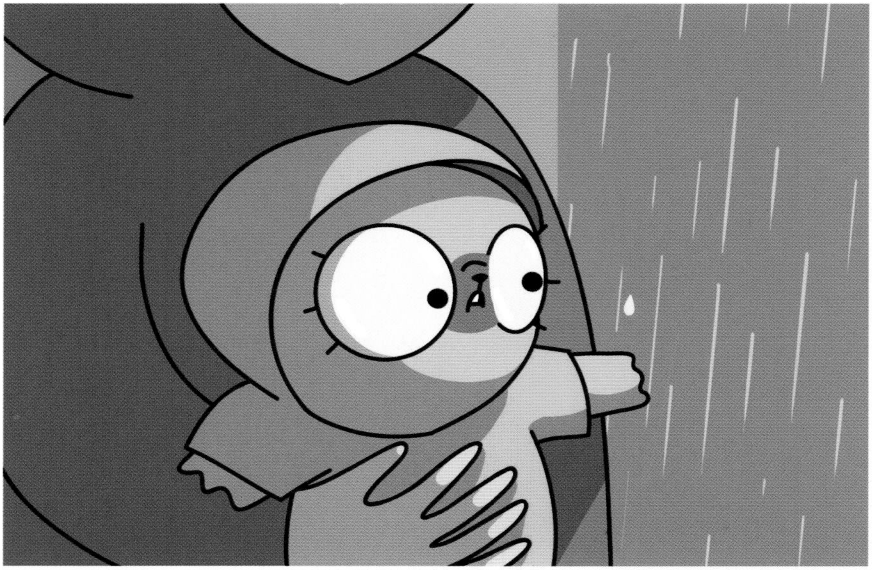

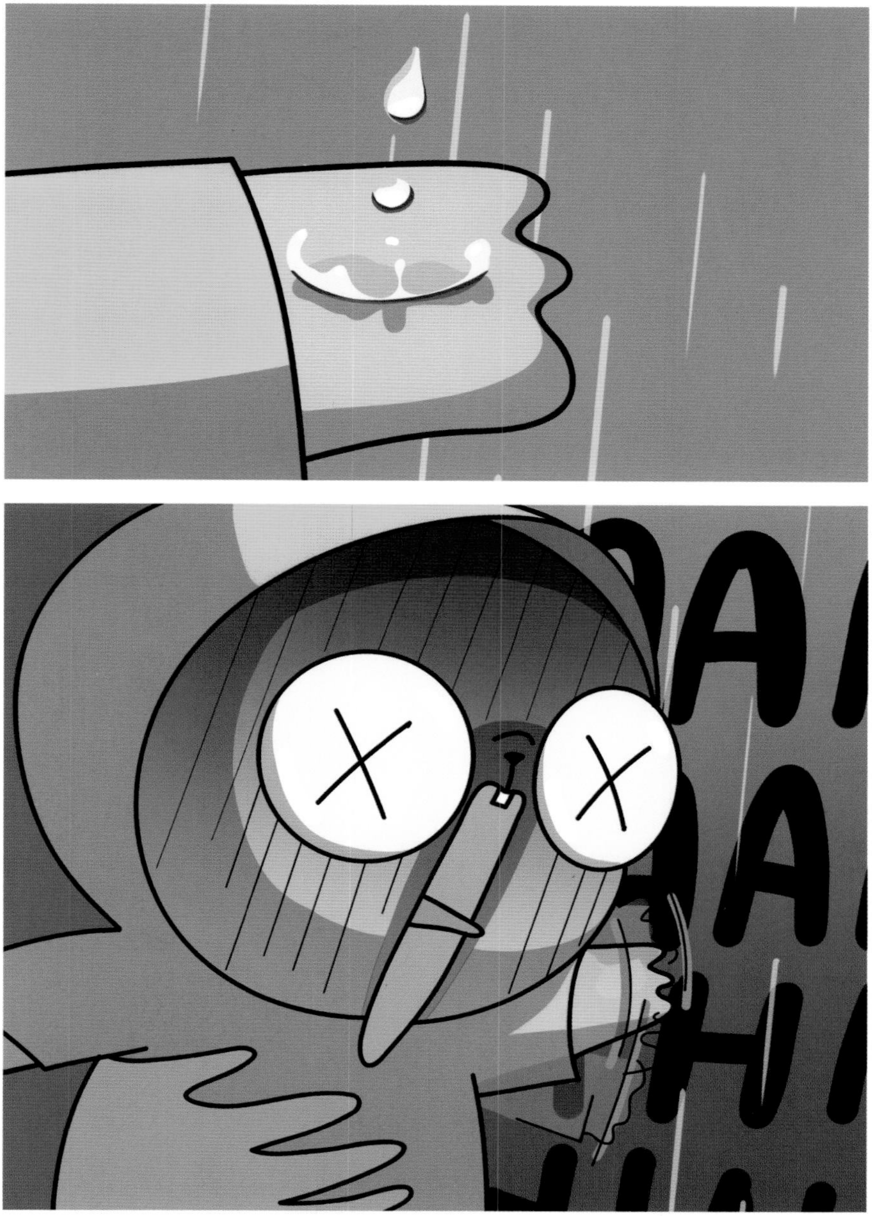

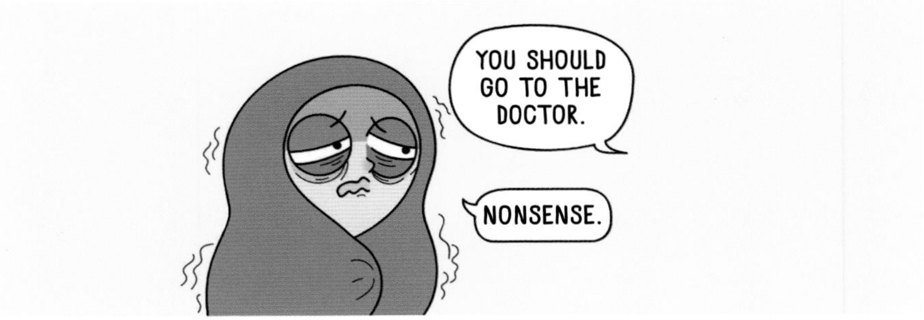
YOU SHOULD GO TO THE DOCTOR.
NONSENSE.

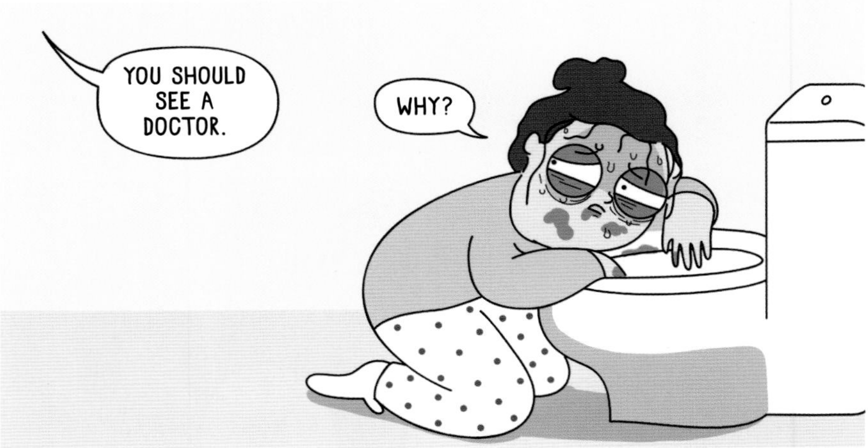
YOU SHOULD SEE A DOCTOR.
WHY?

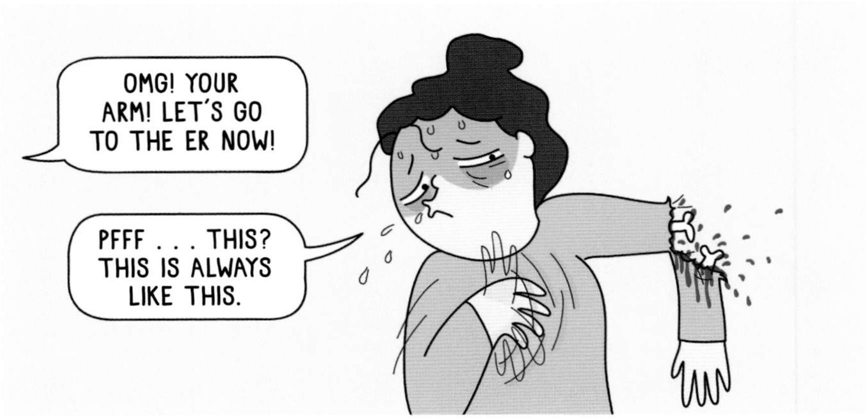
OMG! YOUR ARM! LET'S GO TO THE ER NOW!
PFFF . . . THIS? THIS IS ALWAYS LIKE THIS.

ACHOO
VETERINARY
HOSPITAL

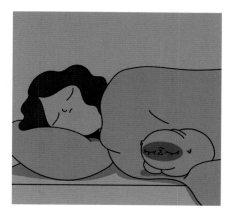

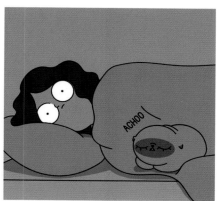

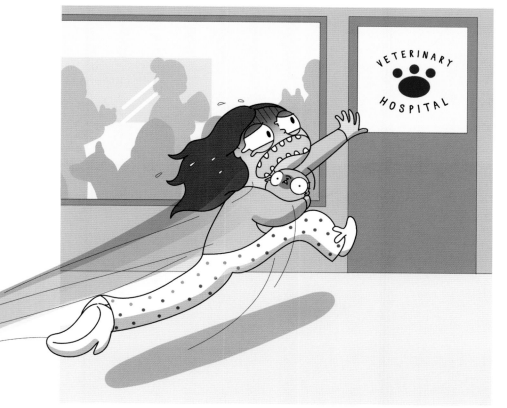

BABIES GROW UP TO BECOME ADULTS.

BUT OTHERS, LIKE MOCHI, JUST GROW UP TO BE BIGGER BABIES.

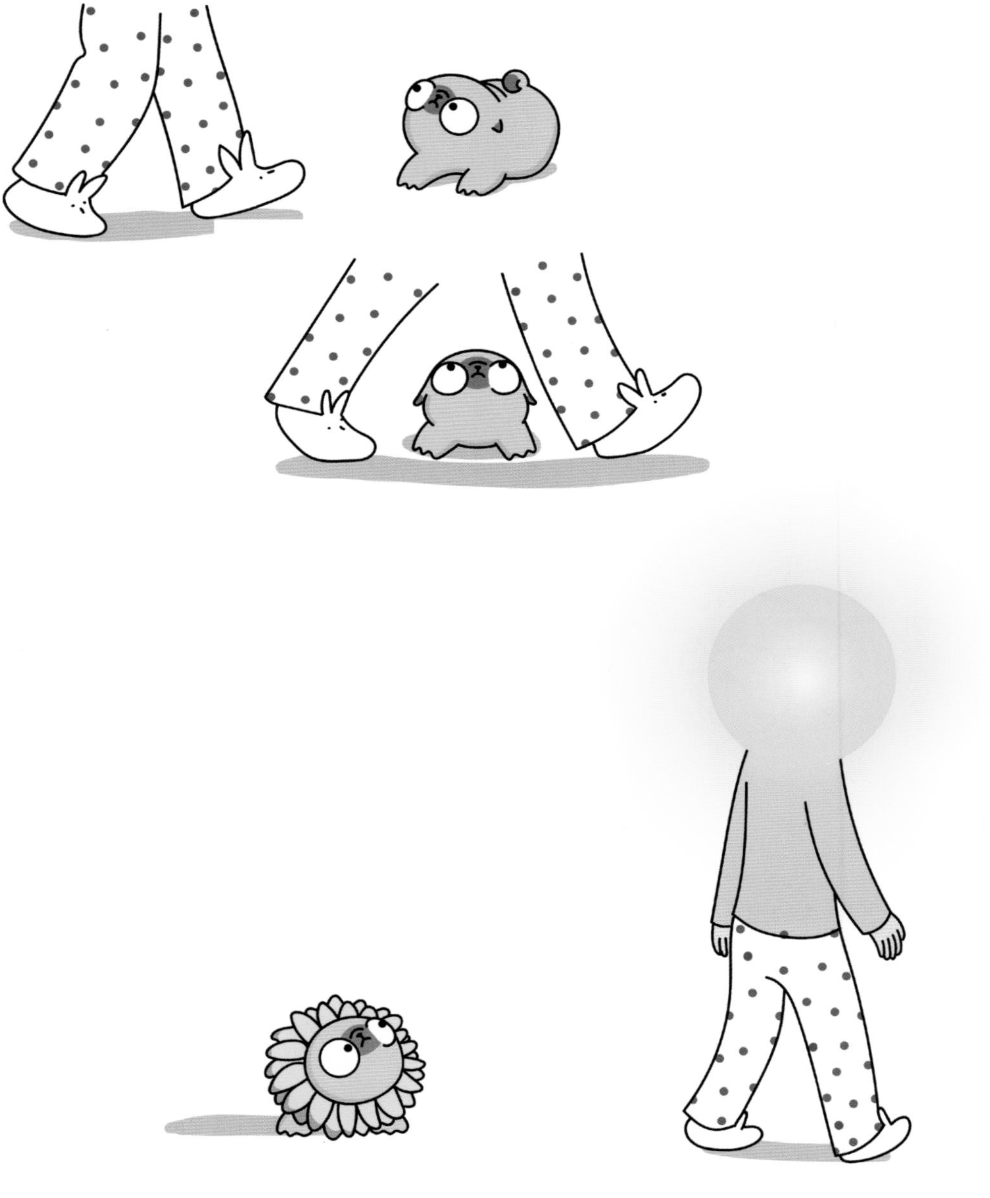

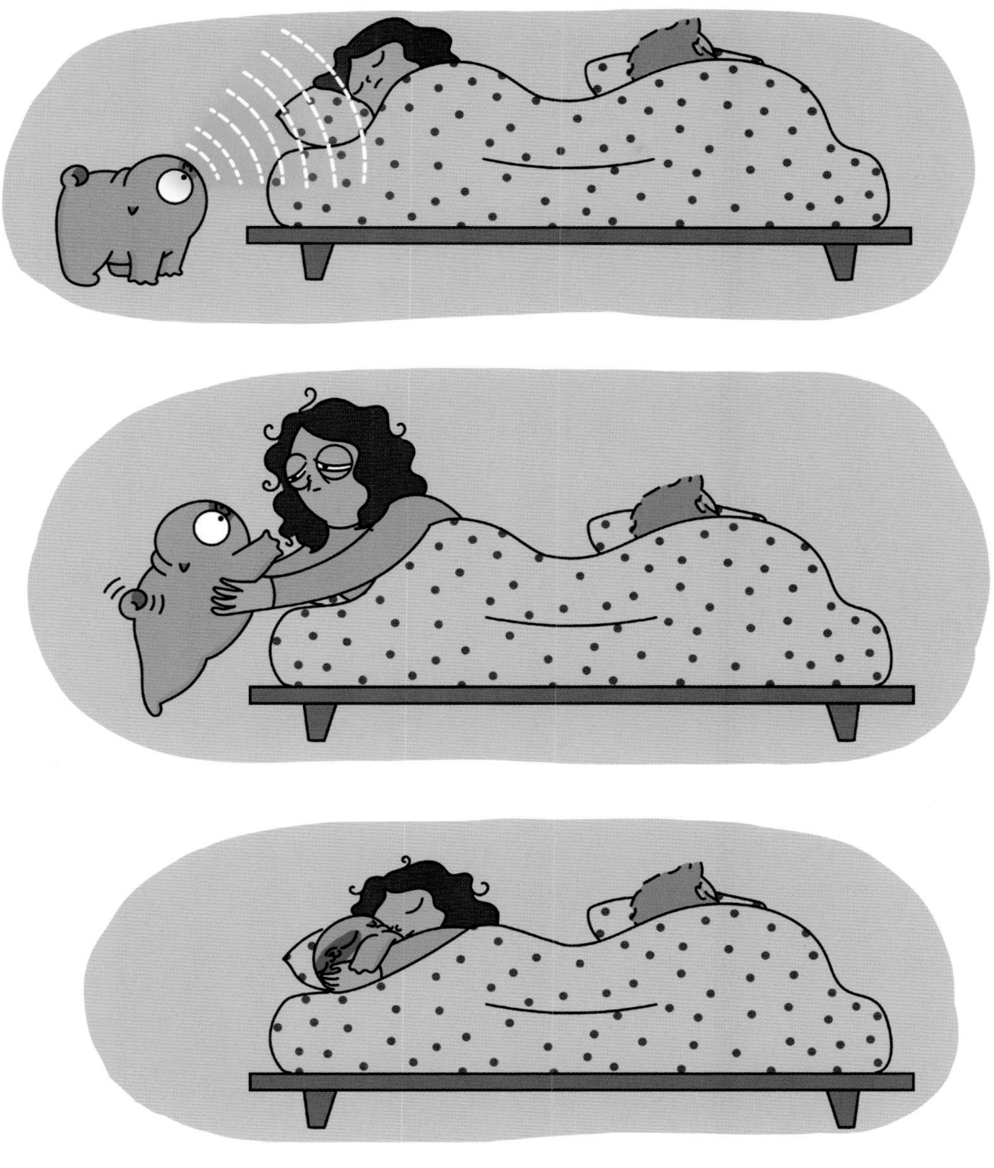

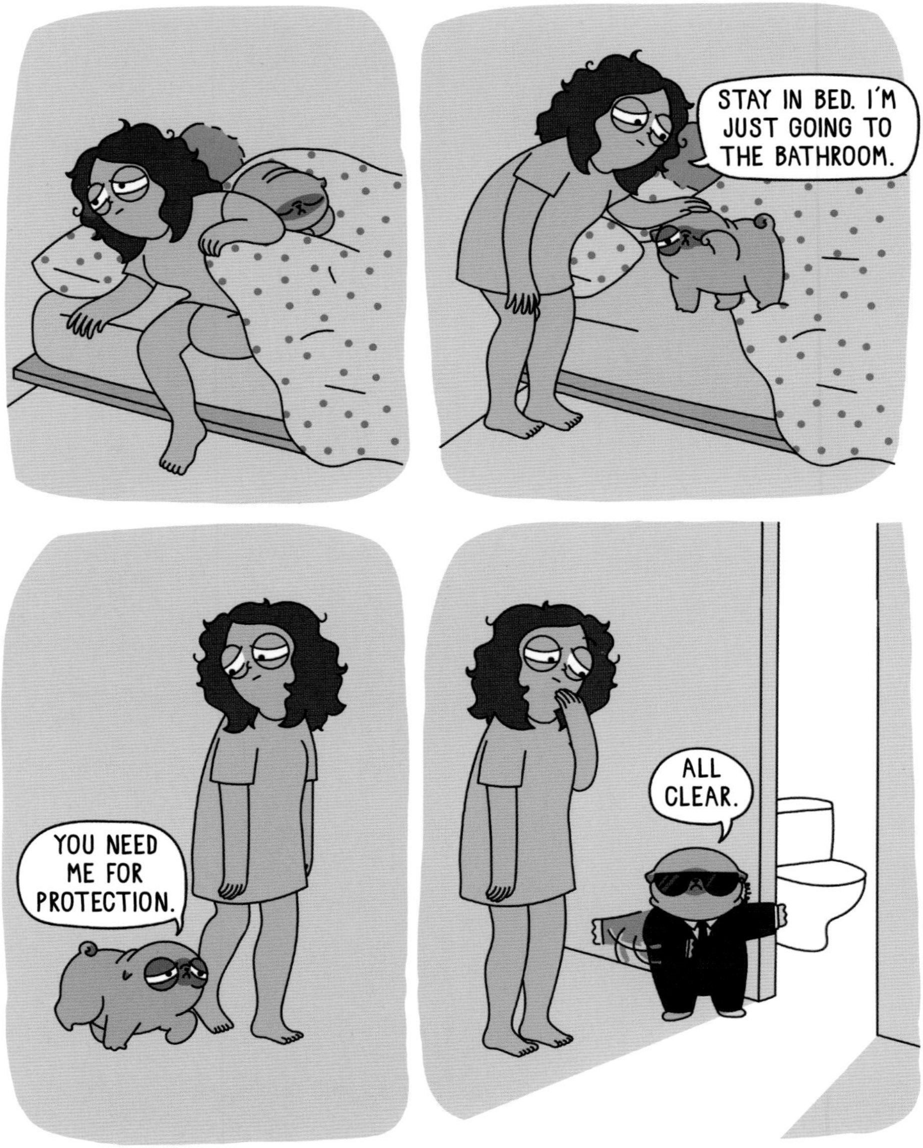
STAY IN BED. I'M JUST GOING TO THE BATHROOM.
YOU NEED ME FOR PROTECTION.
ALL CLEAR.

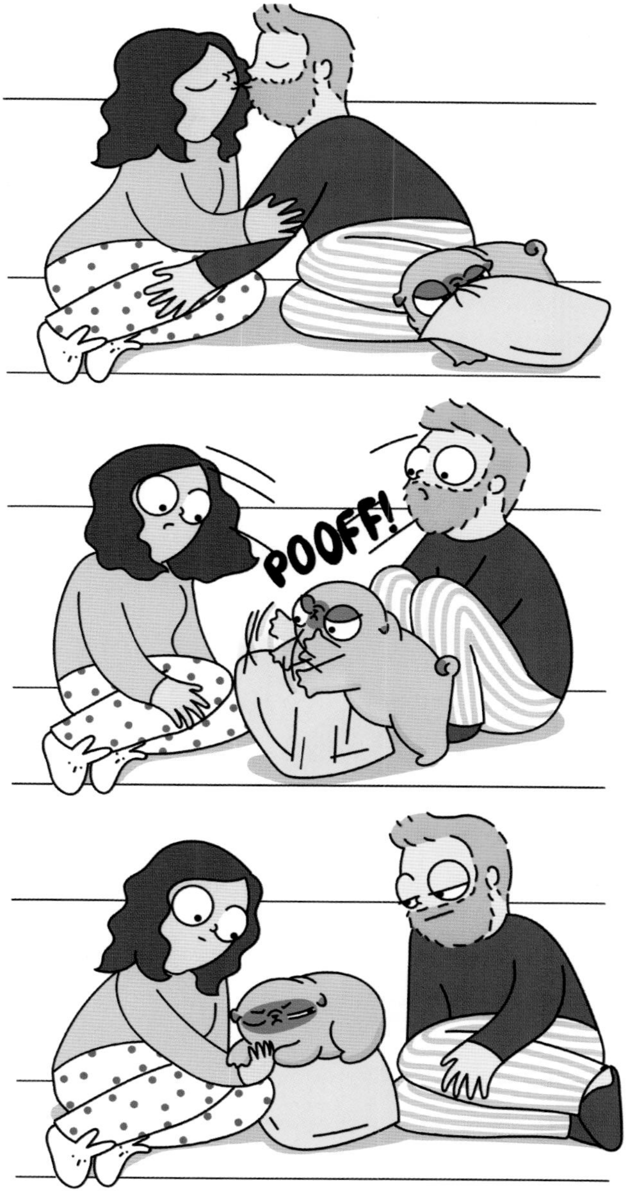
POOFF!

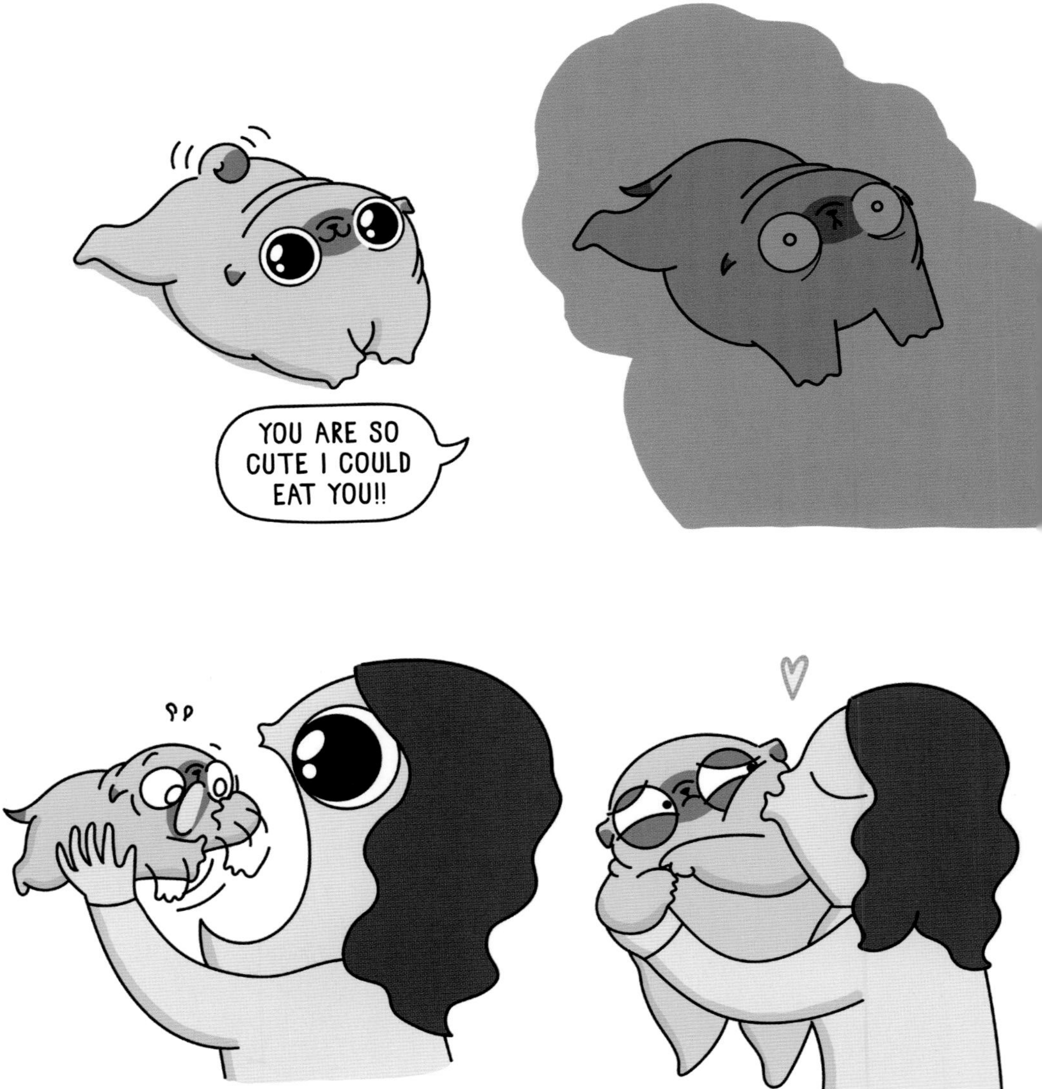
YOU ARE SO CUTE I COULD EAT YOU!!

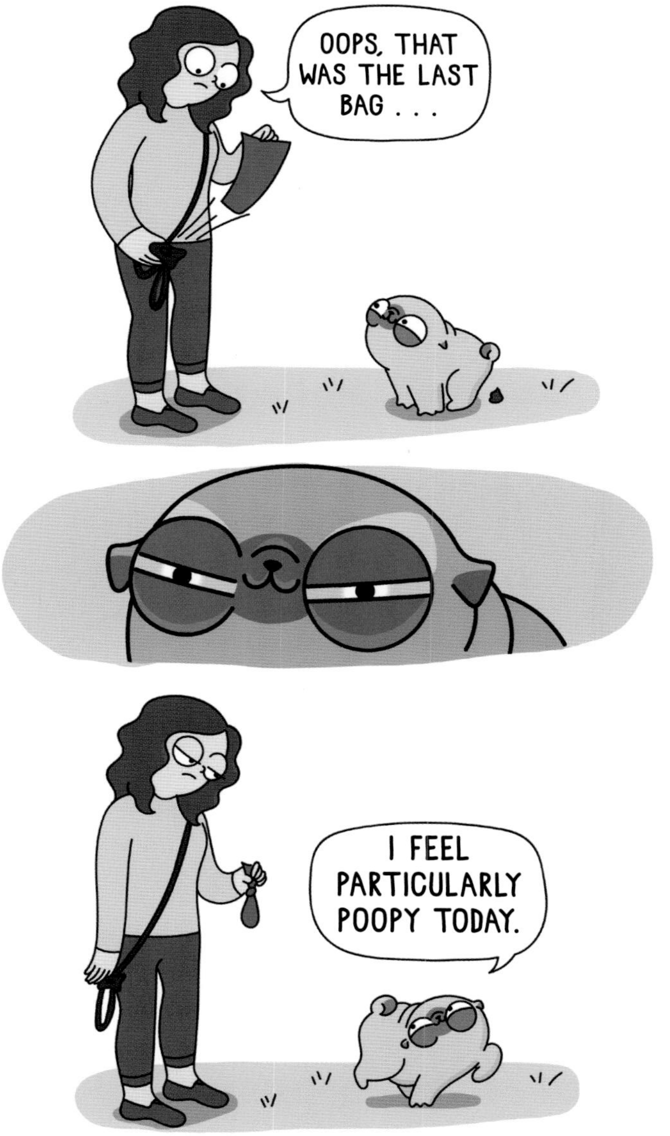
OOPS, THAT WAS THE LAST BAG . . .
I FEEL PARTICULARLY POOPY TODAY.

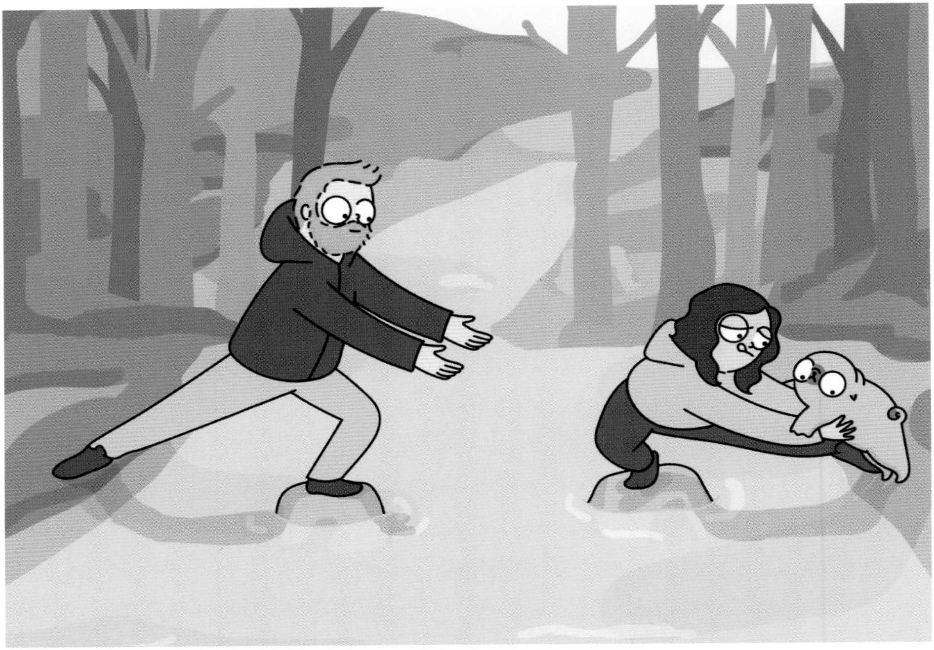

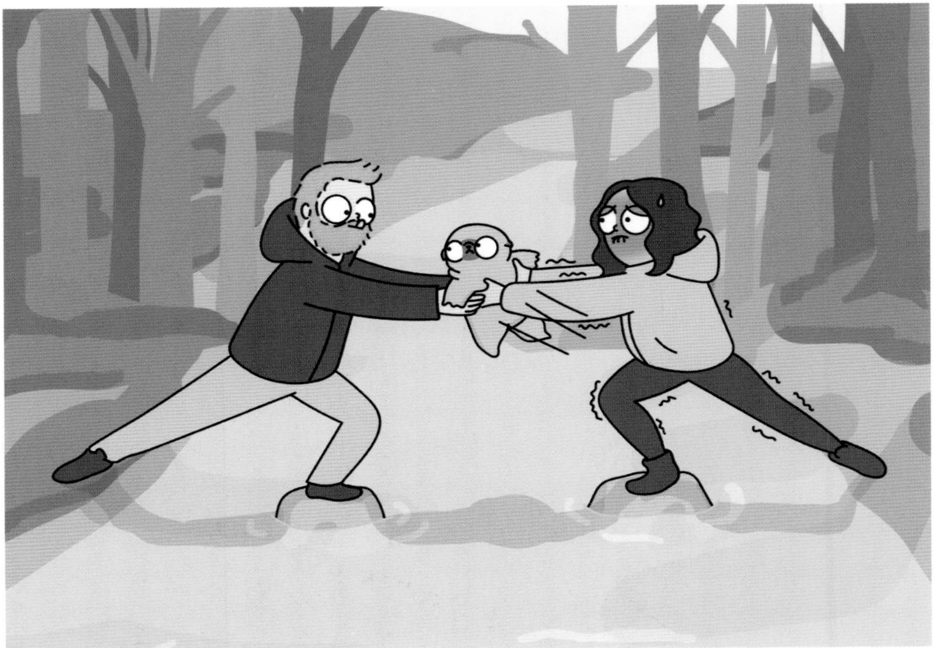

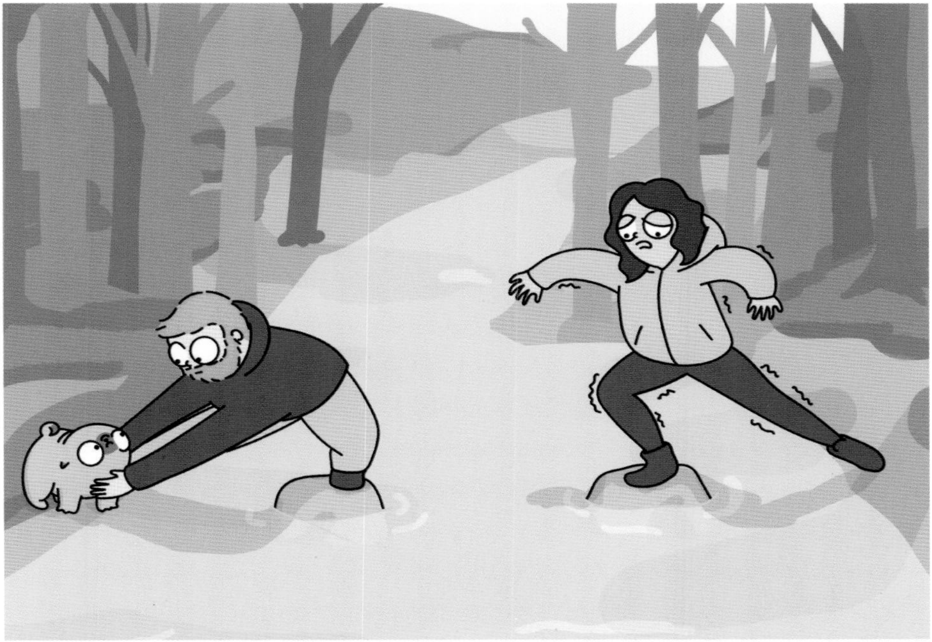

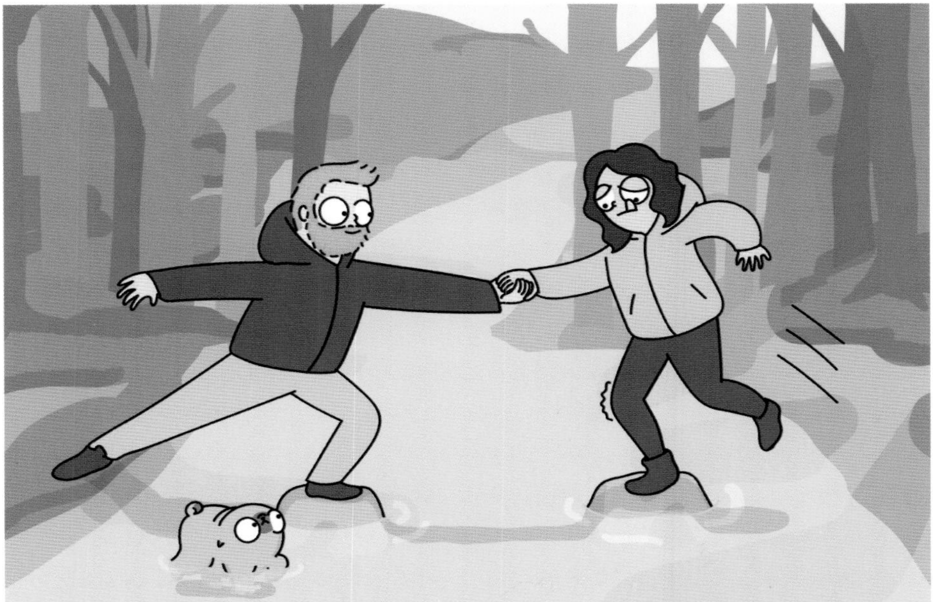

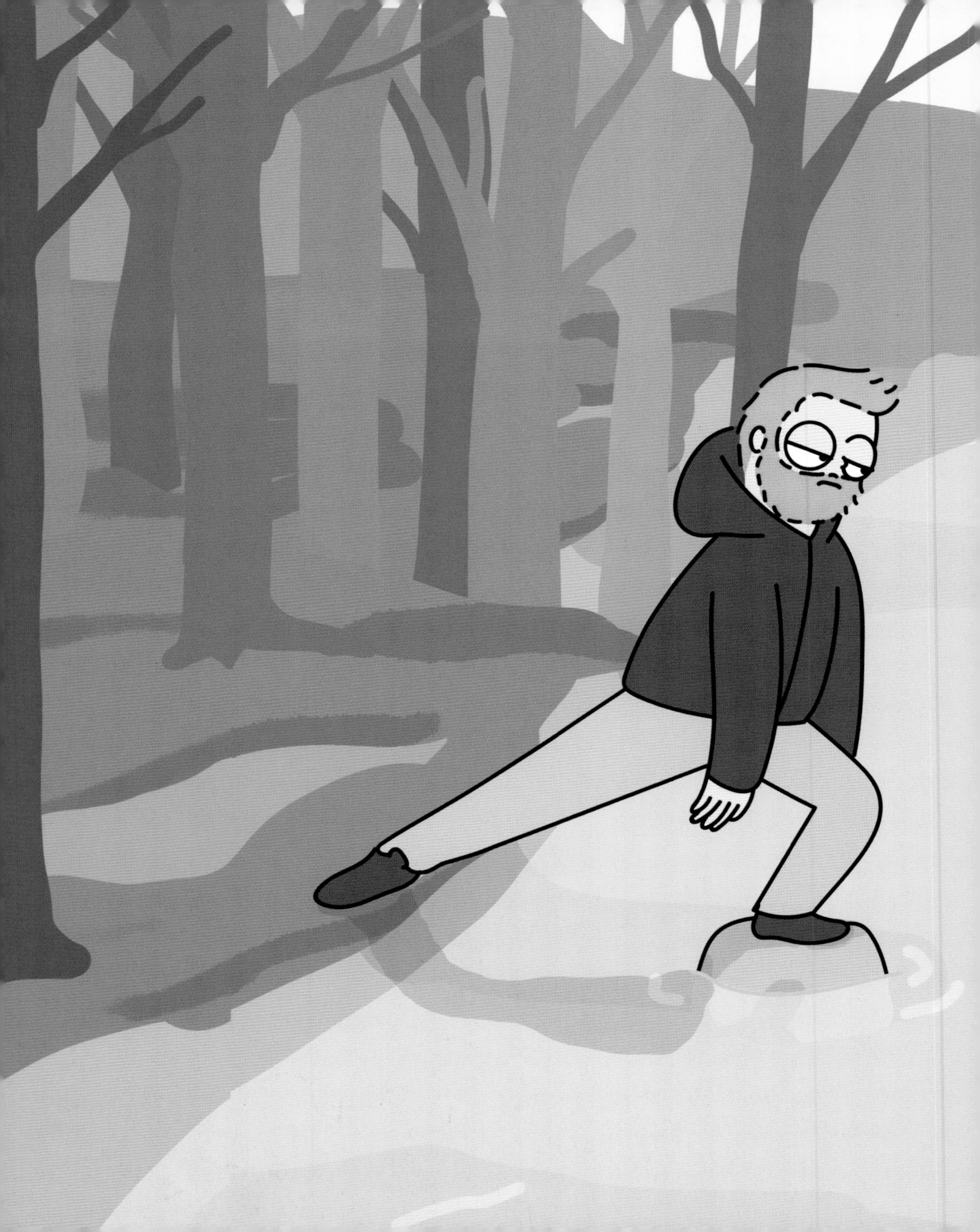

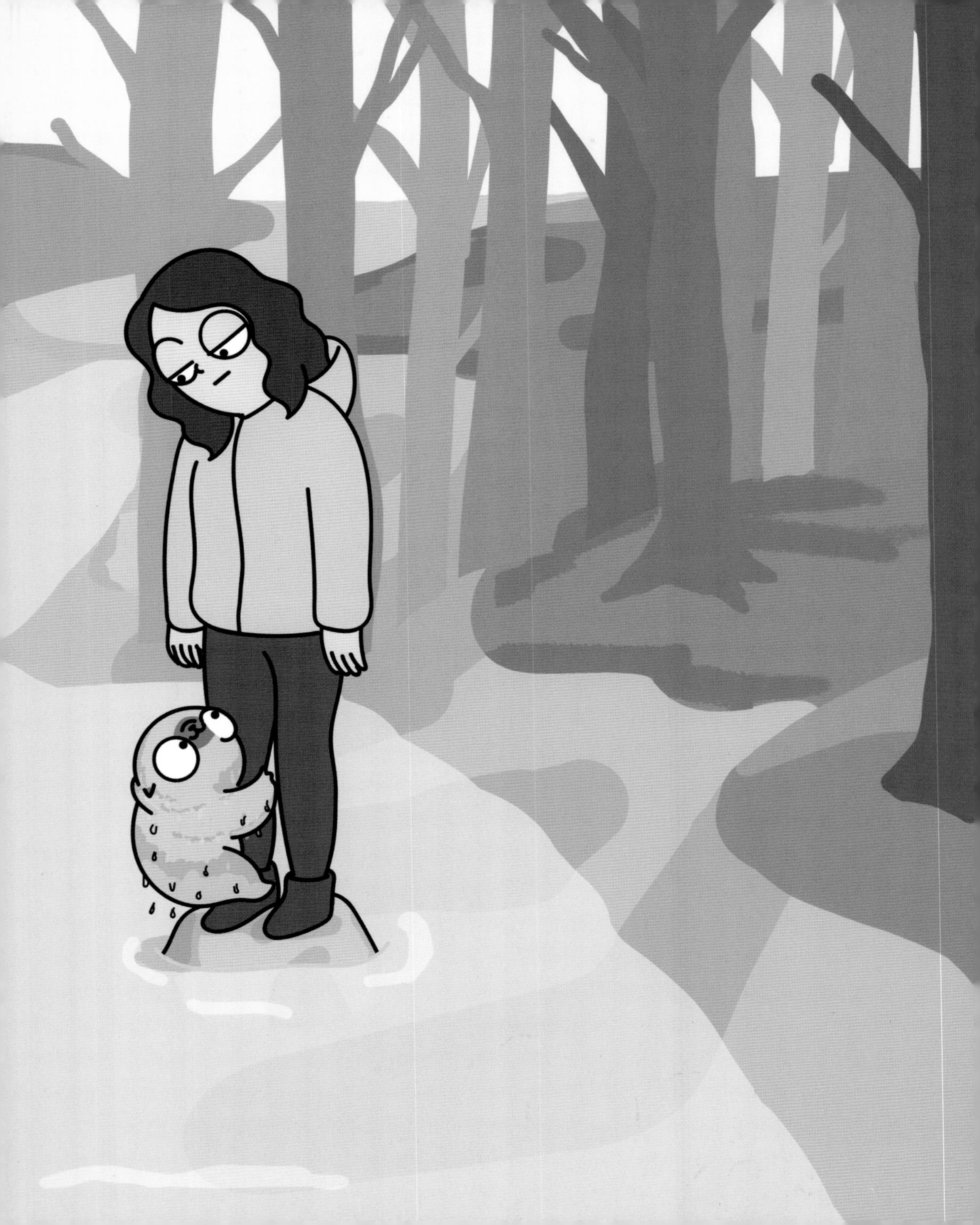

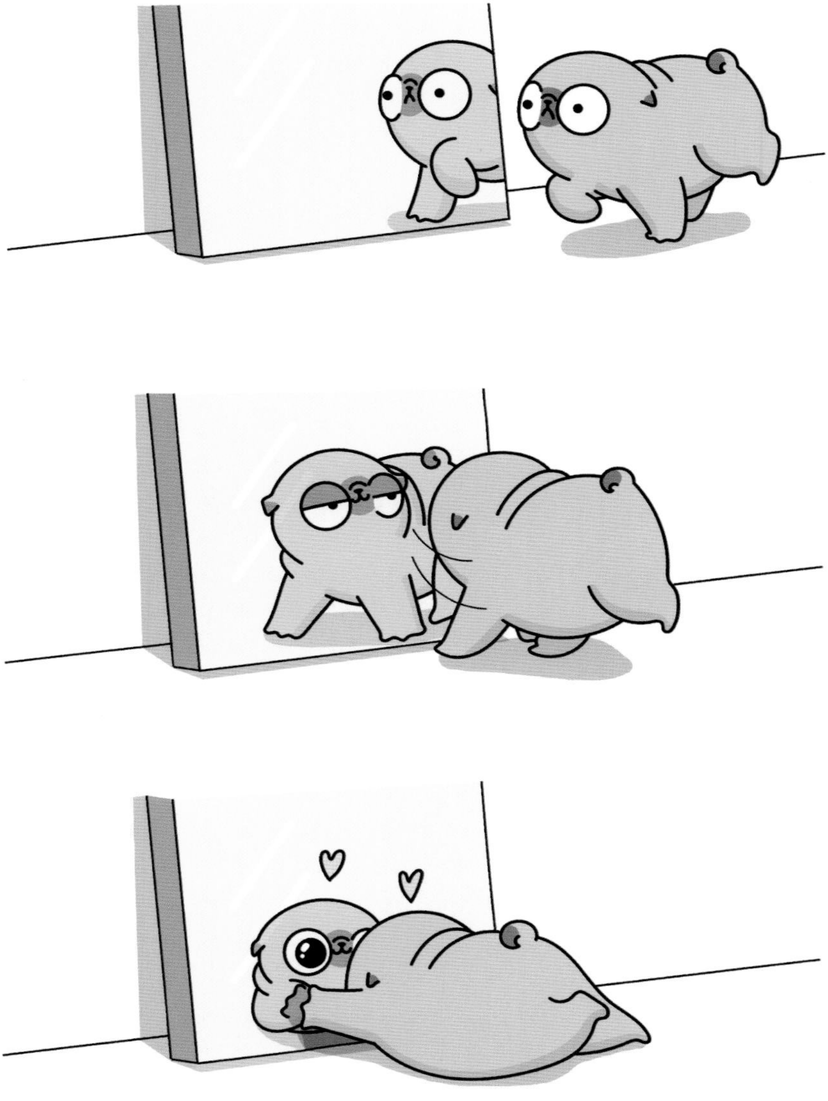

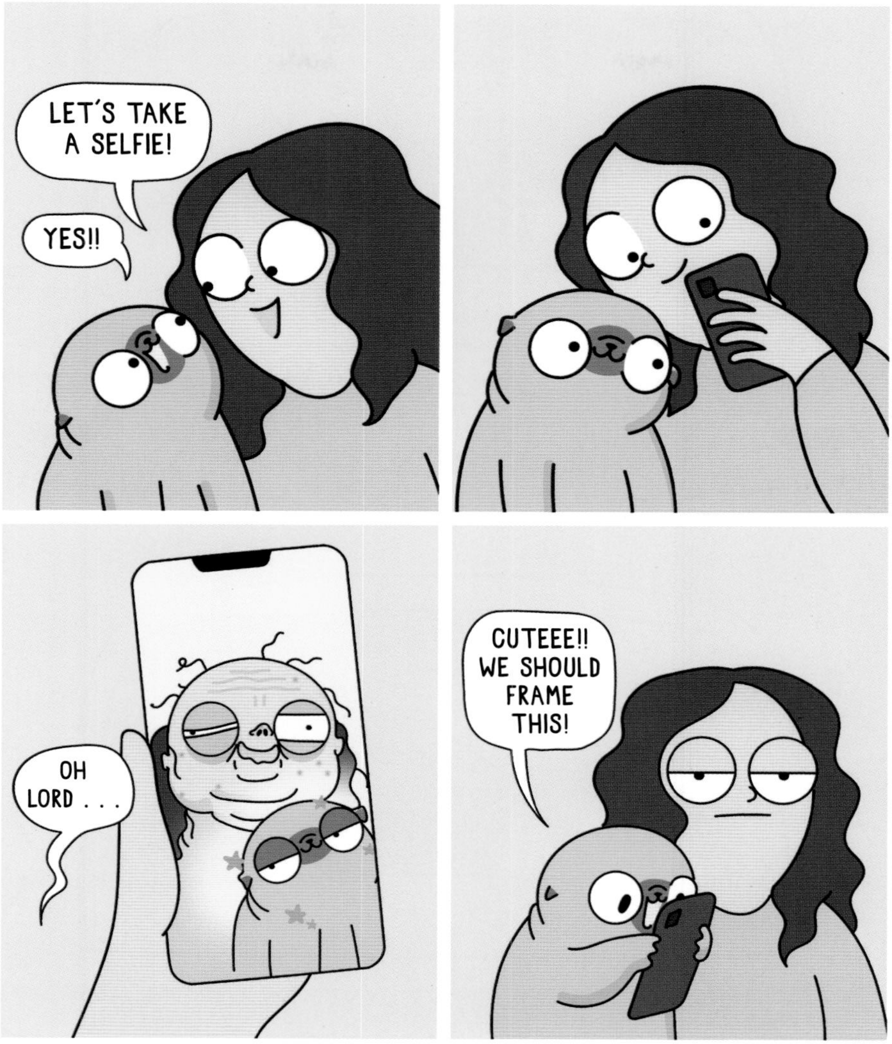
LET'S TAKE A SELFIE!
YES!!
OH LORD . . .
CUTEEE!! WE SHOULD FRAME THIS!

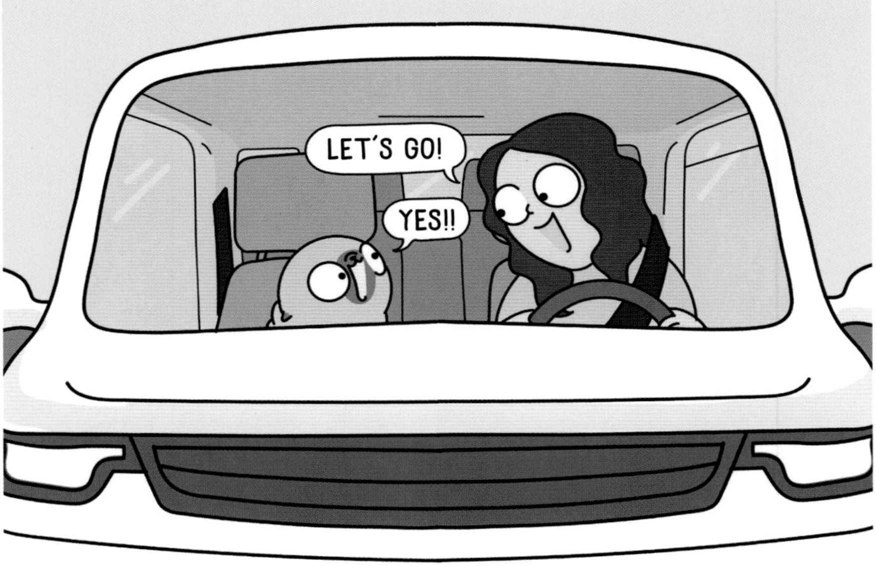
LET'S GO!
YES!!

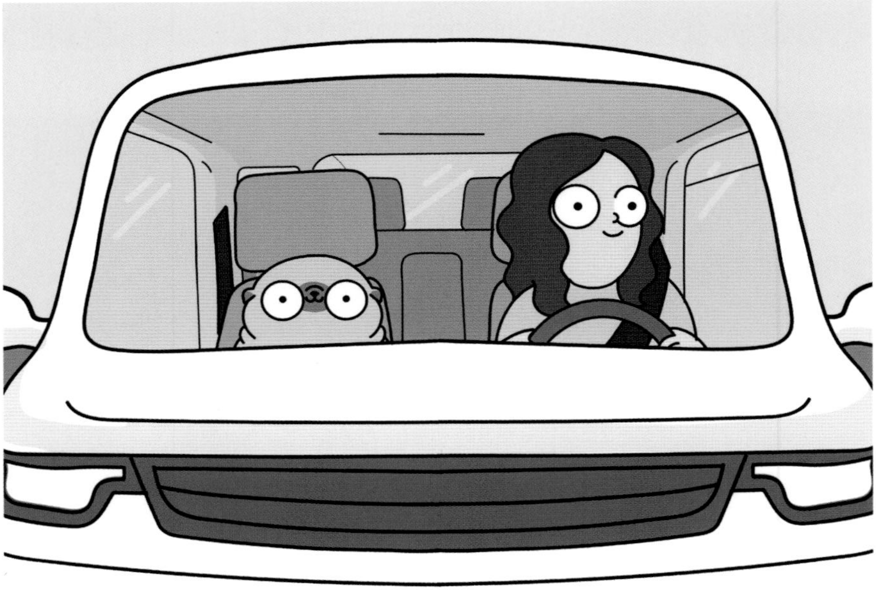

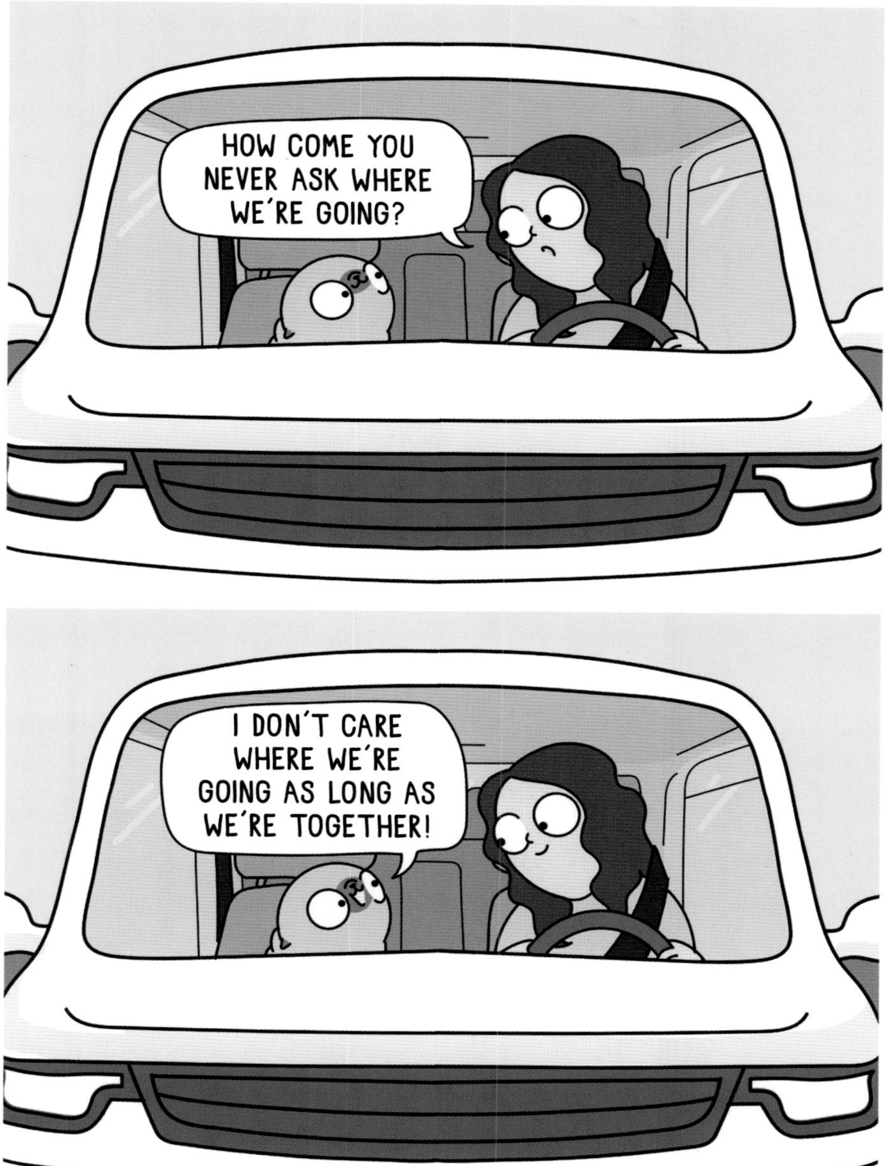
HOW COME YOU NEVER ASK WHERE WE'RE GOING?
I DON'T CARE WHERE WE'RE GOING AS LONG AS WE'RE TOGETHER!

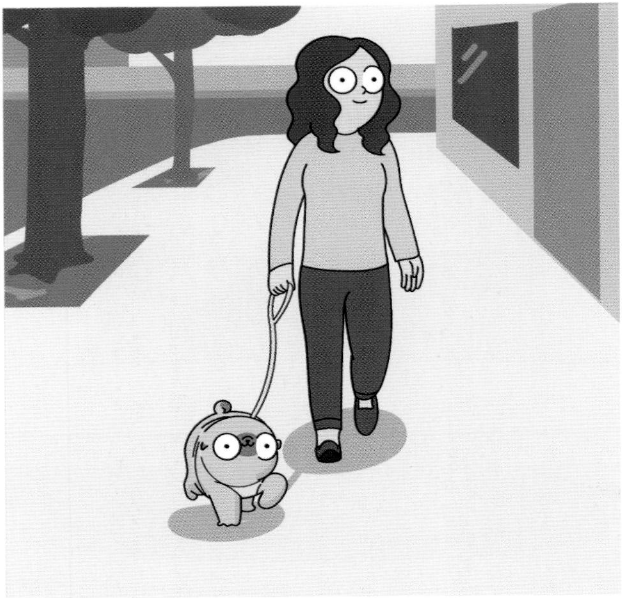

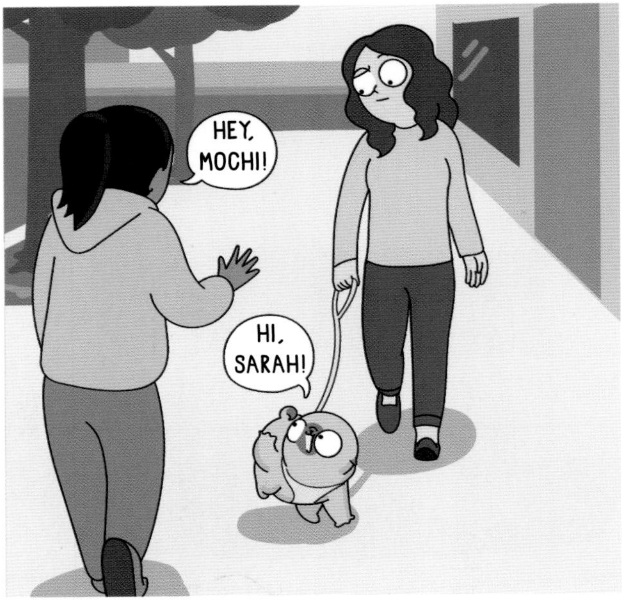
HEY, MOCHI!
HI, SARAH!

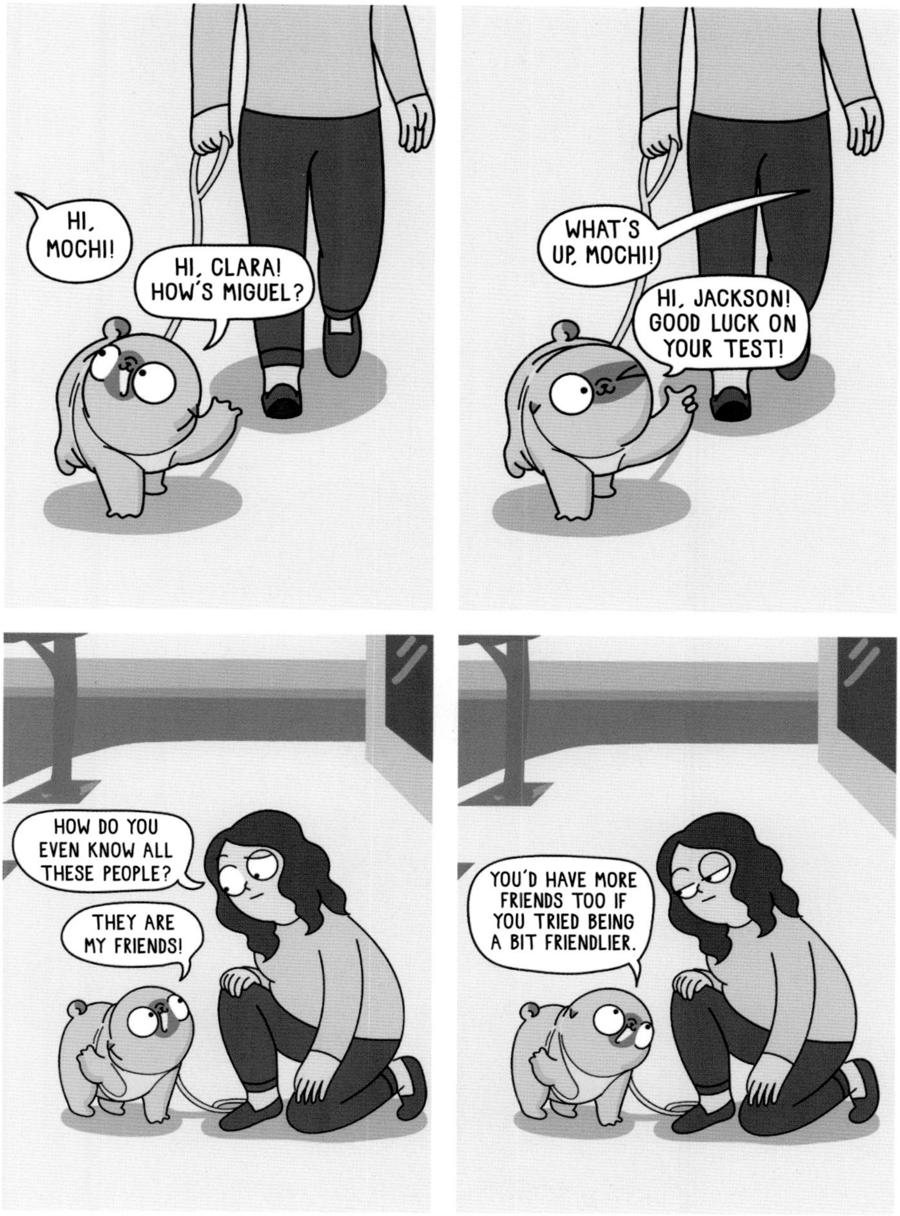
HI, MOCHI!
HI, CLARA! HOW'S MIGUEL?
WHAT'S UP, MOCHI!
HI, JACKSON! GOOD LUCK ON YOUR TEST!
HOW DO YOU EVEN KNOW ALL THESE PEOPLE?
THEY ARE MY FRIENDS!
YOU'D HAVE MORE FRIENDS TOO IF YOU TRIED BEING A BIT FRIENDLIER.

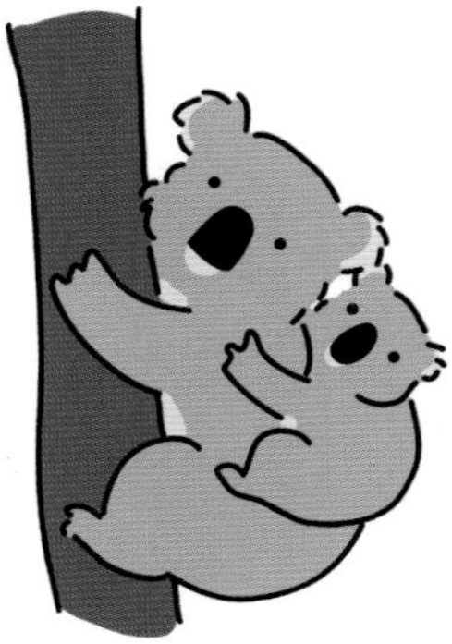

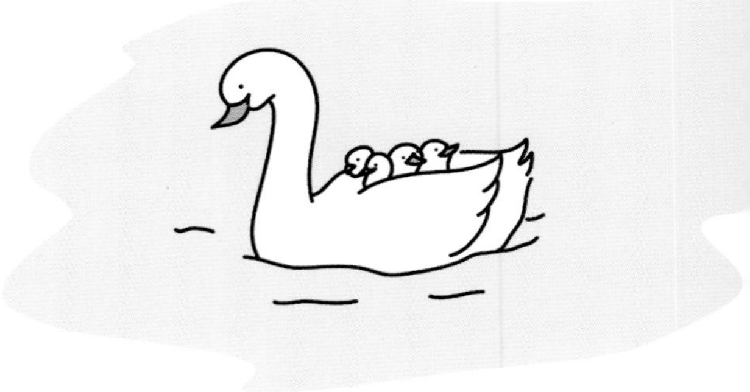

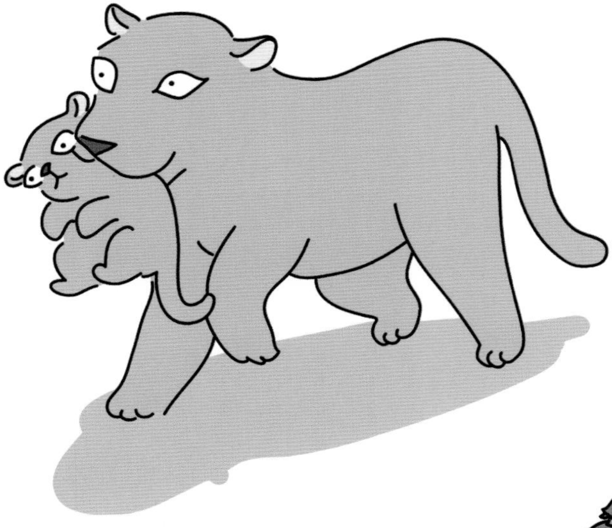

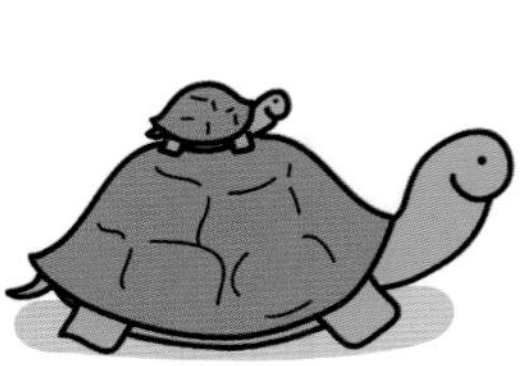

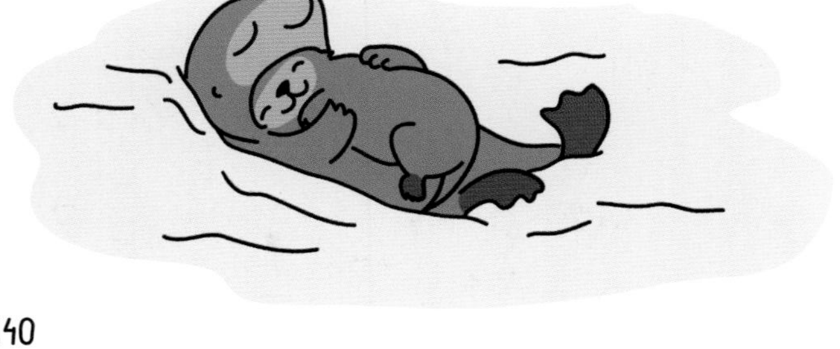

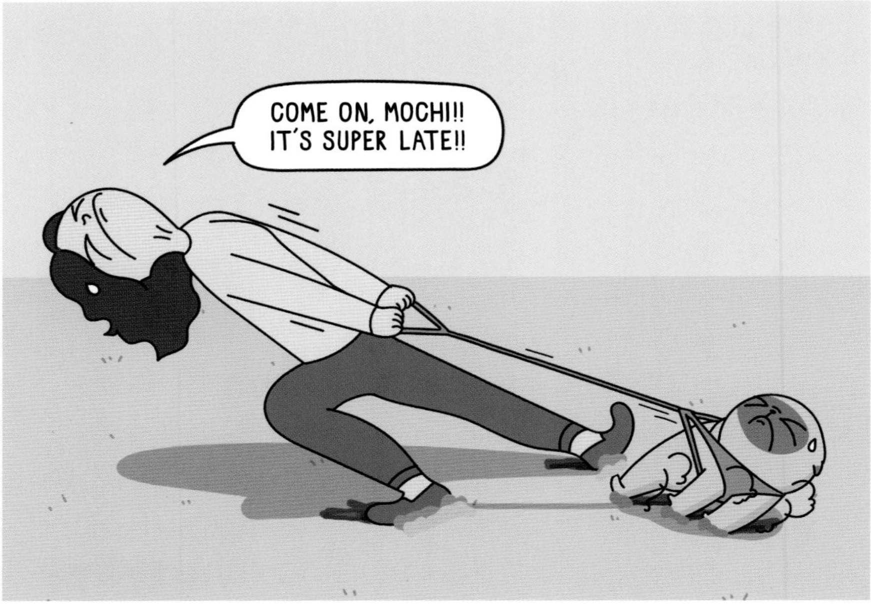
COME ON, MOCHI!!
IT'S SUPER LATE!!

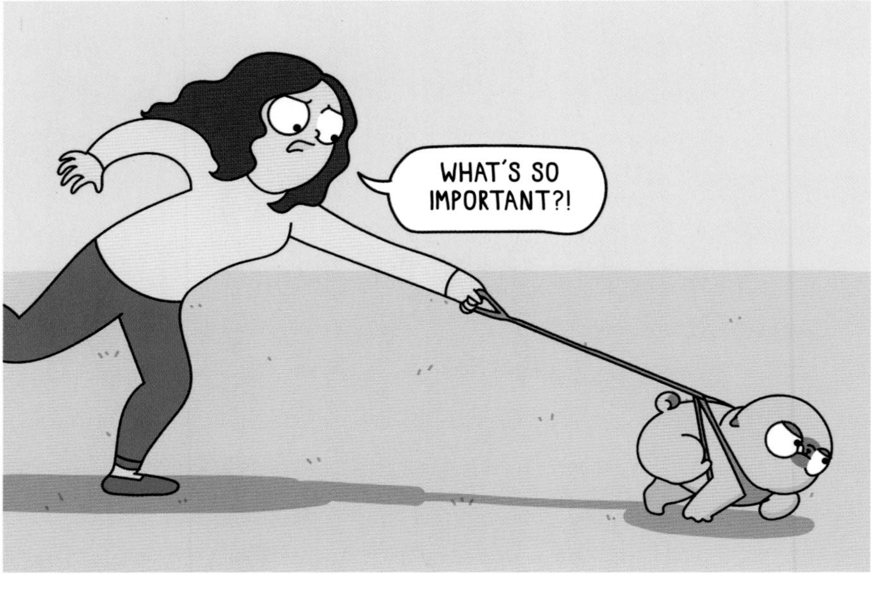
WHAT'S SO
IMPORTANT?!

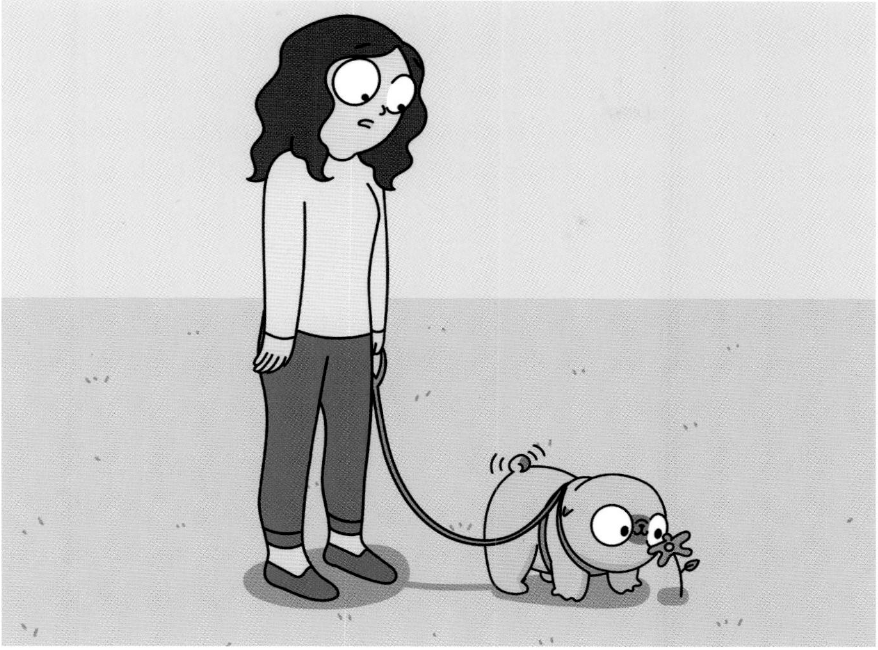

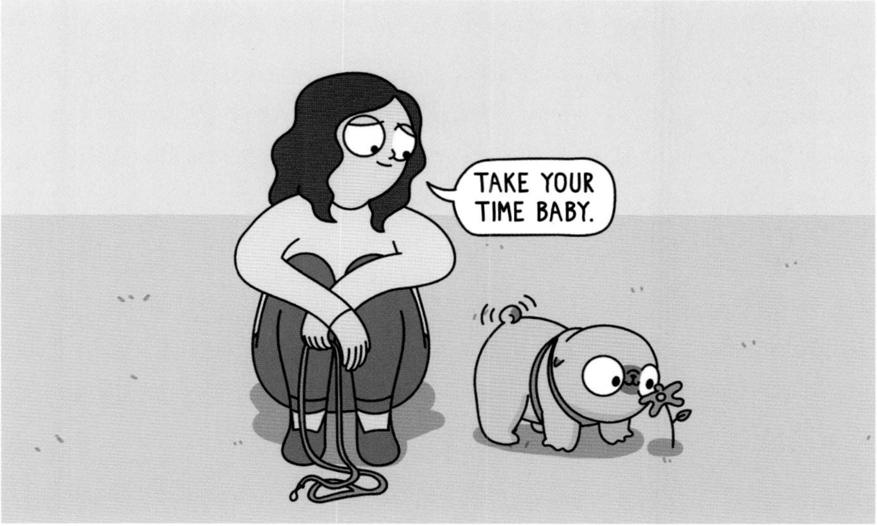
TAKE YOUR TIME BABY.

But it hasn't been all love and laughter . . . one of the worst days of our lives was when Mochi had to have surgery. His vet wanted to do a preventative surgery to check for something that could potentially be serious, and while Mochi was under, do an intervention that would help his breathing and improve his health. So we decided to go ahead with it, hoping it would make Mochi's life better.

This all happened at the beginning of the pandemic. Our vet referred us to a pugs superspecialist at a fancy vet hospital because he was the best of the best. Because of Covid, I couldn't go inside the hospital at all. I didn't even get to meet the surgeon in person, I was only able to talk to him via the phone and e-mail. I thought that because the pandemic was such a stressful time, the surgeon wouldn't be in his best state of mind, so I decided to postpone the surgery. But when I realized Covid was not going to be over in a couple of months, we went ahead and scheduled Mochi's surgery.

The day of, I handed Mochi over to a nurse with a note of his allergies and some important medical information. It was mostly me begging that they don't accidentally kill him during the procedure. Mochi was hospitalized for over twenty-four hours. It was one of the scariest times in my life.

My mind was going crazy with all the things that could go wrong. What if something happened? Why did I put him under if it wasn't a life or death situation? What if Mochi didn't make it? I couldn't eat or sleep. All I felt was an immense silence. I kept looking for Mochi every time I moved my chair, trying to hear his steps following me, but nothing. Absolute, complete, dark silence.

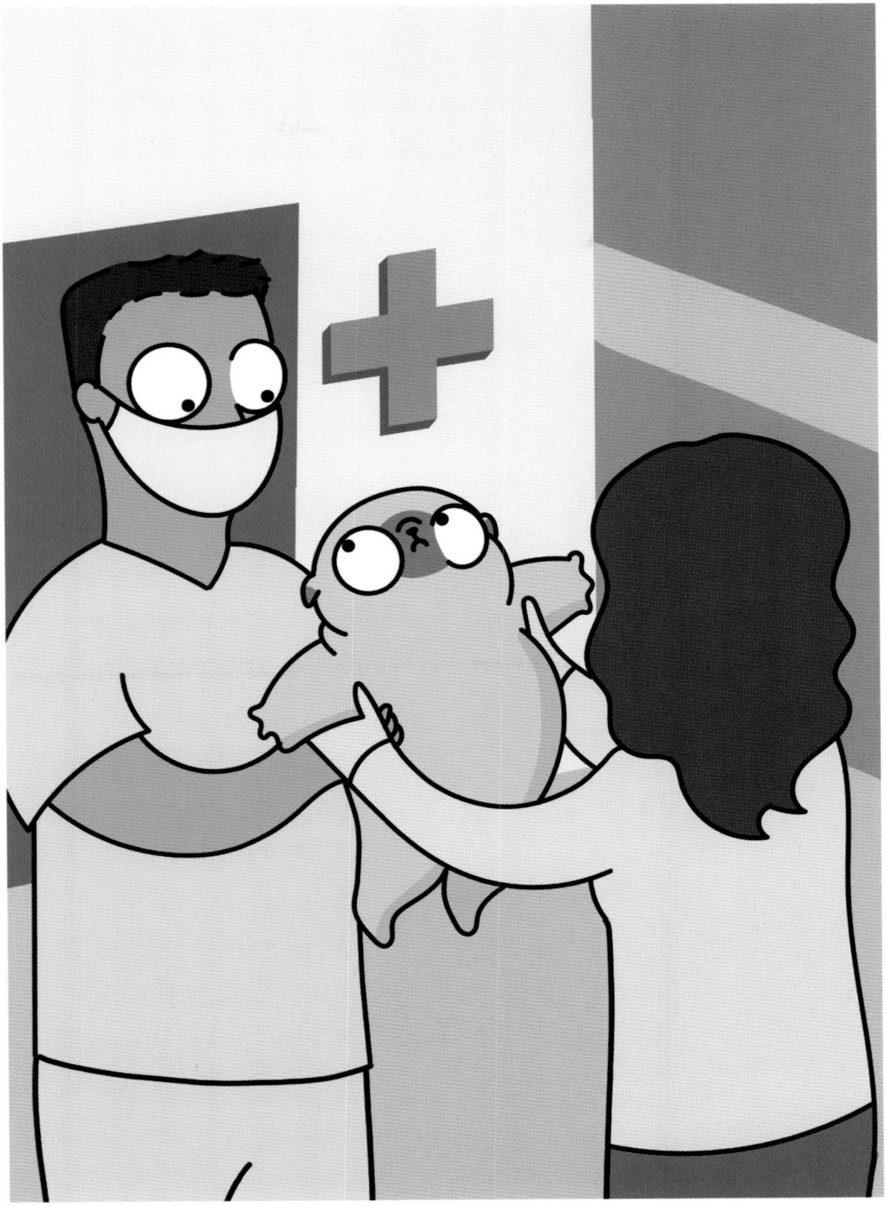

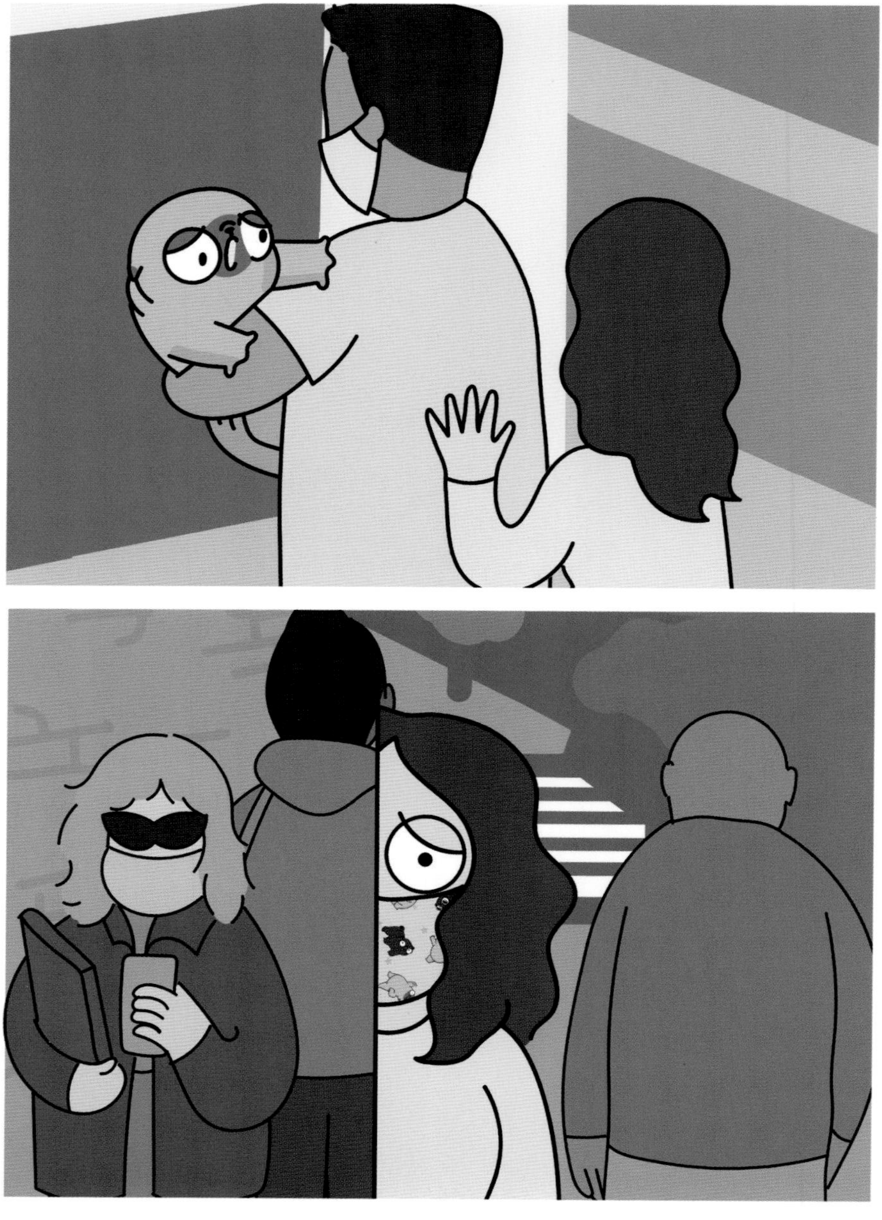

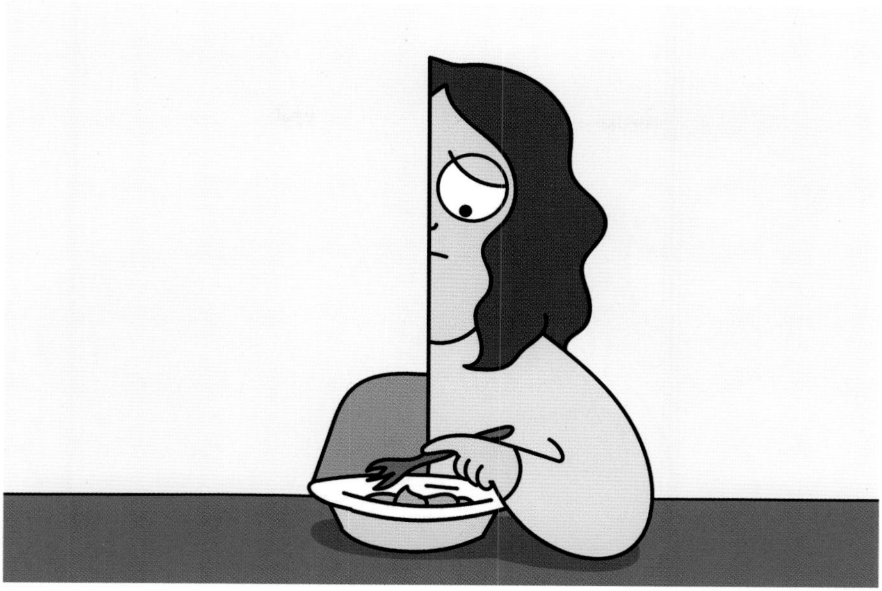

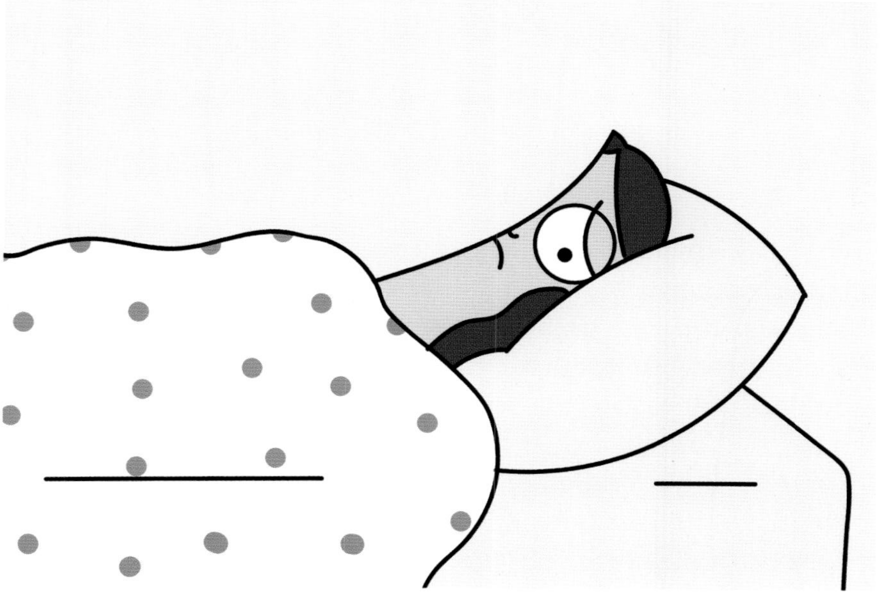

When I went to pick him up, I was so excited!! I've never arrived so early anywhere in my life!! I wish someone would have warned me of how difficult the recovery would be. Mochi wasn't himself for many days! He acted differently, smelled funny, looked odd, and sounded weird. If I didn't know my baby, I would have thought they gave me a different dog! Thankfully, with a little bit of time and a lot of extra love, he got better, and before I knew it, he was back to his normal self.

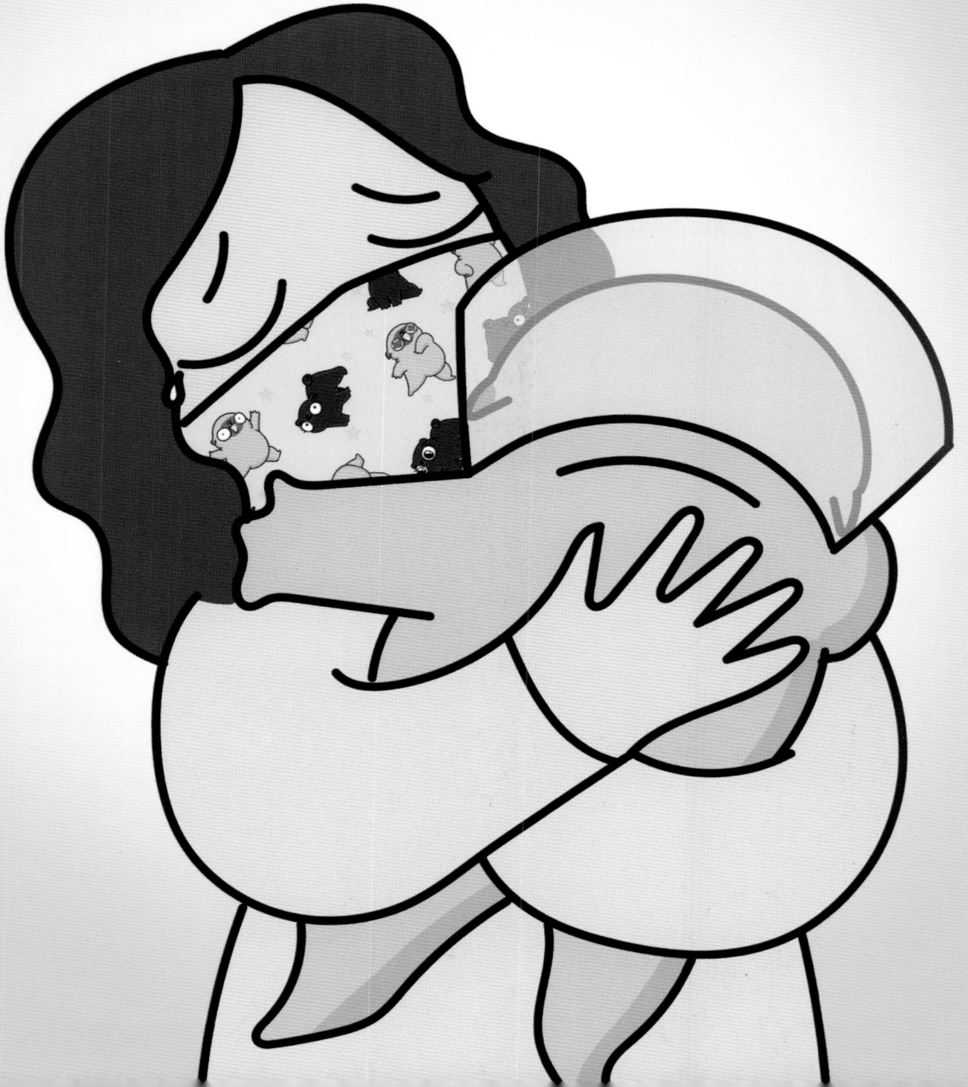

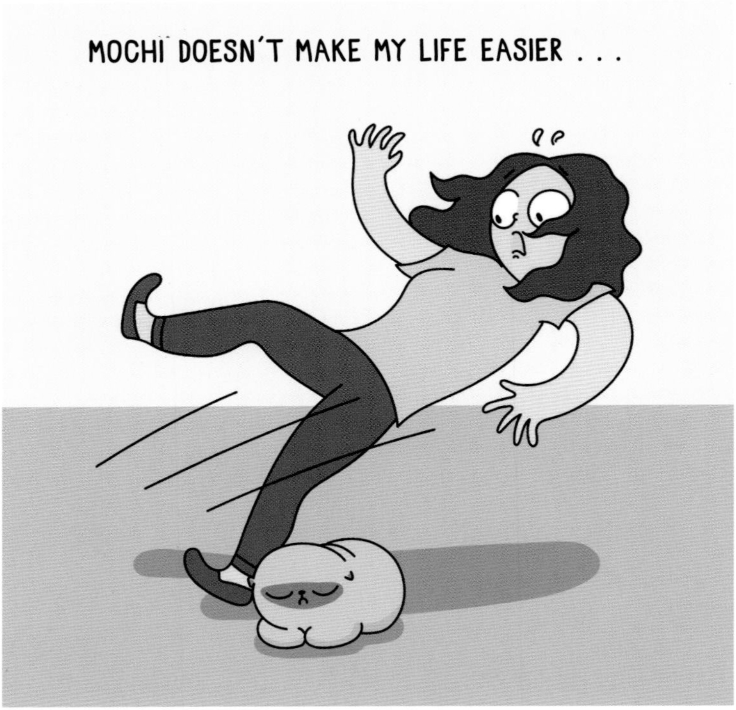
MOCHI DOESN'T MAKE MY LIFE EASIER . . .

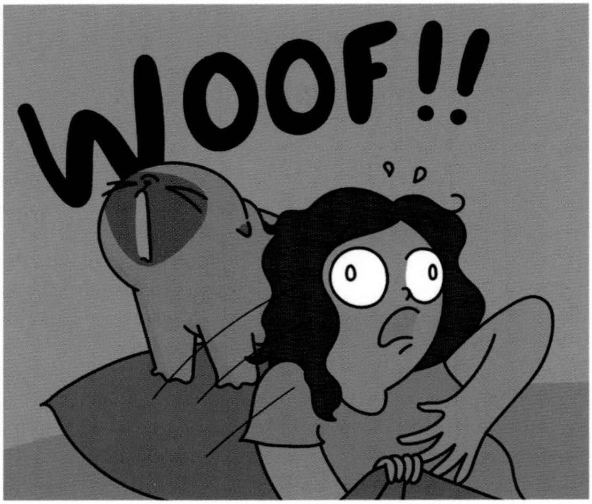
WOOF!!

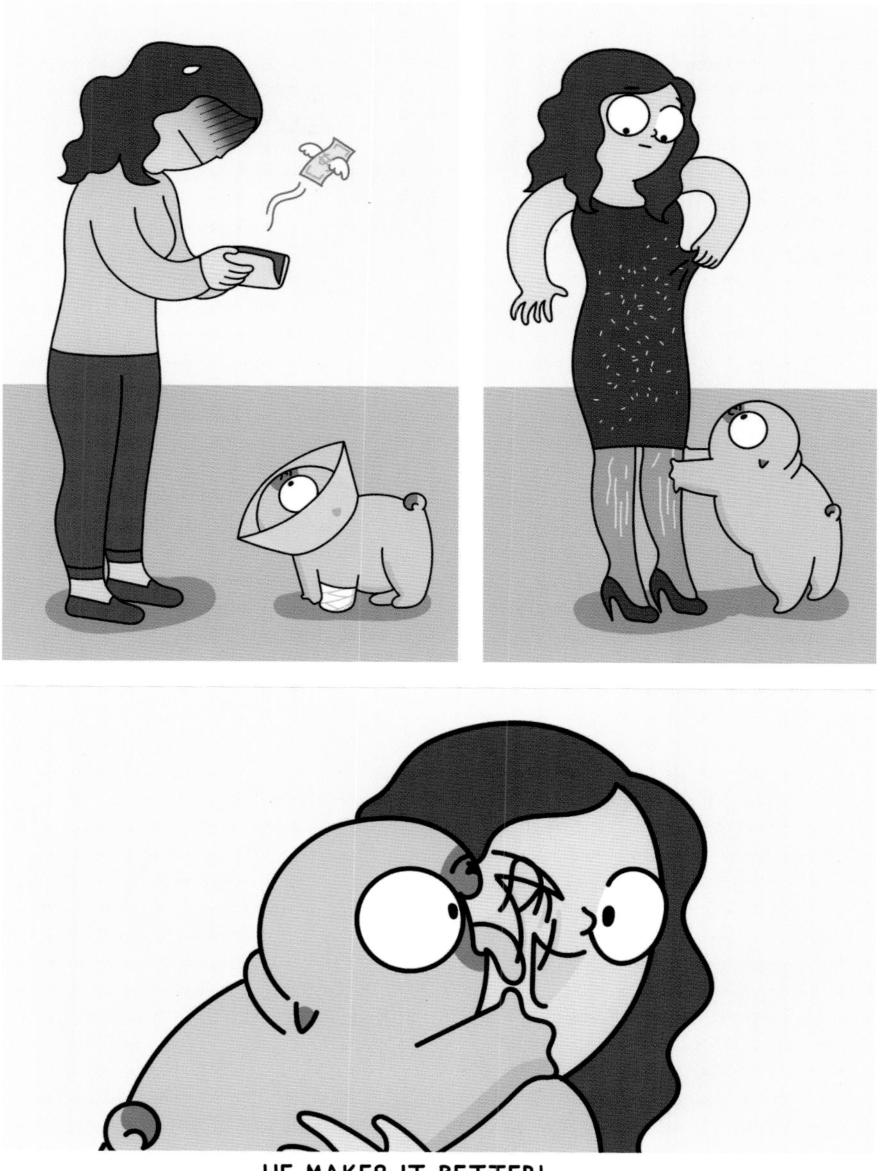

HE MAKES IT BETTER!

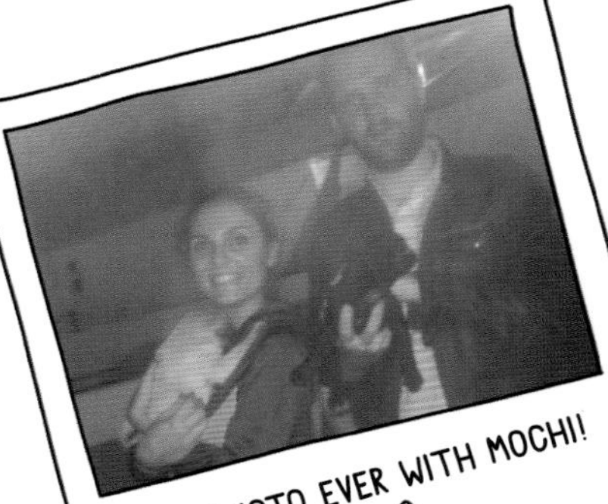

FIRST PHOTO EVER WITH MOCHI!

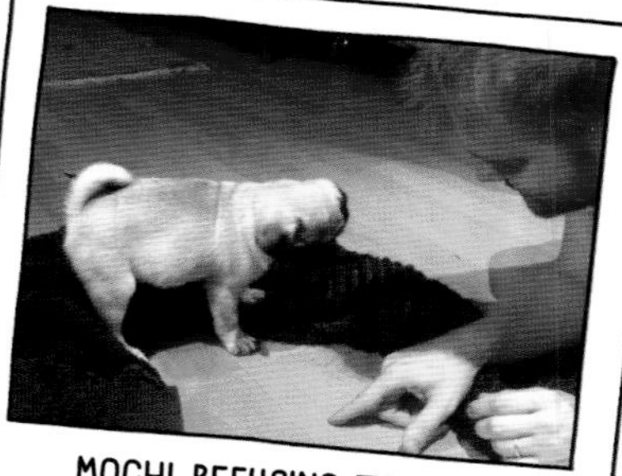

MOCHI REFUSING TO STEP ON THE FLOOR WHEN HE FIRST GOT HOME

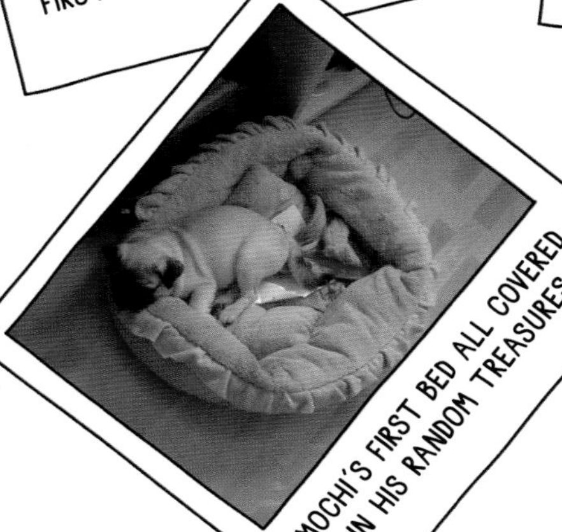

MOCHI'S FIRST BED ALL COVERED IN HIS RANDOM TREASURES

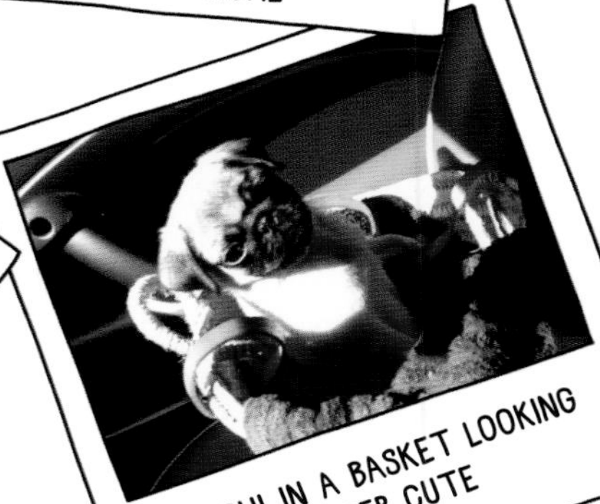

MOCHI IN A BASKET LOOKING SUPER CUTE

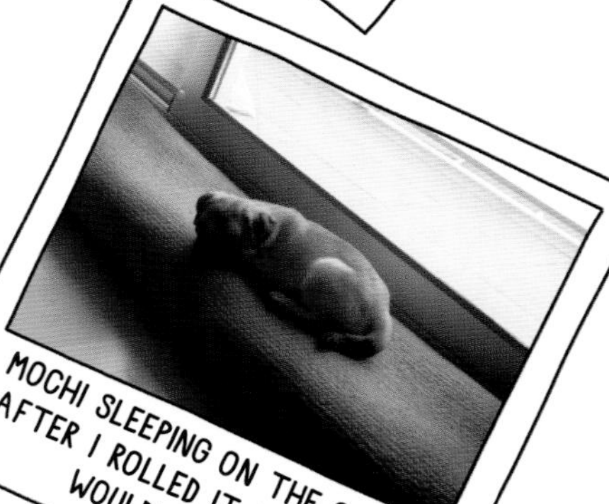

MOCHI SLEEPING ON THE CARPET AFTER I ROLLED IT ASIDE SO HE WOULDN'T USE IT

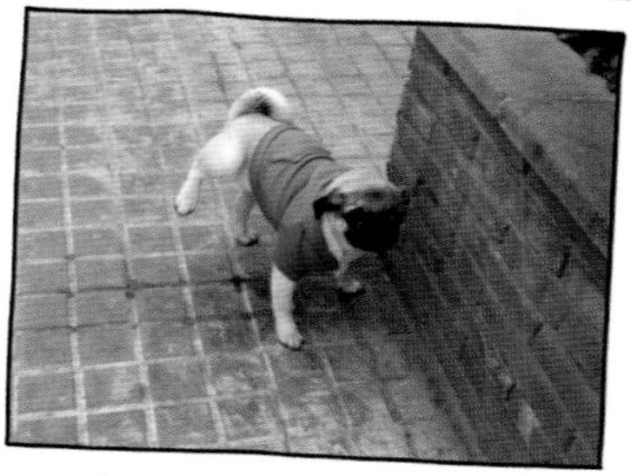

MOCHI ATTEMPTING TO MARK A WALL

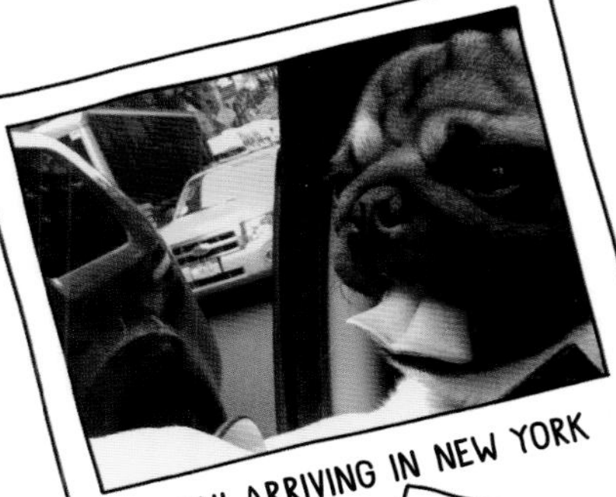

MOCHI ARRIVING IN NEW YORK

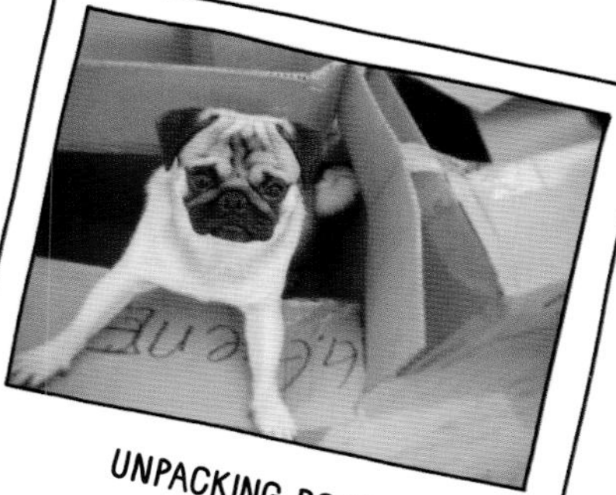

UNPACKING BOXES

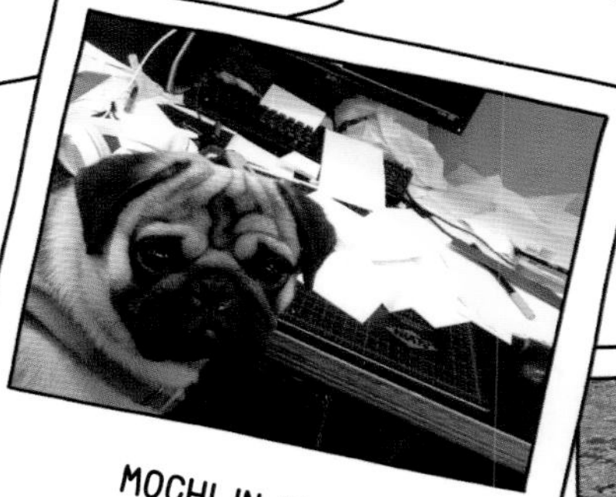

MOCHI IN CLASS

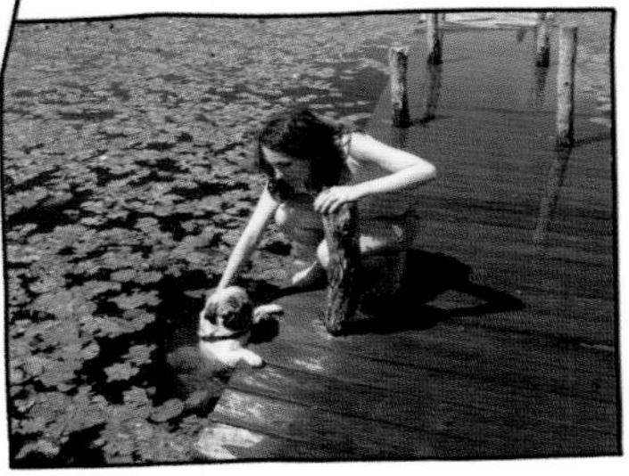

FISHING MOCHI OUT OF THE LAKE

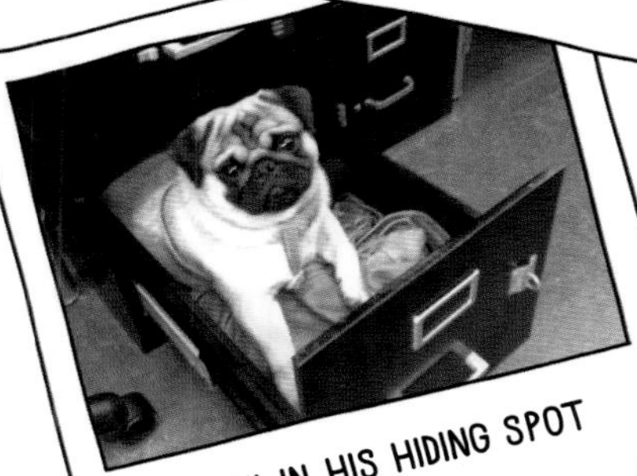

MOCHI IN HIS HIDING SPOT

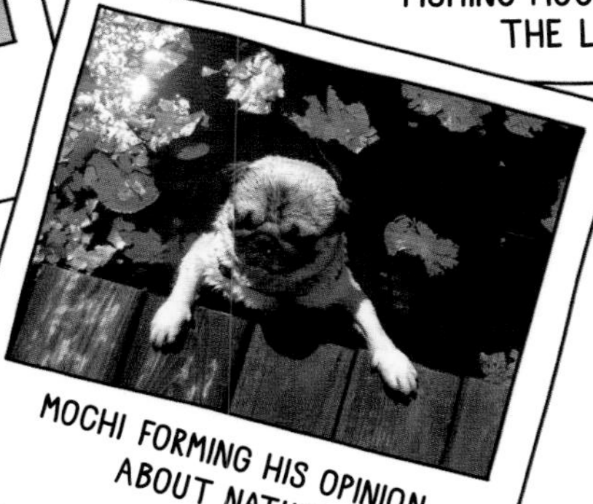

MOCHI FORMING HIS OPINION ABOUT NATURE

Andrews McMeel Publishing
a division of Andrews McMeel Universal
1130 Walnut Street, Kansas City, Missouri 64106

22 23 24 25 26 SDB 10 9 8 7 6 5 4 3 2 1

ISBN: 978-1-5248-7681-4

Library of Congress Control Number: 2022935329

Editor: Lucas Wetzel
Art Director: Sierra S. Stanton
Production Editor: Jasmine Lim
Production Manager: Tamara Haus

Book design and cover by Gemma Gené

www.andrewsmcmeel.com

ATTENTION: SCHOOLS AND BUSINESSES
Andrews McMeel books are available at quantity discounts with bulk purchase
for educational, business, or sales promotional use. For information, please
e-mail the Andrews McMeel Publishing Special Sales Department:
specialsales@amuniversal.com.